Written and Illustrated by
Linda "iLham" Barto

Second Edition 2022
Revised

Text and illustrations copyright 2008, 2020, 2021, 2022 by Linda K. Barto. All rights are reserved. No part of this book may be reproduced or transmitted in any form or by any means, electronic or mechanical, including photocopying, recording or by any information storage and retrieval system, without permission from the author.

For reprint permission and other correspondence:
Linda K. Barto
3806 Grady Williams Lane
Maiden, NC 28650-9535
lindabarto13@gmail.com

Originally published 2010 by
Dog Ear Publishing (IN)
ISBN 978-145750-273-6

Second edition published 2022 by
Lit-by-Linda
ISBN 978-0-578-25723-3

Printing in the USA by
IngramSpark

Sister Linda is doing a wonderful job of presenting various segments of the Qur'an as she feels relevant to contemporary American life. All of us Muslims should help her by encouraging her and suggesting ways to improve. Her technique may become a better tool for introducing Islam to the people of this land, in a language with which they can connect, instead of archaic translations and irrelevant notes.

                Dr. Omar Afzal
                Professor, Cornell University, NY (retired)

FOREWORD

by Shamim Siddiqi

I request that all people of faith take special interest in the parables and prose of our beloved Sister Linda. She uncompromisingly puts the teachings of Islam in correct perspective with regard to the time in which we are living. Linda gives clear direction on inviting people to become obedient to their Creator, while living within their own cultures and maintaining their life patterns, with some adjustments to apply and maintain the values that Islam promotes. We can all learn from Linda's methodology.

The modern world must come to realize that, from the point of guidance in how to act, live, and behave, the original sources of the Torah, the Bible, and the Qur'an are the same, and that the Qur'an is the latest and most perfect model to follow. Although there have been alterations over time in the Bible, it still carries semblances of truth in its contents, reminding the readers that it was sent by the same Creator and Sustainer. In its broader outlook, the Qur'an confirms the truth of the earlier texts.

Sister Linda, through her imaginative approach, has picked up various iota of truth from the Bible and synchronized them with the injunctions from the Qur'an. She presents moments of communion with God's infinite mercy so that His servants may correct their lives in the way He ordains through His latest directives. Her dissertations are reminders that too many are enjoying God's limitless bounties but giving practically no obedience to the Lord of this cosmos, except for some formal, verbal acknowledgements.

If her parables help Humanity to believe, seek truth from God, and surrender to His authority, she would deserve the good pleasure of God on the Day of Judgment. On that day, her parables will recommend to our Lord to pardon her sins and thus pave her way to enter into her abode of eternal bliss. What a joyous day it will be for her! [1]

AUTHOR'S INTRODUCTION

Years ago, on the old homestead, after taking his Saturday night bath, Daddy walked into the kitchen with gobs of his hair in his hands. The rest of his hair looked like melted rubber bands sliding off his head. He said to Mama, "Georgia, I don't know what kind of shampoo you bought, but it sure ain't no count." Unable to read the label without his glasses, Daddy had accidentally used my Nair hair remover. Gradually his hair grew back, and he survived. That's the way this book is. You'll survive it, but it might mess up your hair for a while.

This book is written especially for newly converted Muslims, but it will also appeal to vintage Muslims and anyone interested in learning about Islam from a down-to-earth, American perspective. If you believe that deep ponderings should be left to grumpy scholars with frizzy beards, that loony-tune laughter is not befitting a serious Muslim, and that everything non-Islamic is also anti-Islamic, then you may end up needing a wig. If you are a dogmatic Muslim who jumps up and down whenever a new-fangled perspective is presented, maybe you should take your blood pressure medicine before reading this book. Although this is a serious book, it is often shockingly serious in humorous ways. There are also some tearjerkers that come straight from the heart, and I hope you can feel some of the emotion I felt when I lived those heart-wrenching moments.

"Adventures of a Reluctant Traveler" is my autobiographical sketch, which includes the story of how Islam found me. With that background, I interpret my rural lifestyle through my own understanding of the Universal Qur'an. From my ninety-nine parables emerge conclusions based on my own rustic insights. Please don't pitch a hissy fit if my perspective doesn't match traditional views.

In this book, you'll meet my family. My husband Tom is a loveable creature with a wide grin and a jackhammer laugh. Our son Duston (Dusty) is also a big-grinner and has a laugh that sounds similar to a hot cannonball exploding through a fireworks factory. Our daughter Tana is an off-again, on-again joy-to-terror ride. She can change moods quicker than the contented cat switching her tail under my rocking chair. Our old homestead is in the foothills of beautiful North Carolina. We've lived with all kinds of animals, including goats, chickens, birds, fish, dogs, rabbits, rats, and cats. We love the country life because we can read the Scriptures in nature every day. I hope that you can come in closer contact with nature by reading my parables, and I hope that it's not the kind of nature that you have to scrape off your boots before you walk into the house.

INTRODUCTORY NOTES

Qur'anic passages are from the book *A Universal Message Interpreted from the Holy Qur'an* (Light Switch Press, CO, 2020) by myself and Dr. Ahmed Pandor.

In Biblical passages, I used three versions of the Christian Bible and one Jewish Bible. I may have combined part of one translation with words from two or three other translations and based the final rendering on what I felt was most accurate based on my research.

I have used Scriptures from the Bible as well as the Qur'an in order to show the consonant message of the Holy Books. To a Christian-to-Muslim or Jew-to-Muslim convert, the Bible may still be very much a part of that person, and it should be. Muslims are told, by the Qur'an, to believe in the previous Scriptures as well as the Qur'an. Some critics will complain that I am "equating the Bible with the Qur'an." All I can say is, Go take your blood pressure pills! You may need to get your prescription refilled if you object to the prayers I've used from a variety of world religions. I have, however, adjusted some prayers to give them a universal appeal and make them conform to monotheism.

For those who don't know, the word *Allah* simply means 'God' in Arabic. It's not the moon god, the god of Turkish coffee, or top god on the totem pole; it is the Creator God of us all. Jesus (peace upon him) spoke Aramaic, and he called God *Elah*. Both Arabic and Hebrew are related to Aramaic. I am using the name *Allah* in the Qur'anic passages and in prayers and teachings of Muhammed (peace and blessings upon him). In other places, I have usually used 'God.' 'We,' in reference to God, is called 'the Majestic We' and refers to all the attributes of the One God (blessed and exalted is He).

Names of my neighbors and acquaintances have been changed to protect the guilty.

PART 1
One Wild Lifetime

ADVENTURES OF A RELUCTANT TRAVELER

*Truly, We have imparted clarifying signs,
and Allah guides whom He will to the Straight Way.
(Surah 24: 46)*

There aren't many Muslims in the foothills of North Carolina, so people are usually taken by surprise when I announce that my religion is Islam. Some people act like I'm the anti-Christ; others want to know what an Islam is; many people just act confused and stagger away. For someone like me –a blond, blue-eyed, country cat raised a Southern Baptist in the Bible Belt— to become a Muslim is what folks around here call "a regular curiosity." One lady, on learning my religion, exclaimed, "Good Lord, honey! How did you get mixed up in something like that? I didn't even know we had any of them Islams living around here."

Often, I am asked, "What did your relatives think when you became a Muslim?" Well, to tell you the truth, my relatives all think I'm nuts anyway, so my becoming a Muslim was no more surprise than when I joined the air force, bought myself a motorcycle, or eloped with a man I had known only about eight weeks.

The person most surprised was I. I had been a devout and faithful Christian all my life, and I was perfectly satisfied with my religion. I wasn't looking for anything else, and I didn't want anything else. So how did I come to be standing beside one of Islam's highest religious leaders, saying shahada in the world's fourth holiest mosque, and delivering a message to nearly a thousand Muslims in North Africa?

One of the nicest things anyone ever said about me was, "She's not crazy; she's just really different." In school, I was plain, shy, and not very popular, but I had a great reputation for being "really different." My eighth-grade teacher got the bright idea for a class talent show. A few kids planned a skit about the "Beverly Hillbillies," a popular TV show at the time. Since I was skinny and kind o' goofy-acting, I was asked to be "Granny." I climbed into the attic and assembled a tattered outfit. I masked out two of my teeth with black enamel paint. I had to grin for over an hour waiting for that paint to dry!

We Beverly Hillbillies practiced at the home of the girl playing "Elly May." Elly May's older sister snapped, "You kids ought to be ashamed of yourselves for making that poor, skinny, little girl dress like that."

Elly May answered, "She likes it; she's really different."

In the skit, "Jed Clampett" handed me a wad of Monopoly money. I snatched it up in both fists and started jumping around like an idiot. I was grinning really big to show off my blacked-out teeth. The entire class howled with laughter.

Well, the gal that won the show was smart, beautiful, and popular. She sang, "Where the Boys Are." When she was handed her award, the boy sitting behind me huffed, "Huh! Ever'body knows the best 'n out thar was that stupid ol' Linda Granger." (Granger was my maiden name; my parents are Bill and Georgia Granger.)

Thank God, I'm a country gal! I learned how to make a whistle out of a blade of grass, how to make a flashlight from a mason jar and a summer full of lightning bugs, how to dig for sassafras roots and make tea, how to tell the difference between a skink and a salamander, and how to get a grasshopper to spit his chewing tobacco into my hand (although I never did figure out why I should want a grasshopper to spit on me).

Although we didn't know any better, life in the country was tough. Daddy had quit school in third grade to work on the farm, but even without knowledge of algebra and geometry, he could figure correct measurements and angles for building such things as furniture and cabinets with dovetail and bevel joints. Mama went to the sixth grade, and she expanded her vocabulary by working crossword puzzles. After my sister Toyce ("Toy") was born, Daddy joined the marines to fight in World War 2. Mama faced a difficult struggle to survive on her own.

Toy got three mean brothers before I was born, but I was meaner than all three of them together. Toy said she had always wanted a little sister, but she didn't mean me. I was really different from what she had in mind.

When I was four, we moved into the house that Gran'paw Granger had built. There was no indoor plumbing, and the only electricity was for the light bulbs hanging low from the high ceiling. Daylight peeked through cracks in the walls until we covered the walls with old, paper, letterpress plates that Gran'paw had collected and stacked in the barn. The plates had come from a newspaper publisher, so I could lie in bed at night and fall asleep reading the wall, although the text was backward.

A hosiery mill put a looper in the house so that Mama could work from home. The looper was a bulky contraption with a huge wheel of needles for sewing the toes of socks. As the wheel continuously moved around horizontally, the looper operator's job was to press the toes of the socks onto the needles and, at the same time, keep up with the sewn socks coming back around to her. Mama had to count eleven sewn socks and then tie them together with a twelfth sock. She stuffed all the finished socks back into the huge, green, burlap bags in which they had been delivered. Every week two men from the hosiery mill came to get the bags of finished socks and deliver more bags to be done. Of the two men, one was white, and his name was Blue; the other was black, and his name was Brown. As a kid, I thought that was funny. The bags were always piled along the hallway, and sometimes we had to crawl over them to get from one end of the hall to the other.

Mama washed clothes in a wringer washer for which she was truly grateful. Prior to getting the washing machine, she had to build a fire under a black cauldron in the back yard, and then wash the clothes on a scrub board. Mama also made our clothes and kept them mended.

Every year, we raised a pig to slaughter in the fall with a bullet to the head. We then spent many weeks preparing the meat into sausage, bacon, ham, livermush, pork rinds, etc. We melted the fat, and we always had a barrel of lard in the milk house. Mama made cracklin' biscuits from what was left of the fat.

We also kept chickens for meat and eggs.

In the spring, Mama and Daddy planted fields of corn, squash, pumpkins, peanuts, beans, peas, okra, and tomatoes. We also had apple and pear orchards and a field of blackberries. Mama spent most of the summer slaving over a wood-burning stove and canning vegetables and fruits. I sure miss Mama's blackberry jam and pear preserves! She stored her jars of hard work in the old milk house.

After we got a refrigerator, we didn't need to keep the milk in the dry well in the milk house. One day Daddy decided to fill-in the dry well and pave it over, so there would be more floor space. It was a big hole, and Daddy was having a difficult time finding enough junk to throw into the hole. He finally went berserk and started throwing in everything he could find. I was missing many toys after that—including my little, blue, pedal car, which would be worth a small fortune now.

Gran'maw Granger was a moonshiner, and she had used her homemade whiskey in baby bottles to make the babies sleep soundly. Daddy grew up to be an alcoholic. Whenever he went on one of his drinking binges, Daddy would stay stumbling drunk for a week or two and then pass out across the kitchen floor. He would lie there for nearly a week, and Mama would keep him rolled over on his side so that he wouldn't strangle on his vomit. When Daddy finally did get up, Mama had to disinfect the floor because of his vomit and urine.

One Sunday, after Daddy was almost sober after a week on the floor, I decided to stay home from church and have a Sunday School lesson just for Daddy and me. We read the lesson from the Sunday School booklet, which included Bible verses. After that, I decided to be baptized, and Daddy decided to get indoor plumbing. When I walked to the church altar to dedicate my life to the Lord, Daddy followed me, and he also made the commitment. The indoor plumbing and Daddy's conversion were just the beginning of a better life. We never again had to step over Daddy while he was passed out drunk on the kitchen floor, and we didn't have to walk across the field to go to the toilet.

My baptism was an important event in my life. Baptisms were always at night, and a blue, plastic pool was set up in front of the altar. Lights shown on the water, and the reflections danced on the ceiling. A multitude of colorful flowers and artificial palm trees gracefully surrounded the pool, and a lighted, serene picture of Jerusalem was placed in the background. The scene was beautiful and surreal, like a fantasy.

Serious about my Christianity, I studied the Bible and prayed daily, and I always tried to do the right things. I was still a mean, little brat, but that was mostly a survival tactic. My brothers picked on me so much that I thought I wasn't a real person. I thought I was a robot that Daddy had made from pieces of old plows and other junk in the barn. I had the neighbors' kids convinced of it too, and they were scared to death of me. I liked it like that.

I was raised in a Southern Baptist church in which Ku Klux Klan members were Sunday School teachers and deacons. Even as a stupid, little kid, however, I did not accept the racist message I got from them. As soon as I was old enough to get my driver's license and my own car, I left that church and started visiting other churches. I was in search of a God big enough to embrace everyone regardless of skin color or any other aspect of pluralism.

When I was teenager rambling through the woods, enjoying nature. I climbed over a neighbor's fence and got halfway across the pasture before the bull spotted me and charged. The bull's horns were inches from my scrawny butt as I reached the other side of the pasture. I cleared the fence with a single leap, catching the bottom of my overalls on the barbed wire. At least it was barbed wire, and not that fire-snorting bull, grinning with pieces of overalls in its teeth.

I wandered down to the branch where I stood on a bank and looked down into a shallow bend of water below. I spotted two, black, water snakes swimming in a romantic ballet in a private pool. A sand bar was in the middle of the branch. The water separated as it hit the sand bar, skirted around it, and then rejoined at the other end of it. Wanting to get a closer look at the snakes, I jumped from the bank onto the sand bar. To my shock, the firm-looking sand turned to soup. I sunk like a sack of rocks. My head was under muck in what seemed to be a bottomless pit. I was sinking deeper, and I could feel bones and carcasses swirling against my skin. A bubble of gas must have belched from beneath me, because suddenly I was thrust upward. I shoved my arm into the air above me, but there was nothing for me to grab. Suddenly an unseen force encircled my arm, pulled me from my would-be grave, and flung me onto solid land.

I walked further down the branch and washed a little before walking back home. I almost made it all the way across the pasture before the fire-breathing bull spotted me. I revved-up my robotic energy and beat him to the fence again.

Returning home, I came in through the kitchen door, and Mama was cooking supper. Dripping wet, I had mud, sticks, and pieces of rotted animals stuck in my hair, plus the seat was torn out of my britches. Mama took one look at me and said, "You ought to be ashamed of yourself." I never told her what had happened.

When I turned sixteen, Mama started looking for me a job. I got my first job at a dime store, making a dollar an hour in 1965. It was part-time after school, and it was supposed to have been temporary through the Christmas season, but the boss liked me so much that he made it permanent.

When I turned eighteen, Daddy gave me a full-time job in a furniture factory where he was foreman. My main job was "mark boy." I drew the patterns on the wood for the bandsaw operator to cut. The men resented me at first, but they came to respect me after I proved that I could work just as hard as they did. I handled whatever task I was assigned. Unloading lumber trucks was one of my jobs even though the glued-up blocks weighed more than I did. One block weighed about 120 pounds, and I only weighed 100, but I pulled them off the trucks and stacked them above my head. It was really not possible, but I was always too stubborn to let impossibilities stop me.

The sawdust and scrap wood from the bandsaw went into a huge wheelbarrow, which, when full, weighed about 300 pounds. I had to push that filled wheelbarrow into a field and dump it. It was too heavy for me to dump with just my arms, so I had to put my back under the handles and push it over that way. One day about every three months, the men in the shop would bring their guns, make a circle around the pile of sawdust and scraps, light the pile on fire, and then shoot the dog-size rats that ran from the pile.

One day, when I was dumping the wheelbarrow, a lady that lived next to the shop walked over to talk to me. "I didn't think they let women work in furniture shops."

I responded, "Well, I'm the first."

She said, "I thought working in a furniture shop was too hard, but if a skinny, little thing like you can do it, I can too."

When I left that job, she applied for it. Daddy told me that she worked half a day and then said, "This work is too hard for a woman. You people are crazy!" She went home and never came back.

In high school, I didn't have enough sense to figure out what I was going to do in life. The only thing I had ever wanted to do was drive a dump truck and haul coal. We heated our house with coal, and I looked forward to seeing the truck rumble into our yard, belch its black breath, and dump that pile of dusty coal. That was the coolest thing! When I was eight years old, I begged my parents to get me a dump truck. I was thrilled on Christmas morning when, under the garishly decorated, lopsided, dried-out cedar tree, there was a heavy-duty, metal-cast truck –yellow with red stripes on the sides. I loved that truck! One summer day, I left it under the apple tree. My niece Janis (just three years younger than I) fell head-first out of the tree and smashed my beautiful truck with her hard head. Daddy snatched it up and threw it in the milk house well! I was devastated. I felt that my entire future was crushed and discarded along with that truck.

Days away from high school graduation, I took time to pray about my uncertain future. In the darkness, just beyond the back porch, a vision of soft, white light in the shape of dove's wings, fluttered in front of me. It disappeared as my prayer ended.

The next morning, after the mail had arrived, I spotted the new Southern Baptist magazine on my sister's bed. The picture of the front cover was exactly the vision I had seen. I asked Toy, "What's this?"

She explained, "It's just an artist's conception of the Holy Ghost" (which, in Christianity, means 'the Spirit of God').

I then realized that the vision and the interpretation from the magazine cover were, together, a sign from God that He was always going to be ahead of me in my future.

God kept His promise, and I never doubted His involvement in my life. But there have been times when I thought He was joking. When I prayed for a sign of what to do with my life, I got a postcard that said, "Go Air Force!" I looked up toward the sky and asked, "Just how crazy do you think I am?"

Well, I reckon I was just crazy enough because I enlisted in 1970. I was so skinny that the recruiter made me stand on the scale and eat bananas until I weighed enough to pass the physical and join the WAF (Women of the Air Force).

I had spent most of my youth stomping through the woods around the house, chasing critters or running from them, picking wildflowers, and wading in the branch. Whenever I got to a new air force base, I went on self-guided explorations just as I had done back home. Often, I found myself in peculiar situations. One night, I was exploring a base under its dim security lights. I came to a tall, chain-link fence with a sign that said, "Top Secret Area." I scratched my hillbilly head and thought, 'Well, I wonder what they got stashed in here.' I climbed over the fence and started to take a little stroll. I didn't get very far before a half dozen, vicious, snarling, barking, German shepherd, attack dogs were speeding toward me from all directions. Fortunately, there was a water tower nearby. I scrambled up the tower in a hurry! I was several feet above the ruckus of the dogs when I heard guns cocking. I looked down into a circle of M-16 gun barrels focused on my scrawny butt.

"Hold on thar fellers! I'm one o' yuns," I explained. "I just got stationed here last week, and I was checking this place out. I got lost, and somehow I wound up on this here water tower. I don't know how it happened."

I recognized a good, Southern drawl from the fellow who lowered his weapon and said, "You mean you're one of them thar WAF?"

"Yeah! Yeah!" I was glad to be among fellow hicks.

"Well, Farley," he said to the man beside him, "let's bring her in and feed her some doughnuts."

The guards called off the dogs and escorted me to a little shack full of ammunition and doughnuts. I was offered a chair, and the men circled around me. We talked and laughed for a couple hours before they put me in a jeep and gave me a ride back to my barracks.

I walked from Mather Air Force Base in California to a motorcycle dealer in Sacramento. I bought a motorcycle on the spot even though I did not know how to ride a motorcycle. The next day, the salesman and his girlfriend brought the motorcycle to me at the base and spent a couple hours with me, teaching me how to ride it. After they left, I looked for a wide-open space to practice. I chose the flight line, so there I was dodging B-52's taking off for Vietnam. Suddenly, I was surrounded by military police who promptly escorted me off the flight line. As I passed by the control tower, I could see all the control personnel pressed against the window, watching me, the idiot. I waved to them, and they all waved back.

Tom was a security policeman in the air force. He says it was love at first sight, but my first impression of him was that he was awfully goofy. Every time he saw me, he started walking like he had springs in his britches.

One day, I was riding my motorcycle when I was suddenly being pursued by a military police car –lights flashing, siren wailing. I didn't stop till I got to my barracks. By then, all the other WAF were standing out on the fire escape to see what the heck was happening. I stopped my motor and got off. That goofy cop got out of his car and marched over to me as if he was going to haul me off to the salt mines. Then he grabbed me in his arms and smooched me right on the mouth! The other WAF all moaned, "Awww!" and huffed back inside, as if they were disappointed that I didn't get hauled to the salt mines.

About eight weeks later, Tom and I were married. It was a long Labor Day weekend, and we couldn't think of anything better to do. I told him, "Okay, I'll marry you –but just this once, so it better be good!"

We were married about three weeks before I finally called home. Mama answered the phone. I said, "Guess what, Mama."

Mama said, "Well, let me sit down first."

When she was settled, I explained in four words or less that I was married. There was a long pause. Finally, I asked, "Well, what do you think?"

"I think I'm glad I sat down first," came the astute reply.

Daddy came to the phone. I gave him the news and asked him the same question, "What do you think about that?"

Well, I don't much like it," Daddy drawled.

"Why not, Daddy?"

"Well, you're way out yonder, and I'm way over here, and for all I know you probably married some kind of hippie or something."

Over the years, my parents came to love Tom just as much as they did their own three sons and two daughters and my niece Janis who lived with us.

Tom and I were both discharged during the close of the Vietnam War, but, years later, we enlisted in the North Carolina Air National Guard. I served during two wars; Tom served during three and was among the first to be deployed to the War in Iraq, even though we both objected to that crazy "shock and awe" arrogance.

On being discharged from the air force, Tom and I salvaged the bed of a wrecked pickup truck and turned it into a covered wagon pulled by a Dodge Colt. We wrote on it, "Tom, Linda, and Kittykat" and "Carolina or Bust." We camped our way cross-country from California to North Carolina. We slept in wild areas and cooked on campfires. We learned how to bake biscuits in an old, metal mailbox, and sometimes we found wild berries and other plants to eat.

We actually tent-camped coast to coast three times, and we had many adventures. We were shot at, stalked by coyotes, snipped at by alligators, and one time we even thought we were surrounded by gargoyles.

At Kit Karson pass, melted snow had pooled at the entrance of a cave, and I carefully tiptoed around it to enter. On the walls of the cave was a luminescent algae that crumbled when I touched it. I was enchanted by the algae as I walked deeper into the darkening cave. Suddenly, I heard a grunt and looked to see the head of a grizzly bear poke up. It didn't take long for me to discover that I could actually fly over that puddle at the entrance.

Tom and I hiked a little further, and, in a sink-hole-like depression, we found a pond. It was surrounded by snow, but surprisingly, the water was warm. We were in the wilderness, so I stripped and went skinny dipping. After I put my clothes back on, I looked up at the edge of the depressed area and saw a line of people that had been watching me. Well, I *thought* we were in the wilderness.

A few days later, I was skinny dipping in Ponce de Leon Creek in Florida. It was a warm, sunny day, but that dip was like being submerged in ice water. I found it confusing how deceptive nature could be.

Not long after settling in North Carolina, we bought a speck of woods in a rural area, sketched a design for a house, and started building. Busybodies tried to convince us that such a project could not be completed by just two people. How come? We had read a library book that showed how to do stuff. It took us about eight years, because we never had the money for more building materials as soon as we needed them. Building our own house came with plenty of adventures, including our living in a tent without access to running water and electricity, because we couldn't afford any better at the time. Now we enjoy a modest, country home, and our well taps into a clean, underground river. I thank God for making us foolish enough to think that we could build a house by ourselves.

Tom and I used to drive a church bus. There were quite a few folks willing to accept a ride to church whenever we offered them a good deal, like free watermelon to anyone willing to suffer through an hour of brimstone preaching.

Like many hillbillies, Flossie Finny still lived in a house with a dirt floor and no plumbing. Flossie was on our bus route, and every Sunday, she bargained for the best deal out of having to go to church. We usually promised her a sausage biscuit or a pickled pig's knuckle.

The preaching was hot and heavy one Sunday morning when Flossie became "filled with the Holy Ghost." Flossie wasn't sophisticated, but she did know better than to blow bubble gum on her way to the altar. She took the wad of gum out of her mouth and stuck it underneath the church pew. Without realizing it, Flossie had caught her dress tail in the gum before smashing the wad tightly into the wood grain. To make matters worse, the do-gooder who had given Flossie the gum had done so after Flossie had just filled her cheek with a dip of snuff.

Flossie went running up the aisle, shouting, "Hallelujah!" A long string of nasty, black, snuff-infused, chewing gum trailed behind her all the way to the altar. Everybody was anxious to get Flossie baptized. The preacher dunked her several times, and the baptismal water soon gave evidence that sins really are black.

After starting a family, Tom and I discovered that having brats is often *too much* adventure. Our marriage endured as we stuck together to team-up against the little monsters. It was a survival tactic.

One day, Dusty and I were crossing a street with a traffic cop standing in the middle of it. The cop was waving his arm signals and blowing his whistle. As we passed him, the cop spit out his whistle and told Dusty, "My mama always told me not to play in the middle of the road, and look what I'm doing today."

Dusty thought that was odd. He told the cop, "My mama always told me to sit in the middle of the road and play with a rattlesnake."

In high school Dusty had been selected to represent his school in a soil and water conservation workshop in Raleigh. Dusty arranged to catch a ride with a family from another county. We were to meet halfway to Raleigh, in the little, country town of Harmony. Tom was overseas, so Dusty, Tana, and I took off on our own. We met Dusty's ride in the vacant parking lot of Harmony High School on a lazy Sunday afternoon. Dusty took my keys from the ignition, got his suitcase out of the trunk, and put his stuff in the other family's van.

We said our goodbyes, and then Tana and I waved as we watched the van drive out of sight. Tana and I got into our car and buckled our seatbelts, and I reached for the ignition. No Keys. Dusty must have left them in the lock of the trunk. I looked. No keys. My stomach got a sudden case of roller-coaster-itis as I came to the realization that Dusty still had my keys. He had absentmindedly put them in his pocket, and now the car keys were on their way to Raleigh.

I looked toward the horizon into which Dusty had disappeared. For a few moments, I stood there too stunned to react. Then I just started screaming. "Ayyyyyyyy! Dusty! Why did you do this to me? Whyyyyyyy?" My ribs vibrated from the sound waves of my screams. On this sunny day, I felt thunderclouds and lightning bolts just above my brain. Treetops came alive with the sudden rustle of frightened birds fleeing their nests.

"Okay. Okay." I tried to calm myself. "Think. Think." There was no one I could call. I had no money. What was I going to do?

I recalled a TV news show that reported how young hoodlums could, in three seconds, break into a locked car and start it without the key. "That's what I need! A car thief! —a car thief who is also a Good Samaritan."

Tana was staring at me with her mouth dropped open. "Tana, you stay here," I told her, "and pray really hard while I go get help."

I dashed out into the busy, Sunday afternoon traffic and stopped both cars. "Do you know where I can find a car thief?" The drivers rolled up their windows and sped off.

While I waited for another vehicle, a tattered, old man, carrying a bulging, burlap sack, wandered from the surrounding woods. "Hey, lady," he said as he approached me. "Wanna buy a cooter?"

I ignored his offer of the turtle. "I'm out here trying to find a car thief. Know any?"

"Don't know nothin' 'bout no car thief," he said. "How much will you give me for this here cooter?"

"I don't want your turtle! If you can't help me, leave me alone."

"Ain't no use in gittin' all huffy, lady," he chastised. "He ain't even soup yet."

Somebody must have blabbed something, because the sheriff pulled up. He hauled me and Tana to the jailhouse. We sat there for two hours while I tried to convince him that I wasn't trying to steal cars.

Finally, the sheriff called a locksmith to make a new key. I had a dollar and thirty-seven cents in change —a far cry from the locksmith's bill. The locksmith calmly said, "Oh, that's alright. Here's my business card. When you get home, just send fifty dollars to that address."

Driving out of Harmony, I saw the tattered, old man with the bulging, burlap sack. He was walking along the side of the road. I stopped the car. "How much do you want for that cooter?"

"How much you got?" he asked.

"I got a dollar and thirty-seven cents in good, hard cash," I said.

"For that much money," he said, "I'll give you the cooter and the sack both."

I opened the trunk, and he put the tied, burlap sack inside. I gave him the handful of coins, and he was happy.

Tana and I arrived safely home. I immediately wrote a check and mailed it to the locksmith. He wrote me a letter back and said that he had been bailing out idiots for over twenty years, and I was the first one that had ever come through with the money.

The turtle was glad to get out of the burlap sack and into the skinny creek below the house.

Tana dragged our family through so much drama and trauma that several people have suggested that I write a book just about her soap-opera life. She was gullible and easily swayed, and worthless people often took advantage of that. One time, a man talked her into hiding him in our woods, without our knowledge. She took food and supplies to him for a couple weeks until all heck broke lose.

Although Tana did not have a license, the man coerced her into stealing a car and an ATM card. His plan was to get enough money to buy a shotgun from Walmart and then rob banks while Tana drove the getaway car. We did not have a clue about what was happening until the police woke us in the middle of the night.

As we were talking to the police, the man was directing Tana to a secret location where he planned to keep the car hidden. Tana began feeling uneasy about the situation, however, and drove the stolen car home instead. The man fled into the woods, and we helped the police find him in the darkness. The police did not hold Tana responsible for anything, but the man was arrested. He was turned over to the FBI, from which he was a fugitive. Tana had been hiding a serial killer!

Such episodes became a normal part of our lives. Hardly a week went by without some kind of crisis or drama.

In late summer of 1998, I began having dreams about a country to which I had never been and people I had never met. One night I dreamed that I was a little kid rocking in the chair Daddy had made me. The family was watching a documentary on TV, and the narrator described an Islamic state on the Mediterranean Sea. He explained that it had gained its independence within the twentieth century, and that its government had built homes and schools for the citizens.

Eventually, God revealed to me that the country was Tunisia. Tunisia? I had to look it up in the encyclopedia, and I found that my dreams were accurate. God proceeded to drag me on the greatest adventure of my life —a fantastic, spiritual journey! He began by teaching me many things in my dreams and through the research into which He tossed me. Splat!

At first, I thought that God wanted me to bring "salvation" to Muslims "lost" in what the Church considered a "false religion." Years earlier, Dusty had purchased an old, worn copy of the Qur'an at a flea market. It just sat on a shelf until I took it down and began reading with the attitude that I was preparing myself for targeting Muslims. The translation was that of Abdulla Yusuf Ali, in its original,1934 version. Thanks to Yusuf Ali's insightful footnotes and commentaries, I was able to understand the verses, which seemed strange and foreign to me.

As I continued studying the Qur'an, it started making sense. I didn't expect that! In order to strengthen the armor that the Qur'an was beginning to penetrate, I had to confirm for myself that Jesus is God and the Son of God. I searched the Bible, but I could not find the verses that support the Trinity doctrine. I had many Christian books, but the verses they quoted as Trinitarian could only be interpreted that way by someone who already believed in the Trinity. I made a trip to the library and brought home a stack of books on Church history. I was dismayed to learn how the Trinity doctrine had evolved in an atmosphere of politics and controversy. I was confused. Usually, I can figure things out in a good, bubble bath, but even that didn't help.

Through inspiration, God assured me that He wanted me to take a message to Tunisia, but first I had to unlearn. I had to rethink everything I had been taught and redefine the New Testament message. As I slept, angels pounced on my brain and stuffed it with more ideas and information than I ever wanted. I kept screaming, "Overload! Overload!" But I got no rest from God's persistence.

One day, I was lying on my back in a field and watching the clouds form and change shapes. Suddenly, a breath went into me. I felt differently. I realized that I had received a gift, but I did not know what it was until later. During the night, in my dreams, someone handed me a note, and I was able to read it. Normally, in my dreams, anything written looks like a cross between Russian and Arabic. Scientists say that it is impossible for a person to read in dreams, because the part of the brain that enables reading is in a state of dormancy while a person is asleep. Since that breath went into me, I have been able to get messages in my dreams. For example: I had to get up early one morning to take my sister to the doctor. I set the alarm clock, but it didn't go off. I was dreaming that I was ordering breakfast in a café in South America (although I've never been to South America). The waiter, a young boy, brought my coffee and a note. I read the note in my dream; it said, "It's 6:30." I looked at the clock on the wall of the restaurant and saw that it was 6:30 in my dream. I immediately woke up and looked at my silent alarm clock; it was 6:30 for real –time to get up! God (blessed and exalted is He) gave me this unusual gift and then used it to give me information about Islam and the Qur'an.

The more I read the Qur'an, the more I saw that the message of the Qur'an was the same message I had learned in Sunday School. All truth is God's truth, so truths cannot be in conflict with one another. The truths of the Tanakh (which is the Jewish Bible), the New Testament, and the Qur'an are all one truth —God's truth.

I have always believed that all religions of light have consonant values of honesty, integrity, charity, compassion, generosity, justice, and fairness. We can find these values in the Abrahamic religions, in the teachings of Buddha, in the ancient traditions of the Native Amer-Indians, and in any other religion that encourages truth and understanding. When we can focus on the things that make our religions alike and appreciate and respect the things that make our religions unique, we can begin to realize the dream of global peace.

Nothing is created, however, without God (blessed and exalted is He), so the most important thing for people to do is to individually submit their whole selves to God and build personal relationships with Him. Kabalism, the mystic teachings of Judaism, says that God is a verb. God is not a passive verb or a state-of-being verb, however. He is an action verb! When a person submits his or her whole self to God, God swings into action. He works to change all that is ugly in that person's life and to create a life that is pure and holy.

It was a struggle to come to a new understanding of the Bible, but, after investigating the origins of Church doctrine, I no longer felt comfortable with some of the Christian views. I began learning about Jewish interpretations of the "Old Testament" and about Islamic perspectives. Congruent with unlearning and relearning the Bible, I began accepting the message of Islam, but I have never discarded the Bible. I still love the verses that I memorized as a child, that inspired me during dark hours, and that guided me throughout my life. God has not given me a conviction to reject the Bible, but rather to come to new understandings as I seek His guidance on a higher plane.

As I studied the Qur'an and Islamic philosophy, I gained, not only respect, but also genuine love for the religion. I did not have much trouble saying the name *Allah*, but referring positively to Muhammed (peace upon him) was awkward. I had always heard that he was "a false prophet, a violent man of the sword, and a madman whose delusions made him think that God spoke to him." Unlearning the false Muhammed described by the Church and putting faith in the true Prophet of Allah was a slow process.

After months of angels' shooting basketball with my brain, I was ready for the message God wanted me to take to Tunisia. Finally, God revealed to me, in my dreams, the message He wanted delivered. It was the simple message of Jesus' Gospel: "I tell you this truth: no one can see the Kingdom of God unless he is born again. I tell you the truth: no one can enter the Kingdom of God unless he is born of water and of the Spirit" (John 3: 3, 5). ["Born of water" refers to the physical birth. If you hear a pregnant woman say, "My water just broke," you may need to become an action verb yourself!]

Leapin' lizards! God had used my brain for play-dough, kicked me out of bed at two a.m. to jot down notes, and sent Jonah's whale to chase me around the bedposts just for that? Everybody knows you have to submit your whole life to God, be forgiven of your sins, and become renewed by His saving grace. Right? Well, apparently not everybody understands that message. I later met a Tunisian man who told me, "Tunisians like God; they just don't pay much attention to Him. They are Muslims because their heritage is Islam, but most of them have not experienced Islam as a personal and spiritual way of life."

I thought God would choose someone else to take the message after I had prepared it, but the Christian organizations I contacted did not believe in my dreams, and they tried to discourage me. When God inspired me to make the journey myself, I thought God must be joking. I was just getting old enough to act like I had a little sense, and now it seemed that God wanted me to go off half-cocked again. I reminded God that I couldn't speak the language, I didn't have money for the trip, and, for crying out loud, I was just a little hillbilly! God wouldn't let me get back to my normal nightmares of monsters from outer space, demented robots in the attic, and mutant bugs taking over the world. I just kept dreaming that Islamic stuff and wrestling with angels.

To top it all off, one of my customers offered to pay for most of the trip. Doggone him! He called and asked, "Linda, have you ever thought of going to France to see the Louvre and Orsay museums?"

I said, "I'd like to do that, but I'm not able to able to afford it."

He said, "Well, go ahead and make plans for this spring, and I will pay for you and Tom to travel and spend a week in Paris." Tunisia is just a few rock-skips from France, so I didn't have much of an excuse to get out of going to Tunisia.

Finally, in May 1999, Tom, Tana, and I took off for the other side of the world. We made no arrangements; we had no contacts, no reservations, no travel guide, no plan, no itinerary, nothing —not even any sense.

After landing in Tunis, we must have looked desperate as we spun around wondering, 'Now what?' A gentleman at the airport offered to help us. Tom asked, "Do you speak English?"

He answered in Arabic, "La, ana kalimArabeewaFaransawee, illa mush Engileezee."

I had tried to learn a little conversational Arabic before the trip. Even though the part of my brain that learns languages had apparently shriveled, I did understand him. I told Tom, "Faransawee, Tom! Faransawee! Hoowa-kalimFaransawee."

Tom, who did not know a word of Arabic, ignored me. The Tunisian looked at me as if I were the wildest thing he'd ever seen. I finally realized I was speaking Arabic to Tom. I started laughing, and the Tunisian laughed too. I then explained to Tom in English that the man spoke French. Tom speaks a little French, so eventually we were escorted to a hotel in Tunis.

The next morning we took the train to Carthage. People on the train, noticing that we had no sense, helped us get off at the right stop. But then, there we were with no idea of where we were going or what we were doing, so we just started walking. The first person we saw was a fisherman. Prior to our trip, I had gotten the message translated to Arabic, and I had made it into greeting cards. We shared with the fisherman the message that you must be born again, which quoted the Qur'an as well as the Gospel. He was glad and stopped what he was doing to spend the entire day with us.

He took us to the famous ruins, but we did not realize we were supposed to buy tickets. We were walking around, taking photographs, when the museum director came running out of his office, waving his arms, and shouting something in Arabic. I tried to explain in pieces of hillbilly Arabic that we didn't have any sense. When he realized that we must be crazy Americans, he was so excited that he would not accept payment for the tickets. He begged us to come with him, and he showed us many relics salvaged from the Carthage ruins. He had us climb with him straight down into a deep, dark tunnel to show us where the archaeologists were currently digging. He had only the remnant of a candle to light the way. The candle was so short that it looked like the flame was coming from his fingernail, but it didn't faze him at all.

Before we left the ruins, I shared the message with the museum director.

He became so overjoyed that he was giggling.

We also visited a beautiful, historic cathedral. Underneath it, archaeologists had been tunneling to find ruins of ancient, Grecian culture. It was quite awesome and even surreal.

The fisherman took us to his aunt's house where we were greeted with kisses and wishes of peace. None of the family spoke English, so we mostly just smiled at each other. On our departure, the family presented each of us a gift from their modest possessions.

Because of all our baggage, we decided it would be easier to rent a car instead of trying to lug everything around on the trains. We got a car the next morning and began driving. The country's landscapes were like Bible story illustrations, and everywhere we went people smiled, stared, and giggled. After school, children led their donkeys, burdened with huge water containers, miles down dusty roads to the nearest waterholes for the next day's supply. The children all seemed happy despite what Americans would consider destitute poverty.

We stopped to visit the ancient, Roman ruins of Dougga, which cover many acres and are amazingly well preserved. Intricate designs of colorful tiled floors lay in the dust as if reminiscing over the magnificence of their day. We could almost hear their secret stories echoing among the columns so bravely standing like soldiers against the enemy of time.

We arrived in the city of Kairouan and were instantly famous. We were escorted to a hotel, and, as we ate supper at the hotel's restaurant, people waited for us outside. We were quite tired, but we didn't want to disappoint them, so we went wherever they took us. Almost everywhere we went, we were given hot, mint tea served in shot glasses. There was always a platter of dates, raisin-filled pastries, and confections rolled in crushed nuts. Sometimes we were served glasses of delicious, creamy, strawberry juice.

Soon we were being escorted through the dark, narrow, city streets. The group of Muslim men with us grew in number. They chattered excitedly as they led us deeper into the maze within the city's fort-like walls of huge, baked-mud blocks. The streets often turned into tunnels, and we had no idea where we were. When the men wanted us to crawl through a black hole in the wall, I began to worry about their intentions. Were they going to shrink Tom's head and sell Tana into belly-dancing slavery? Would I have to spend the rest of my life in a strange country, hunkering with a tin cup and a constant dribble of hillbilly adventures?

One of the men, noticing my hesitation, said, "It's okay; it's okay." He grabbed my arm and pulled me into the blackness. I followed the sound of his footsteps until I saw the rectangle of light for which we were heading. We walked into the light and were suddenly in someone's living room. An old man the color and texture of a raisin sat cross-legged on the floor as he burned incense and recited Qur'an. His shriveled wife lay on a mat on the floor and was content to listen. She had broken her leg and wanted me to bless her. I knelt on the floor beside her, held her hands, and stumbled through bits and pieces of almost all the hillbilly Arabic I knew: "Alhamdul'Allah. Asalam alaykum. RamatAllah." She responded with a toothless grin, and we left a few dinars to help with her medical bills.

One of the men we met was introduced as "the imam". I was immediately disappointed and confused. In my dreams, I had seen the face of the imam to which I was to present the message, but this imam did not look anything like the man in my dreams. When I told him that I had come to see him with a message from God, he looked as if he were about to go into shock. He did not speak English, but as one of the other men explained my story in Arabic, the imam's eyes filled with tears, and he was so overcome that he couldn't speak.

In order for Tunisians to believe my story, God had inspired a painting, which I had framed and brought for Tunisia. The painting was in the hotel room, so I explained that I needed to bring it to the imam the next day. The other men assured me that they would take me to the imam if I would meet them at the Great Okba Mosque in the morning.

When we arrived at the mosque, a young man met us, and took us on another long trek through the city streets. We were suddenly in a home where we were seated in front of a small table spread with pastries, plums, and coffee. Two young men questioned us about why we were there, and they discussed it between themselves in Arabic. Finally, they went to get the imam.

When the imam arrived, it was a different man from the one I had met the night before. I didn't understand. Across from me, he sat erect and stared suspiciously. I thought he seemed like a king who only needed to direct his thumb down, and I would lose my head. He was older and his features less remarkable than in my dreams, but the depth, wisdom, and mystery of his penetrating eyes were unmistakably the same as that of the man with whom I had spoken in my dreams.

He understood no English, but his son (one of the two who questioned us) interpreted. "We are Christians from the United States, and I came with a message from God," I awkwardly explained.

He was not impressed. "Christians cause us nothing but trouble!" he scoffed.

I had a copy of the Qur'an, and I pointed to a portion, which he read aloud in Arabic. It said, "...Those who love Muslims most will be found among those who say, 'We are Christians,' because among these are scholars and devout parishioners,[2] and they are not arrogant" (Surah 5: 82).

"We are not the arrogant ones," I told him.

Finally, the imam nodded, and I continued. I explained that God (blessed!) had given me dreams and revealed a message from Jesus that I should take to Tunisia. The imam maintained his solemn expression. I felt so inadequate, and his unwavering stare made me think that I might be as crazy as everybody said I was.

Not being very successful at words, I finally decided to show him the painting. I unveiled it, and the imam's face changed. It suddenly glowed to match the sunny yellow tunic he wore. A gentle smile erased the intense stare.

"Tihibhada?" I asked. ("Do you like it?")

He answered simply by placing his hand over his heart.

I explained the painting, which shows the Great Okba Mosque. God is symbolized as a lamp, and out of the light is a shooting star. The star symbolizes a repentant person who has received New Life by the power of God's Spirit. The tail of the star is made of three bands of color, which represent mind, body, and soul. I gave the imam the Arabic translation of the message, and he read every word aloud.

> God is symbolized as brilliant light from a lamp of luminous oil (Al Noor 24: 25). Like a new star bursting into existence, a lost soul can be ignited and changed by God's eternal power. In the Gospel, Jesus (peace!) invited sinners to experience New Life: You must be born again —not physically, but by the Spirit of God.
>
> "...Allah will change the evil of such persons into good..." (Al Furqan 25: 70). The soul is purified and colored by the Spirit of God filling the believer like sweet incense. To experience a spiritual transformation is to receive the full measure of God's amazing grace and to know His magnificent power to instill peace, joy, and love.
>
> Muhammed (peace!) taught, "To go out in the morning in the

way of Allah and to go out at dusk in the way of Allah is better than the whole world and all it contains." Such a close walk with God requires that each believer submit the whole self —mind, body, and soul— and our lives should reveal what is righteous and holy.

As People of the Light in a dark world, we must peacefully and gently proclaim, "...He will provide a Light so you may walk on the Straight Way, and He will forgive you of your sins..." (Al Hadeed 57: 28)

The greeting within the card said, "May God's grace embrace you, so that your soul is daily refreshed. Most assuredly God loves you!"

The imam said something in Arabic to his son, and then left. The son explained that his father, Imam Abdel Karim, wanted me to present the message to the imam. Huh? I thought I just did. Now, they were telling me to see someone else, and he would be the imam. I was so confused.

The imam returned with two boxes of fresh, date pastries he had just bought as a gift for us. He extended his hand to say goodbye before he left for a meeting in Tunis. I never saw him again, but I loved him because I could see that he was truly a good and holy man.

We were constantly being approached by people wanting to make money off us. Several people kept inviting us, "Come to the Berber Festival! You're just in time; it's the last day." We finally figured out that there is a Berber Festival whenever a tourist can be abducted and held down long enough to look at every carpet in town.

Several city dwellers wanted to take us to interpreters and others who could help us spread the message. Looking back, I think perhaps they were sincere, but at the time, we thought they were just trying to find ways to get our money. We couldn't go anywhere without people ganging around us. We went to take pictures of the mosque, but we could not even get out of the car because of the crowd that quickly gathered. The scene caught the attention of the police, and we thought we would be arrested —especially when we drove off with people hanging on the car handles and bumper.

We went to the street market, but it was just as bad. I recognized the market from a dream I had before leaving home. In the dream, I was trying to get away from a man wanting to sell me a snake while I was sitting on a bench under trees on a sidewalk. In reality, we bought pastries, and we did sit on a bench under trees on a sidewalk. Instead of a man with a snake, however, there was a man with a shoeshine kit. He squatted down at my feet, made faces and weird noises at my dirty shoes, and started to clean them. I was annoyed because of the way he acted, and I just wanted to eat my pastry in peace. I told him I didn't want him to polish my shoes. He grabbed my ankle and put my foot on his shoeshine box. I set it back off. He yanked it back up. I yanked it back down. I kept saying, "La, shukran, la" ("No, thank you, no"). Tom also told him in French that I did not want the shoeshine. The man kept grabbing my ankle, and I kept yanking my foot away until I finally got up and left with my half-eaten pastry. The man called us, in English, "Stupid Americans!"

A shoeshine was two dinars, and somehow the man had managed to semi-clean one shoe during the battle over my foot. He kept following us, wanting a dinar for the one shoe. I suppose I should have just given him the money, but he was very rude and harassing. He upset us so much that we finally just headed back to our hotel room.

Men would turn all the way around to look at Tana, a pretty, teenage girl with beautiful, blue eyes. Tom and I had to keep her close between us, because young men were always coming up to touch her face and hair and to say, "I love you." One young man made a beeline toward her, saying, "Buenos dias, amiga." We were offered ten thousand camels for her, but we did not have a way to get them home. She said, "Well, at least now I know how much I'm worth."

We were ignorant about Middle Eastern culture and Islamic manners. Tana wanted to go for a swim at the hotel's patio pool. We did not know there would be a problem with her modest, one-piece, skirted swimsuit. As soon as she took off her robe and jumped into the pool, all the local men within "swimsuit" hearing distance brought chairs and set them up around the pool for the show. It was embarrassing for Tana, and Tom became angry. He went to the hotel manager who called security to get rid of Tana's audience.

Well, that did it! I decided that those people really did not care about the message. I thought they only wanted whatever they could get out of us, and that they were playing some kind of weird game. We couldn't understand why, after meeting "the imam," we had been led on a long, mysterious trek to see another person called "the imam," and then had been told there was still someone else who was "the imam."

I told Tom, "Tomorrow morning let's just leave Kairouan and try to enjoy the rest of our trip as a vacation, because I don't understand what's going on here."

Immediately after he had agreed, three people entered the pool area. If it had not been for the ruckus over Tana's swimsuit, the hotel manager would not have known where we were when the visitors asked for us. I recognized the imam's son and the son's friend, and there was a young woman with them. She was the son's sister.

Just before leaving on the trip, I had a vision of a yellow rose on desert sand. I wasn't sure what it meant, but I recalled that the Bible mentions a desert rose in reference to a woman. When I saw the young woman, I realized that she was my yellow rose and a sign to reassure me of God's plan.

Our three visitors explained that they were in the mosque for afternoon prayers when they each individually received inspiration to come to the hotel and tell us not to leave. They assured us that they would meet us at the mosque that evening and we would finally meet the Grand Imam Supreme as the Grand Imam had said to do. We finally began to understand that there are many imams with different positions of leadership. (Did I mention we didn't have any sense?) I had not dreamed about the Grand Imam Supreme; he was a surprise. We were later told that his position was one of only six in the world at that time. His name was Abderehmen Kalif.

That evening we were escorted to the mosque. We were told that the imam would see me after the opening prayer. Until then I had thought we were going just to meet the imam; I didn't realize we were going to a service. Hundreds of people began arriving by foot, motor scooters, bicycles, and donkeys. Some came from nearby homes in the city, others came from the distant hills and deserts, and many had traveled most of the hot, dusty day to come to the service.

Surrounded by massive walls, the main arena of the mosque was an outside court in which the floors were laid with white marble. Women congregated near the back and off to one side under huge pillars supporting the porch encircling the open court. The men jammed together up front. There were stacks of woven-reed, prayer rugs under the porch, and, while everyone's shoes joined the mounting pile, someone brought rugs for Tana and me.

Before the prayers, Imam Kalif, who spoke no English, sat on the floor with Tom and, through an interpreter, asked about our beliefs. The wise imam had an aura of majesty tempered with sincere humbleness and gentleness. Tom told him about our devotion to God, our trust in Jesus, our belief in the Bible, and our new acceptance of the Qur'an. When Tom shared some beautiful Bible verses from memory, the imam was visibly pleased. Afterward, the imam directed the interpreter to me. The interpreter sat with me on the prayer rug as I told him about the dreams, the painting, and the message.

During the service, everyone knelt on his or her prayer rug. It's a little like hunkering with God (blessed!), and everyone prostrated just like the Bible described Abraham and Jesus doing. After many prayers and praises, I was told that the imam would see me after the lessons. People separated into small groups, like Sunday School, and studied the Qur'an. During that time, the imam was available for private counseling. Men, women, and children came to him with their problems, and he advised, prayed with, and blessed them.

After about an hour of lessons, I was told the imam would see me after the preaching. We sat attentively even though everything was in Arabic, and no one interpreted for us. After preaching came responsive readings from the Qur'an. Everyone, including small children, recited with exuberance in perfect synchronization, pronouncing every syllable distinctly and loudly. A symphony of voices combined into one huge spiral of praise rising into the night. I looked into the star-specked sky and expected it to peel away to reveal angels ushering the spiral into Heaven. It was truly magnificent.

As my heart pounded with the rhythm of the Qur'an, I finally took time to gaze at the tower guarding the mosque. It was the tower from my painting, and the crescent moon nestled behind it just as it did in my art. I was sure there must have been guardian angels standing on its corners.

After nearly four hours of congregational activities, I was told that the imam would see me after another praise and worship service. I was happy to enjoy this unique experience before being able to see the imam privately after everybody had left. I would give him the message and the painting, I would leave, and he would present the message at his own discretion. At least, that's how I had it figured.

The praises began with a slow, steady, low, "Alhamdul'Allah, alhamdul'Allah, alhamdul'Allah." The repeated phrase grew faster and louder until the walls resounded with praises of their own. The very sound of *Alhamdul' Allah* became a world around us and within us. We were one with each other and with God. Every phrase was chanted with the same enthusiasm, beginning low and growing strong. And God was there!

Finally, I was told it was time to…. Speak to the imam? Well, yes. And to the nearly one thousand Muslims waiting for me to present the message. What? Hold the camels, Ahab! I was terrified.

"First," a young lady said, "you must say shahada."

I had already come to believe that the Qur'an was truly revealed by God and that God's messenger was Prophet Muhammed (peace and blessings upon him). I did not feel that accepting Islam would negate my belief in Jesus (peace upon him, and may he bring peace). I had already become a Muslim at heart, so, when I was given this beautiful and excellent opportunity to say my shahada, in Arabic, in front of a thousand Muslims, in a foreign country, in one of the greatest mosques in the world, of course I said, "Huh-uh! No way, José! I ain't gittin' up in front of all those people!" I wrapped my arms around one of those marble pillars and hung on, crying, "Mama!" The women had to peel me off that pillar and drag me to the front.

I heard a familiar voice. Tom was already saying his shahada! I thought, 'I reckon they wrestled him down too!'

After the women made me presentable ("You have to look like us," they said), I found myself wrapped in white and standing beside the Grand Imam Supreme with hundreds of people staring at my mouth, which was gaping open. I looked at the imam, and he stared into my mouth as if he were pondering whether he should reach in and pull out the words. I looked back across the audience. The crowd stared at me in such awestruck silence that I thought there must have been lobsters crawling out of my ears.

Finally, I heard words slowly tumbling from my mouth. "La illahilla Allah; Muhammed rasul Allah," I said in hillbilly Arabic. After I got it all out, everyone, including the imam, sighed a long-held breath of relief.

Now everyone was staring at me again. I stood there, too dazed to think about what I was supposed to do. Finally, one of the lobsters whispered, "Show them the painting, stupid." Oh, yeah.

I lifted the veil from the painting, and the crowd responded with a collective, "Ahhhhh."

I handed the imam the translated message, and he read it aloud as I stood beside him. Many people cried and praised God.

The imam took my hand and slowly said, "God bless you," in perfect English. He had memorized the words after asking Tom what he should say after I delivered the message.

I must have blacked out because the next thing I remember is being back on the prayer rug for dismissal. Later, people gathered around us to both thank us and congratulate us.

We were given a tour of the entire mosque. We entered the sacred hall of prayer and stood among gleaming columns of pink and black marble. The floor was covered with one hundred sixty-two squares, each bearing a different geometric motif. The imam's pulpit was an impressive and intricate structure sculpted out of wood from Mesopotamia. Above us hung a massive chandelier originally lit by olive oil, but now updated to hold tiny, electric bulbs. The mosque itself was truly a wonder of art. I imagine that an immediate sense of purity and holiness seizes the soul of every believer who enters.

Tom asked about the niche. He had read that every mosque has a niche in the wall for the Ramadan lamp. He was told that this was the only mosque in the world without a niche. Tom asked where the lamp is placed and was told, "On top of the wall, just like in the painting." Tom told our escorts that I knew nothing about the wall or the Ramadan lamp when I painted the picture. Everyone was amazed, and someone said, "That's another part of the miracle you brought us."

The Great Okba Mosque was begun in 670 CE and built around a well. During the services, a bucket drawn from the well was passed around with an ancient clay cup. Everyone used this same cup to quench his or her thirst during the evening. Before we left, we were presented the cup, which now has a special place in our living room.

Even though it was quite late after the services, people were so excited about the message that they wanted us to visit their relatives who were not able to attend the presentation. Before returning to our hotel room, we promised to return the next day for more visits.

Early the next morning, we were greeted with hugs and kisses, and tables spread with pastries, fruits, yogurt, and Arabian coffee. The people were very generous and kept giving us things —fans, eyeliner, prayer beads, baskets, all sorts of things. They even took the rings off their own fingers to give us. It's a poor country, and they have so little that we did not want to take their things, but we were afraid of offending them if we did not accept the gifts.

The only thing we had to give in return was prints of the painting, and everyone was overjoyed to have an art print and copy of the message. The worst feeling came when I ran out of prints and had to see the disappointment on people's faces when they learned that I didn't have any for them.

Even though people invited us to stay longer and offered their homes to us, we had a plane to catch, so we finally had to say goodbye. We drove along the coast of the Mediterranean Sea and stayed overnight in Hammamet. There were many opportunities to share the message. After apparently running out of the art cards, I was surprised to discover another batch in my suitcase, so I was able to continue my ministry throughout the entire trip. No one rejected the message, but everyone who heard my story praised God (blessed!). We know that God planned our every move; otherwise, we would never have been successful. Nothing we did was of our own power, but the power of God moving in front of us just as He had promised through the vision of dove's wings when I was a teenager.

We made our way back to Tunis, and, just before departing Tunisia, I decided to get my shoes cleaned. The soil was a fine, powdery, gray dust. My black, suede-like shoes were covered with it. I propped my foot up on one of the shoeshine stands that lined the streets of Tunis, and the shine man went to work. First, he custom mixed the polish to match my shoes. Since my shoes were solid black, that should not have been difficult. When he was finished, however, my shoes perfectly matched the gray Tunisian dirt. I paid him the two dinars and went away laughing. Those shoes were never black again.

To me, the most incredible part of this story was that people in Tunisia accepted the simple message I gave and believed that it really came from God. Nobody threw tomatoes at me or called me a "hick".

When Christians ask me why I gave up Jesus for Muhammed, I tell them I didn't give up anything. Now I have both. Jesus (peace upon him) is still important to me as a spiritual guide, friend, and brother, and I am encouraged and influenced by the life of Muhammed (peace and blessings upon him). I did not have to stop being a Christian in order to become a Muslim. I simply added layers of light to the light I already had. In other words, I got promoted!

Eternal Lover of Your Children,
Bring us into Your life,
Make us sharers in Your love and transmitters of it.
Help us to become serene and patient
In the midst of our frustrations,
But at the same time, make us heroic adventurers,
Brave, gentle, tender, but without fear
And with radiant faces.
[Rufus Jones (1863-1948), Quaker minister]

May God's grace embrace you so that your soul is daily refreshed. Most assuredly, God loves you!

PART 2
Ninety-Nine Parables

1. NEW LIFE

What is of you must perish; what is of Allah will endure.
On those who patiently persevere,
We will certainly grant their reward
in response to the best of their deeds.
To any man or woman who performs righteously and has faith,
We will give New Life —a life that is good and pure.
On such people, We will grant their reward
in response to the best of their deeds.
(Surah 16: 96-97)

One day near the end of summer, I found a fat, lime-green caterpillar decorated with shiny, gold spots. It was so splendid that I put it in a little box to keep till Dusty came home from school. As a budding photographer, he would want to take a picture of it. By the time he got home, however, the caterpillar had spun itself into a cocoon inside the box. I kept the chrysalis (the pupa and cocoon) inside my greenhouse for safekeeping until the butterfly could make its great escape.

One could say that a chrysalis is just full of itself. The pupating life within the cocoon is dependent upon the earth's resources, but it is not an active participant in the world around it. The chrysalis is a world locked within itself. Until the pupa transforms into a new life form, it will not grace the world with its beauty, and it will not serve its purpose in pollinating flowers during its interaction with the natural environment. After emerging from the pupa, the butterfly is like an entirely different creature. It's as if an old house was taken apart, and a new house was built from the old materials.

In the same way, a person can be spiritually transformed and may emerge as a new creation of God. The person who has not committed his or her life fully to God has not begun to reach his or her potential as a true child of God. Before a person's spiritual wings can take flight, the chrysalis must vanish, and the beauty of God must burst forth in all its wonderful array.

The difference between the insect and the person is that the insect's development is involuntary while the person has a choice. People often choose to clip their wings and remain in a dormant, pupating state. They never realize how fulfilling life could be if they escaped the cocoons of their self-centered motives and entered the service of God.

A baby is born pure and innocent, with a soul already dedicated to God, but the Evil Whisperer (Satan) gets busy right away. As needs and wants of the physical world become more important to the physical self, the child begins to disassociate from the spiritual realm from which he or she came. The lure of the world becomes stronger as the spiritual awareness becomes more distant. It becomes necessary for a person to reconnect with the spiritual realm.

Who has not given into temptation at some time or another? Who does not face a moment in which he or she must make a firm decision whether to follow the Straight Way? Even a person raised in a religious family must, at some point in life, make his or her own personal commitment. At that moment of affirmation, a person is changed and receives New Life. He or she may be a sinner mired in the muck of a struggling world, or he or she may be a good person who is already following God's commandments. Becoming wholly dedicated to God is an emergent process whereby the believer strives to regain the perfection with which he or she was born. It is, as the Scripture says, the disappearance of everything that is you so that you can become filled with everything that is God (blessed and exalted is He).

New Testament writers explained it this way: "Do not conform to the standards of this world, but let God transform your spiritual being, and then you will be able to know God's will" (Romans 12: 2). "Your spirit and thoughts must be made completely new, and you must acknowledge your new self which is created to reflect the character of God and reveal a life that is righteous and holy" (Ephesians 4: 23-24).

When a person receives New Life from God, a life that is good and pure, he or she does not simply live by God's Word; rather, God's Word lives in him or her. God not only lives within the believer's heart, but the believer lives within the heart of God (blessed!).

Jesus said, "I tell you this truth: No one can see the Kingdom of God unless he [or she] is born again. I tell you the truth: No one can enter the Kingdom of God unless he [or she] is born of water [the physical birth] and of the Spirit [of God]" (John 3: 3, 5).

By the physical birth, each soul is given the opportunity to succeed in this world of struggle. Eventually, he or she must experience a new beginning by reconnecting with the innocent child within him- or herself. A person must ask the infant soul to remind him or her of that pre-existence within God's numinous reality.

If you have not yet been born again by submitting your whole self to God (blessed!), may today bring your moment of decision in which you receive New Life!

> Let only that little be left of me
> Whereby I may name You my all.
> Let only that little be left of my will
> Whereby I may feel You on every side,
> And come to You in everything,
> And offer to You my love every moment.
> Let only that little be left of me
> Whereby I may never hide You.
> Let only that little of my fetters be left
> Whereby I am bound with Your will,
> And Your purpose is carried out in my life,
> And that is the fetter of Your love.
> [Rabindranath Tagore (1861-1941), Bengali mystic]

2. THE GREATEST LOVE STORY

> Consider the glorious morning light.
> Consider the still of the night.
> Your Lord has not forsaken you, and He is not displeased.
> Truly, the hereafter will be better for you than the present.
> Soon your Lord will give that which will please you.
> Did He not find you as an orphan and give you shelter?
> He found you wandering, and He provided guidance.
> He found you destitute, and He made you independent.
> Therefore, do not treat the orphans harshly.

> Do not turn away the beggar.
> Proclaim the blessings of your Lord.
> *(Surah 93)*

When my favorite aunt realized that cancer would soon win the battle she had been fighting for years, she gave me her necklace, a delicate chain from which dangled a sparkling, handsomely cut topaz set in gold. Her husband had given it to her on their first anniversary, and it became as special to me as it had been to her. Aunt Tootsie died soon afterward when I was in my teens.

A few years after I was married, our house was burglarized. Among the sentimental treasures stolen was the topaz necklace.

I have the kindest husband in the world, and Tom took it upon himself to gradually replace some of my stolen jewelry. At a rock and mineral show, Tom discovered a flawless, intensely blue topaz. He purchased it and had it cut in the same pear shape as Aunt Tootsie's had been. After the stone was polished to perfection, Tom took the gold, college ring from his finger and had it melted to make the setting for the stone. It was an excellent reproduction, and the extra love that went into it made it even more special than the original.

At an arts and crafts festival, a jewelry-maker complimented me on my necklace, and I told him the history. His eyes pooled with tears, and he remarked, "That's the most beautiful love story I've ever heard."

There is an even better love story in the Qur'an. Surah 93 offers hope for all those whose hearts have been burglarized and whose treasures seem lost to the bandits of a dark world. Among us are many enemies who seek to rob us of our dreams and bribe us into clipping our wings in order to trudge along in the mire of an evil society.

Abdulla Yusuf Ali wrote that Surah 93 "seems to have been revealed in a dark period in the outer life of the holy Prophet, when a man of less resolute will might have been discouraged. But the Prophet is told to hold the present of less account than the glorious Hereafter which awaited him like the glorious morning after a night of stillness and gloom."[3]

Yusuf Ali also describes the Surah as pertaining to each person wandering in a life of sin before being adopted by our Guardian Lord: "Our holy Prophet was himself an orphan ... [but] each one of us is an orphan in some sense or another, and yet someone's love and shelter come to us by the grace of God. .... Spiritually we all belong to one of these three classes in one sense or another: orphans, (beggars), and victims of poverty. We all receive God's grace and guidance in some degree or other. We all owe it as a duty to (others) to be kind and helpful to those less endowed in any respect than ourselves."[4]

We are all created by God, and thus He becomes metaphorically a Father/Mother/Guardian/Creator, but in the spiritual sense, we are not all God's children. Although each person is born a child of God –a perfect creation of the Perfect Creator— to remain so is a matter of personal choice. Jesus explained that anyone not submitting to God becomes a child of the devil, the father of lies (John 8: 42-47). Every sin a person commits is a lie about God (blessed!), because each person was created to reflect the goodness of his or her Creator.

Jesus taught that all believers have the right to be called children of God –not children reproduced physically but created spiritually. He emphasized that "God is spirit, and He must be worshiped in spirit and in truth" (John 1: 11-13; 4: 24).

When a person submits his or her whole self to God, not only is that person forgiven, but also God adopts that person into the family of believers. Through a spiritual metamorphosis, a person ceases being an orphan without hope to being an adopted child with wings sailing upon the very breath of God.

As an adopted child, you will find your true purpose in the service of the One True God as you help others break away from the cocoons keeping them from spreading their wings. A child of God is one of many lights helping others to find the Straight Way. Jesus said, "You are like light for the whole world. ...(Y)our light must shine before people, so that they will see the good things you do and praise your Father in Heaven" (Matthew 5: 14, 16).

> O Allah, enlighten my heart, my eyes, and my ears.
> May light be on my right and on my left.
> May light be above me and below me, before me and behind me.
> O Allah, I turn myself to You; I resign myself to You.
> I entrust myself to You, I submit myself to You.
> I hope for Your mercy, and I fear Your wrath.
> No refuge and no peace exists except with You.
> *[Prophet Muhammed (peace and blessings upon him)]*

3. BUGS AND ALL

Whoever submits his/her whole self to Allah
and lives righteously has secured the most trustworthy grasp.
With Allah is the termination of all accounts.
(Surah 31: 22)

My brother described his family's camping trip during which everyone had to pick out the bugs landing in the beanie-wienies. "I ate my bugs," added my nephew.

The buggy beanies were a fair simile of how God accepts a new believer. When a person submits his or her whole self, bugs and all are lifted up to God to be transformed by His amazing grace. The sinner doesn't have to pick out the bugs or fix anything first. He or she begins a spiritual journey in which God fixes things according to His timing.

When you submit your whole self to God, give Him your best china and silverware, but give Him your dirty dishes too. Let Him pick out the bugs, wash your dishes, and fill them with fruits that never rot and never lose their flavor. Whether you just have a few bad habits or are involved in severely decadent behavior, trust in God completely, and He will raise you from a spiritual infant with a messy bib to a beautiful, spiritual giant whose face radiates the glory of God's eternal light.

Some people experience sudden changes when they submit to God (blessed and exalted is He!). That's the way it was for my daddy. Although course and abrasive in many ways, Daddy was a hard-working, family man who kept the lid on a stash of love and sensitivity in an unmarked mental box. When he was drunk, however, he transformed into a monstrous, evil creature seething with anger and rage. A painful memory for me is the image of Mama as a crying and helpless lump curled, bloody and beaten, on the floor. Daddy finally changed, but he did not have to stop drinking *before* coming to God (blessed!). When Daddy made the decision to live a righteous life, by God's grace, he immediately stopped drinking. Our home life improved tremendously, although Daddy still had a problem with his temper and stubbornness. His journey to spiritual perfection was a long, difficult struggle, but God accepted him just as he was and helped him find the way. Daddy stumbled and fell many times, but God (blessed!) always picked him up and never expected a bug-free apartment in Daddy's whole-self housing development.

Other people may not have sudden-change experiences, but the changes may come gradually. Some people may even have to get help for problems that separate them from God's grace. Daddy never had to go to Alcoholics Anonymous, for example, but, for another person, such support and guidance may be part of God's plan in that person's spiritual journey. Whatever the road has to offer, you can be sure that old experiences will seem new, and new experiences will seem providential as all the bugs are worked out of your spiritual senses.

> Take, O God, all that I am
> And make it holy and pleasing in Your sight.
> Grant me patience as I struggle
> Through the constant process of refinement.
> Teach my soul to see, hear, touch, taste, feel, laugh, and love
> In amazing ways as I experience
> New adventures in my daily walk with You.

4. THE WORD IS BUGGED

> Truly, Allah does not mind using parables about anything.
> It doesn't matter if the parable is about a gnat or something bigger.
> Believers know that it is the truth from their Lord.
> Unbelievers say, "What does Allah mean by this story?"
> By it, He causes many to stray, and He guides many.
> He does not cause anyone to stray except those who are mean.
> *(Surah 2: 26)*

When I notice egg sacs of praying mantises in the woods, I try to ensure their safety, and, on occasion, I've watched them hatch. One day I saw a praying mantis laying eggs. Our family thought it was exciting. Dusty took photographs, and Tana called a friend over "to see something really cool."

When the friend, Seth Pool, arrived and saw that all the excitement was over an insect, he was aggravated. "You called me all the way over here just to look at a stupid bug?"

The fascination with one of God's tiny wonders was unfathomable to Seth Pool, but, to us, Seth Pool looked like the idiot. The insect was spoken into being, just like the more majestic creatures. We all share the life-giving force of God's Word.

Both the Bible and the Qur'an use metaphors, similes, and parables to express God's Word, but only those who seek truth will be led to understand their meanings. One might say that the Word is *bugged* in order to catch those without sincerity in their hearts and who do not seek true guidance and wisdom.

When Jesus (peace upon him) was asked why he spoke in parables, he explained, "Knowledge about the secrets of the Kingdom of Heaven has been given to you [believers], but not to them. Whoever has [understanding] will be given more so that he will have abundance, but whoever has nothing will lose even the little bit that he has. The reason I use parables is because they look without seeing, and they hear without listening. …. Their minds are dull, and they have plugged their ears and closed their eyes; otherwise, they would see with eyes [spiritual insights], hear with ears [spiritual understanding], and use the wisdom of their minds, and they would repent, and I would heal them [with the truth of the Gospel]" (Matthew 13: 11-15).

In the Jewish Bible, David (peace upon him) is quoted, "The Lord has spoken one thing; I have heard two" [Psalms 62: 12 (62: 11, Christian Bible)]. A parable has the obvious, literal meaning, but there is also the deeper, spiritual meaning that many people miss. A believer must spend time in communication with his or her Lord to receive the guidance needed to find the gossamer wings of God's golden bugs. If you find a gnat in the Word today, fly with it on the wind of God's breath.

> I want to ride a huge blue wave to Your Presence, Lord.
> A stiff blue wave like a giant meringue that blasts through walls.
> I want to arrive on the breath of a tree in heavenly regions.
> The click of a twig as it falls to the ground in a breeze, Lord,
> Flung to the ground with leaves, flat as the earth, Lord,
> Flashing like glass, fast as a flash of light,
> First flight of bee to Your fragrant flower, Lord,

In first morning light.
[Adapted from selected verses from
"Plea" by Daniel Abdul-HayyMoore (USA)][5]

5. FAITH WITHOUT BAKING POWDER FALLS FLAT

Those who have faith and do good deeds are going to Paradise.
They will live there forever.
(Surah 2: 82)

    I like to bake from scratch, but, with time as a constant joker, I usually have to resort to store-bought cake mixes. I pulled many flat cakes from the oven before I realized I needed to add fresh baking powder. A cake mix may have sat on the store shelf for longer than I sat on my butt while writing these stories. No matter how much faith I have in a cake mix, I have to add my own good deeds: fresh baking powder, a little *real* vanilla flavoring, a dash of cinnamon or cardamom, and oat milk or juice instead of water.

    Spiritual faith is like that too. Once you have repented of your sins, you have to add baking powder to your faith by doing what is right. No true religion teaches that a person can attain salvation by faith alone after living a Mardi Gras life of sin. A New Testament writer explained, "Faith without good deeds will not lead to salvation. A person with wisdom and understanding will prove him- or herself by a righteous life of good deeds done in humility" (James 2: 14; 3: 13). A Jewish proverb teaches, "Those who strive to do good, kind deeds are those who attain life, success, and honor" (Proverbs 21: 21).

    God will accept you, bugs and all, but you can't stumble around in stinky diapers for long. After you have learned the Straight Way, trade in your training pants for the clean, pure garments of holiness. Your faith is worthless if you continue to pick up hotties at the local bar, spread dirty jokes, and smoke those stinking cigarettes. Once you have given your whole self to God (blessed!), you have no right to pollute your mind, which is rightfully God's;

your body, which is rightfully God's; or your soul, which is rightfully God's. Don't fall flat, but allow God to raise you up to an acceptable transformation.

> God, bless my bread to sustain my life.
> God, bless my head to think my life.
> Bless my arms and legs and feet,
> To work my life and not mistreat
> The time that You have given me.
> Keep me busy like a bee.
> Bless my hands to do my work
> As I labor without shirk.
> God, bless me and live in me.
> Be my Potter and shape me.

6. RECONCILIATION WITHOUT COMPROMISE

Allah wants to lighten your burdens because humanity was created weak.
Concerning your differences, the decision is with Allah.
Such is Allah my Lord! In Him I trust. To Him I turn.
(Surah 4: 28 and Surah 42: 10)

At a restaurant one day, I noticed a woman dressed similarly to me, in a colorful blouse and long skirt. She noticed me too, and we exchanged smiles. She sat near the door, and, as I was leaving the restaurant, she said, "I love your scarf; it looks so stylish."

I noticed the yellow, butterfly pin on her shoulder and said, "I like your butterfly. I ought to rip it off you."

She laughed and said, "I think we are both free spirits."

As I was getting into my car, the woman came running from the restaurant and across the parking lot. She was carrying her butterfly in her hand. She trotted to the car and, with a big smile, handed the pin to me. I accepted it, and then I took the butterfly clip holding my scarf in place and gave it to her in return. It was a gratifying moment in which two strangers found a common thread just because of our free-spirited style of dress.

It hurts my feelings when other Muslims criticize me for not wearing a traditional hijab and jilbab. I think my hillbilly clothes are just fine! In becoming a Muslim, I did not have to make any big changes in my clothes because I didn't dress like the hoochie-coochie in the first place. I kept my personal identity in my style of clothing, but I added stronger threads of modesty and humility.

When a person accepts Islam into his or her heart and becomes a changed person, his or her life may change a little or a lot depending on how rotten he or she was before. If you are a new Muslim, you will likely find yourself having to reconcile your newfound faith with your previous beliefs and your American lifestyle. If you are a Jew, you may have to reinvent your life as you honor your family's Jewish traditions and observances while following the guidance of Islam. If you are a Christian, you will have to unlearn Church doctrine and reevaluate the message of Jesus. It's a journey without a time schedule other than the one God has planned just for you, so do not let others rush you on your way or confuse you with conflicting dogma.

Evaluate your lifestyle and find solutions that do not compromise the guidance that God has provided. How should the swimming or gymnastics instructor dress in order to be modest yet appropriate for her job? How can the restaurant owner honor the Islamic rules concerning food without forcing his religious beliefs on his customers? Should the storeowner stop selling tobacco products? Should the jewelry store owner stop selling crucifixes that humiliate Jesus by representing him as dead, naked, and disgraced? How can an accountant be successful without supporting the usury practiced by some of his clients? Should the owner of the ABC store sell the store, which would continue making intoxicants available, or should he accept the loss of closing it and destroying the contents? Must a professional hair stylist wear her scarf to work? Can the cheerleader keep her position and still dress and act in a fashion honorable to Islam? Would the student be involved in gambling or charity if he sold raffle tickets to raise money for new band equipment? How should the sole Muslim in the family interact with Christian family members during holidays such as Easter? An endless list of such questions faces the new Muslim. Immigrants from Islamic countries face similar questions as they adjust within the American way of life and the freedoms it affords.

We should each offer encouragement, advice, and prayer, but never criticism and dogmatic opinions that only make the journey more difficult. Let everyone seek God's guidance for the sake of His glory as Islam continues making steps toward becoming established in mainstream America. Every society has its own culture, traditions, style of clothing, and lifestyles, and America has great diversity in all these. Islam is a religion for a diverse people, and, insh'Allah, Islam will find its own way as American Muslims reconcile – without compromise— culture and faith.

"The whole object of Islam is love of Allah, and not the servitude of an unhappy and flustered slave. It is a joyful release of the soul, an awareness of blessedness and grace; it should not be the terrible guilt-ridden burden of trying to get this detail or that detail in one particular way that will not cause criticism from one's peers in congregation" (RuqaiyyahWarisMaqsood).[6]

May we not argue and become divided as we try to assess God's will in matters in which modern lifestyles must be modified in order to wear the beautiful garments of old-time religion.

> Say, "O Allah, Creator of Heaven and Earth,
> Knower of all that is secret and public,
> You will judge among Your servants
> concerning those matters about which they differ.
> *(Surah 39: 46)*

7. THE COLOR OF GOD

> Our dye is of Allah, and who can dye better than Allah?
> We worship Him!
> *(Surah 2: 138)*

In high school, a boy in my algebra class asked me to go with him to a school dance. The evening of the big day, he knocked on the front door. I opened the door and invited him in. Daddy took one look at Delbert and then belted out a tirade of laughter. Delbert was wearing a shocking pink shirt, a purple tie with huge, pink polka dots, a red-orange suit coat, lime green pants, and mustard-yellow suede shoes.

"What a pretty boy!" Daddy said when he finally could catch his breath. He hollered for Mama. "Georgia, git in here and look what a pretty boy Linda got for herself."

"Bill, quit laughing at that poor lil' ol' boy," Mama scolded as she entered the room. She took one good look at Delbert, and then she too became silly with laughter. Delbert's face flushed a color that blended perfectly with his orange hair and red freckles.

Delbert was a fine boy who liked to dress snazzy-like. There was nothing wrong with Delbert, but I did try to talk him into taking me somewhere where nobody knew us.

Color is a wonderful thing, and the psychology of color is fascinating. A soft blue or sage green has a calming effect. Peppy red and spicy orange lend excitement. Yellow is a happy color.

People can be funny about color though. In a department store, another shopper picked up a hat and asked me, "What color is this?"

"It's burnt sienna," I answered.

"Well, that sounds like a good color," he said. "What is burnt sienna?"

"The color of red mud," I told him.

He quickly put the hat back on the shelf. "Well, I don't think I'd like that," he decided.

As an artist, I like color, and I like to wear colorful clothing. I think that, as the Master Artist, God likes color too. Sunsets look like finger paintings in the sky, and I love the way the treetops are brushed with the gold of morning. The tiniest bug is cloaked with color, and polished pebbles form a magnificent mosaic underneath the clear water of a mountain stream. A tail feather from a red-tail hawk is a treasure for the hiker who finds one on her trail. Colorful and amazing creatures have been discovered roaming the deepest ocean floors where only God can freely walk. We have been blessed with a living-color world!

As a sign of His promise not to again destroy the world with water, God created the rainbow. The primary colors —red, green, and blue— of the rainbow, however, combine to make pure, white light. In the same way, a person is a colorful, unique individual, but, when he or she combines all the spiritual colors of God, he or she emanates the purity and holiness of God (blessed and exalted is He).

Abdulla Yusuf Ali explained that "the Arab Christians mixed a dye or colour in the baptismal water signifying that the baptized person got a new colour in life."[7] The red dye symbolized being "washed in the blood of the Lamb," which reflects the Christian belief that Jesus' blood on the cross paid for the sins of the world.

Although Muslims do not perform a formal baptismal ceremony, when one accepts Islam, the new Muslim should take a private, symbolic bath. He or she should ponder God's grace in washing away old sins so that the believer carries no burden into his or her New Life with God. Yusuf Ali reminds, however, "Our higher baptism is the 'Baptism' of God by which we take on a colour (symbolically) of God and absorb His goodness in us."[8]

The Muslim who strives for perfection should seek daily, spiritual baptism. The personal, morning prayer should include repentance for any sin lurking in his or her soul, and it should include a request that God bathe him or her in God's wonderful colors –all the colors of goodness. His colors should be reflected in our spiritual lives as we perform da'wah through being intelligent, sensitive, and compassionate people. When we show others that we respect them as unique individuals created by God (blessed!), the pure, white light of God shines as a beacon in this world of suspicion and prejudice.

> Wash my soul and purify my mind, hands, and feet.
> May I reflect Your love to everyone I meet.
> Color my eyes with Your white light so I may see
> The beauty of life and people surrounding me.
> Color my lips with love, courtesy, and kindness
> So that it is Your true nature that my words express.

8. WHERE IN TARNATION ARE YOU?

> O Believers, do not approach the ritual prayers while you are intoxicated.
> Wait till you can understand what you are saying.
> Do not come in a state of ritual impurity,
> with an exception for when you are traveling.
> Wait until you have washed thoroughly.

> If you've been sick or on a trip, or if you've just been to the toilet,
> or if you've been involved in intimate touching,
> and you can't find any water, resort to clean sand,
> and use it to rub your faces and hands.
> Allah blots out sins and forgives again and again.
> *(Surah 4: 43)*

Sometimes Gran'maw Mitchell would yell out the back door, "Whur in tarnation are you younguns?" The word *tarnation* means 'eternal damnation', but it is used to signify annoyance.

I was actually in tarnation one day. It was during a hot August afternoon, and I was smearing tar. The heat made the tar extra gooey, and I got tar all over my hands and arms and even some on my face. Cooking in the sun, the tar made my skin burn, and the fumes stung my eyes. At the end of the day, I had to scrub with kerosene and then soap containing sand-like particles. Even after all that scrubbing, some of the tar remained until it just wore off.

Sin is like that. You can't get rid of it by yourself. You can try to put your 'wild oats' or 'indiscretions' behind you, but only God's grace can wash away your sins completely. If a person does not offer sincere repentance and then live righteously, he or she may do time in tarnation.

Wudu is the ritual cleansing that Muslims do to prepare themselves for salat, realizing that only God's grace can truly cleanse the guilty soul. After conscientiously making the intent of wudu, a Muslim washes face, hands, arms, and feet three times. The nose and mouth are also rinsed out three times. The first washing loosens grime, the second cleansing washes grime away, and the third scrub sanitizes. The head and ears generally just collect dust that falls on them, so they may just get a once-over. If there is no water available for wudu, sand cleanses by scrubbing off dead skin cells and opening clogged pores.

There is a direct spiritual connection to the wudu ritual. The first washing symbolizes repentance; the second, forgiveness; and the third, righteousness. If one repents and receives forgiveness, his or her forgiveness is perfected for eternity through the performance of good deeds. Like tar wearing off gradually, one's life of righteousness will wear away the effects of sin, which will be replaced with goodness.

A person chooses whether to present a smiling or frowning face, what deeds his or her hands do, what his or her arms bear, and where his or her feet lead. What a person actively inhales is a choice as he or she naturally turns away from a smell that is repulsive and actively smells that which is pleasant. Some people defeat their natural instincts by forcing their bodies to accept cigarette smoke and the smell of whiskey, for examples. We also collectively share the guilt of poisons put into the air by carelessly used pesticides and other chemicals. Spiritually, people also defeat their natural instincts of turning away from repulsive activities and being attracted to the numinous perfume of righteous activities. The nose knows when something is just plain rotten! We are also responsible, not only for whether we put nutritious or fattening foods into our mouths, but also for the words from our mouths. Jesus said, "It is not what goes into the mouth that makes a person [ritually] unclean, but what comes out of the mouth" (Matthew 15: 11). A true believer must not dishonor God by defiling the prayerful tongue with cursing and vulgarity.

The once-over of the head and ears is a reminder that we cannot always control what is fed into our ears and minds by those around us, but we must do what we can to cleanse ourselves of evil inculcations, and then trust God to do the rest.

Sometimes a person cannot attain the Living Water that God offers because he or she has a buildup of constricted ideas that have become mental blocks. In that case, a good scrubbing with mental sand —a kind of unlearning— will open one's clogged mind so that new understanding can be attained.

The ritual of wudu should mentally prepare the Muslim for coming before God (blessed and exalted is He). If wudu is performed as a mindless ritual, you are missing the point. When Muslims perform wudu, they must mentally scrub away the evil influences that surround us, distract us, often weaken and tempt us, and sometimes even seduce us. When our minds and hearts are ritually pure, we are prepared to enter into God's presence as people sharing the same spiritual color of God that unites us all.

<blockquote>
O Allah, set me as far away from my sins
As the east is from the west.
O Allah, cleanse me of my sins
As a white garment is rid of its dirt by washing.
O Allah, wash away my sins with water, snow, and hail.
[Prophet Muhammed (peace upon him)]
</blockquote>

9. HOMETOWN HOSPITALITY

(This concerns) the pacts made with the Quraysh for their protection.
[These are] during winter and summer journeys [for the trade routes].
   May (the Quraysh) worship the Lord of this House [the Ka'bah].
He nourished them against hunger and safeguarded them from fear.
      Woe to the worshipers insincere in their prayers.
      They want only to be seen. They deny simple aid.
Alif. Lam. Ra. This book of Scriptures is perfected and clarified.
   It is from the One who is Perfectly Wise and Fully Aware.
        You should worship none but Allah.
     I [Muhammed] am sent from Him for your benefit,
        to warn and to announce good news.
Seek the forgiveness of your Lord and turn to Him in repentance.
   He may award you a satisfactory life for an appointed time
   and bestow His abundant grace on all who are meritorious.
But if you reject Him, I fear for you the penalty of an awesome day.
   To Allah you will return, and His power extends over all.
(Surah 106, Surah 107: 4-7, and Surah 11: 1-4)

    As Tom and I were traveling cross-country, our vehicle pulled a homemade camper that resembled a covered wagon, built onto an old truck bed. We had a sleeping bag and some supplies in our covered wagon, and, by most people's standards, we were 'roughing it'.

    Late at night, somewhere in the eastern part of Texas, we pulled off the side of the road, crawled into our covered wagon, and slept till the whizzing of passing trucks roused us the next morning. We climbed out, stretched, and yawned. From a nearby farmhouse, a couple brought us each a cup of coffee fresh-brewed from southern hospitality. They even invited us to join them for breakfast.

    Such hospitality should be part of every Muslim's character, and it should be extended to Muslims and non-Muslims alike. As I understand it, Surah 106 was revealed early in the Prophet's ministry, before full knowledge and understanding had been made available to the Quraysh tribe. Yet the verse extends both permission and invitation for the tribal members to peaceably and comfortably worship at the Ka'bah.

In order for Islam to grow as an American religion, a seedbed must be prepared of small-town, community Islamic centers where people can worship with their neighbors. First-time visitors must be able to feel among friends in a welcoming and comfortable environment. Visitors must not feel alienated, confused, and unwelcome.

It is understandable that immigrants want to flock with others who share the same cultural background, language, and similar interests. When such camaraderie is done at the exclusion of others, however, the Islamic center becomes more a social club than a place of worship. Language barriers should be avoided, and every person must somehow be accommodated. The equal right and access for everyone to worship comfortably must be recognized and realized, regardless of gender, race, culture, or language.

After hearing the story of my conversion, a woman who was raised Muslim told me, "I felt envy because I can never experience what you encountered on your journey to Islam. Hearing your story, however, inspired me to become a born-again Muslim as I renewed my faith, and I will try never again to take my Muslim heritage for granted."

All Muslims should daily renew their faith and openly invite sinners to seek unconditional forgiveness. We should not require that a non-Muslim first put on a prayer cap or scarf, learn another language, change his or her lifestyle, or change cultural behaviors. "Seek the forgiveness of your Lord and turn to Him in repentance..." should be our invitation. We must not complicate what God has made simple.

Some potential Muslims have been rejected because they weren't dressed properly and didn't know the Islamic traditions and courtesies. A visitor wearing inappropriate clothing to a mosque must not be met with disdain and rejection. Ignorance should be met with kindness and accommodation. The center should keep a few inexpensive robes and scarves available. If proper clothing is not available and the visitor's attire is intolerable, the visitor should be taken to a room (or otherwise accommodated) where he or she can be counseled privately and respectfully.

What if a visitor does not know the prayer ritual? Someone should befriend the guest and explain the traditions. If the visitor is interested in Islam, someone should volunteer to be a coach.

What about after the service? Someone should be appointed as a welcoming agent for each guest. It the guest is willing to share his or her phone number and address, a phone call should invite the guest to return. A greeting card could be sent to thank the person for visiting. Literature about Islam should also be offered, and questions should be invited.

Muslims in America must do more to propagate Islam in a friendly environment where visitors do not feel as if they've walked into a foreign dimension.

Every spiritually active person is on a journey, and no one should judge based on where that person is at any given time on that journey. While we see a person only as he or she is today, God (blessed and exalted is He) sees the final person –the person at the end of the journey. When a person is actively seeking God's will in his or her life, we must remember that God (blessed!) is not yet finished with that person. We must trust God's timing and accommodate the traveler at every rest stop.

"Come as you are" should be the welcoming message of the mosque. "Leave with God" should be the joyous farewell.

> O my Lord, may everything that I do start well and finish well.
> Sustain me with Your power.
> And in Your power, let me drive away all falsehood,
> Ensuring that truth may always triumph.
> *[Prophet Muhammed (peace upon him)]*

10. SANDALS AND ELBOWS

> It is He who has bestowed upon you the Book.
> In it are fundamental Scriptures, which are the Book's foundation.
> Other Scriptures are vague.
> While seeking discord, those who are perverse
> concentrate on the vague portions and search for secret meanings.
> No one knows the true meanings, however, except Allah.
> Those who are steadfast in knowledge say,
> "We believe in its entirety, which is from our Sovereign Lord."
> Only people of understanding will grasp the message.
> *(Surah 3: 7)*

One of the things a new Muslim convert learns is that Muslims are quite adept at driving one another crazy.

"You can't wear that dress to the store because the sleeves don't go all the way to the wrists."

I have ugly, pointy elbows (great for self-defense), but that loaf of bread really doesn't care, and neither does anyone at the store.

"Your prayers aren't any good if they're not Sunnah."

Tell it to God! He has answered my prayers all my life, and He is patient as I try to learn the Sunnah examples.

"You can only wear molded plastic sandals on hajj!"

Yeah, I'm so sure Muhammed owned plastic sandals.

"That scarf isn't good enough; your bangs are showing."

If my bangs inspire lust, somebody needs serious counseling, and it ain't me, babe.

"You can't make paintings of animals; it's idolatry."

I've been an artist since I could hold crayons. Not once have I bowed to and worshiped anything I've drawn.

"You can't have a birthday cake; it's not Sunnah."

If my husband wants to bake me a cake, anyone objecting should know that I am trained in hand-to-hand combat, and I can fight with one hand holding cake.

Good grief! If I wanted to be burdened with picky rules that have nothing to do with my spirituality and my devotion to God, I would have started my own religion and made up my own silly rules.

A friend called me once to have me help him remember why he became a Muslim. "I went to one mosque," he said, "and they told me my pants were too long. I cut them off, but when I went to another mosque, they told me my pants were too short. I think I'll just give up and go back to church. And I'll take with me that fellow who had to dye his red beard black because Muhammed didn't have a red beard."

A new Muslim who is bombarded by criticism and exaggerated dogma may become discouraged. He or she should be gracious to the critic, and then not worry about it. Seek God's guidance, study the Qur'an and Sunnah, and then use your own judgment. If you try to live like everyone else tells you that you should, you'll stay confused and upset. If God (blessed and exalted is He) wants you to change something about your clothes, behavior, or lifestyle, He will smack you upside the head in His own time.

By the way, Muhammed never used a cell phone. Throw that thing in the river! Just kidding! Muslims should encourage one another and help one another grow spiritually. A closer walk with God is more important than sandals and elbows or even cell phones.

Muslim intellectual Dr. Omar Afzal opines, "Many Muslims profess, but don't really believe, that all is permitted except what is specifically prohibited in the Qur'an. Many acts were added under the 'sin' category by extension of someone's inference. A good example is that one cannot wear a half-sleeve shirt during prayers or pray without a cap. In many parts of the Muslim world, one cannot pray in pants or wear a necktie. Using paper napkins was declared a sin because of 'wastefulness'. Of course, a Muslim community, by a collective decision, may forbid and give up certain acts that the Messenger (peace upon him) did not like or that his Khulafa [representatives, agents] deemed unfit for a good person. The discussion will continue, and we hope that both sides will take the arguments seriously but calmly. We need more input from new reverts to open our eyes. We need to remember that the basic point of Islam is to submit yourself to God and do every deed, however insignificant, only to please Him, and He will gladly hold you in His arms despite all that might look sinful or incomplete to others."

The Prophet (peace and blessings upon him) said, "Religion is very easy, and whoever overburdens himself in it will not be able to continue in that way. So you should try not to be extremists, but try to be near to perfection and accept these good tidings that you may be rewarded. Gain strength by worshiping in the mornings, afternoons, and during the last hours of the nights."[9]

> Our Lord, let our hearts not deviate from truth
> now that You have guided us,
> but grant us mercy from Your divine presence.
> You are the Bountiful Provider.
> Our Lord, You will assemble Humanity
> for a day about which there is no doubt.
> Allah never fails in keeping His promises.
> *(Surah 3: 8-9)*

11. WHEN IDIOTS PRAY

> Your God is only Allah. No god is there except Him.
> He comprehends all things in His knowledge.
> Truly, Allah knows all the hidden things of the skies and Earth.
> Truly, He has full knowledge of all that is in our hearts.
> *(Surah 20: 98 and Surah 35: 38)*

"Can you draw something and make it look like a picture?"

"How do you make cartoons jump around so you can get them on TV?"

As an artist, I often get telephone calls that make no sense at all. Many people don't know enough about art to even know what terms to use. They have no idea how to express themselves.

"I got a poem I wrote, and I want you to take it and make it look like a page."

What the heck does she mean?

When my son Dusty worked for an electronics store, he also had a volume of terrible telephone tales.

"What do I do with this cord?" a customer called to ask.

"What cord, sir?" Dusty asked.

"The one I got in my hand."

"Sir, I can't see the cord in your hand. Where did you get it?"

"It came from your store! I bought this box," the customer explained, "and I got every cord stuck somewhere except this one, and I can't figure out where to stick it."

Many sentences later, Dusty had coached the customer into setting up the "box", a telephone-answering device. There was one step left.

"Now you just have to plug the telephone cord into the machine."

"I can't because the phone cord is stuck in the wall," the frustrated customer whined.

"I realize that, sir. First, you must remove the telephone cord from the wall, and then —Hello? Sir? Hello?"

Idiots! We're surrounded by idiots!

What happens when someone's prayer makes no sense? A sinner who has lived far from God may be awkward at prayer. His or her prayer may not begin with a reverent approach; it may not contain proper lines of praise or use the appropriate words in expressing remorse and repentance. Do you think God looks over at Gabriel and says, "I don't know what that idiot is trying to say"? Certainly not! God (blessed and exalted is He) does not have to depend on our communication skills in order to hear the prayers of our hearts. Every soul knows how to pray regardless of the idiot housing the soul. When a sinner repents, God hears the voice of the soul, and every syllable is precious when the heart is sincere.

When a sinner submits the whole self to God, he or she begins a journey to reach a goal of perfection in prayer and righteous living. It is not up to us to determine where a new believer should be at any time during the journey. We should encourage, strengthen, support, and assist, but leave the directing up to God (blessed and exalted is He).

> How should I pray?
> Teach the art of prayer to me, so that I may devote myself to You.
> Should I meditate upon the wonders of Your creation?
> Should I give thanks for the wisdom of my elders?
> Should I praise You for Your many gifts to me?
> Should I reflect on all the things I have done wrong?
> Or should I simply wait until You speak to me?
> Tell me truly: how should I pray?
> *[Zoroaster (6th century BCE), monotheistic reformer (Persia)]*

12. UNITED IN PRAYER

> In the Name of Allah, the Most Gracious, the Most Merciful!
> Praise belongs to Allah, the Lord of the Worlds!
> The Most Gracious, the Most Merciful!
> Master of the Day of Judgment!
> We worship You. We seek Your help. Show us the Straight Way,
> [Show us] the way of those on whom You have given Your grace.
> [Show us the way of] those who do not anger You
> and do not go the wrong way.
> *(Surah 1)*

Allan Fowler was in dire misery with agony and strife. My daddy told Allan that he needed to turn his problems over to the Lord. Allan offered a timid prayer: "Lord, I ain't never been much of a praying man, and I hardly know what to say, but if You're up there and if You're listening, I sure could use Your help right about now."

Nobody has to stumble through such an awkward prayer. There is a perfect example in the Qur'an.

Bism'Allah, al Rahmaan, al Raheem. This model prayer begins with the acknowledgment of God and His attributes of grace and mercy. The sound of God fills the believer at once with reverent fear and overwhelming calm. There is power in His name —the power to bend a sinner's trembling knees, the power to breathe hope into the empty pit of despair, the power to instill courage when the realization of apparent disaster has gripped the spirit with crushing force. Allah. Allah. Allah.

Alhamdul'Allah, RabeelAlameen, al Rahmaan, al Raheem. We offer praise to God, and our meager words are joined by an infinite number of voices over the eons of time, and a constant symphony permeates creation for the glory of God (blessed and exalted is He).

MaleekyYaum al Deen. Not only do we acknowledge God's power, justice, and glory, but also, by pondering for a moment the Day of Judgment, we join God in His plan. We each take time to say, "Here am I, use me for that day when all corruption will end and all creation will be restored to Your absolute specifications."

Iyaaka na'boodoo, wa iyaka nastaeen. By acknowledging God as the only one worthy of our worship and of our complete confidence, we reject all other forces that continually threaten to rip us from God's grasp. These are not the pagan gods of Muhammed's time but are more sinister idols appearing in the lively and colorful wrappings in which modern society has dressed them. Sexual freedom, recreational drugs, social drinking, swingers' clubs, adult entertainment —these are some of the sophisticated names for the vile gods of the modern world— the gods that beckon our submission, worship, and praise.

Ihdeena al Siraata al Mustaqeem —siraata al latheenaan'amtaalaheem, ghayeer al magdoobeealayheemwa la al daaleen. The Straight Way seems a dull path to the slaves of sin —those people trapped and blinded by their gods. They are ever assisting Satan as he lays his snares in the shadows that surround the

Straight Way. Only by the power of God's will are we able to keep our eyes on the goal and our feet set firmly on the path. The world is treacherous, but God is the Most Gracious, the Most Merciful, and He is able to keep us in His good favor.

Surah 1 is spoken in the first person plural instead of from the perspective of 'me.' Even when a person prays alone, his or her prayer is united with the prayers of all believers, and, like strands of a rope, they keep our faith strong in the constant tug-of-war we are waging with the evil forces that surround us. Alhamdul'Allah! Ameen.

> Our Father in Heaven, blessed is Your name.
> May Your kingdom be established
> And may Your will be done on Earth as it is in Heaven.
> Grant us the sustenance we need for today.
> Forgive us for our sins, and help us to forgive those
> Who have committed evil against us.
> Do not lead us into difficult trials, but protect us from the Evil One.
> [Matthew 6: 9-13, a prayer of Jesus (peace upon him)]

13. THEN DO IT SO-SO

> Attend obediently to your ritual prayers, especially the central prayer.
> Stand in humble worship before Allah.
> If you have any concerns, you may pray while walking or riding.
> Whenever you can pray comfortably,
> remember Allah in the way He has taught, which you didn't know before.
> (Surah 2: 238-239)

"Mama, the cat had babies on top of my homework!"

"Is my lunch ready? The school bus is here."

"Where's my other sock?"

"My tummy hurts."

"Honey, I'll be late getting home from work. Can you get my uniform from the dry cleaners?"

"No, I have to stop a train to deliver a painting to the engineer."

"Daddy, why can't we see air?"

"Aunt Toy is on the phone; her shoe is stuck in the toilet."

"Daddy, how do astronauts go to the bathroom?"

How can a person ever get into a consistent prayer routine? There are hundreds of things pulling us in all directions. We are distracted even from our distractions. Getting into the habit of praying five times a day is perhaps the most difficult thing for many new Muslims, and it is especially difficult for those of us who are not near a mosque from which the adhan is announced. It's easy to get involved in work or school or other activities and forget the time or be unable to stop the activity and prostrate in prayer. God has made it easy for us, however, by the examples given in the passage. If you cannot prostrate and/or cannot recite prayers and Qur'an aloud, do whatever you can whenever and wherever you can. Amer bin Rabi'ah reported that he observed Muhammed (peace and blessings upon him), offering prayers, without regard to direction, while riding his camel.[10]

There is an old saying, "If you can't do something right, then don't do it at all," but the ayat says that if you can't do something right, then do it so-so. God is so easy on us that we have no excuse for not doing the right thing – even if it is just so-so.

Of course, we should pray as God taught us whenever we can. The early morning prayer can be difficult, but when the roosters awaken me, I slither out of bed, say my two rak'ats, and then slither back into bed and ignore the roosters.[11] In the winter, I have warm socks and a robe handy so I won't use the cold as an excuse.

Of course, if you oversleep by accident, just say the morning salat whenever you awaken. There are a few reports in which the Prophet (peace and blessings upon him) overslept and missed the morning salat. He didn't make a big deal of it; he just prayed when he got up. I do that sometimes myself. Even when I get up in time, my morning prayers are often late due to crazy, morning distractions.

The routine of salat is a whole-person exercise involving mind, body, and soul. Muhammad Asad wrote a beautiful entry in his autobiography, in which he explains why Muslims pray as we do:

> ...one day I asked the hajji, who understood a little English, "Do you really believe that God expects you to show Him your respect by repeated bowing and kneeling and prostration? Might it not be

better only to look into oneself and to pray to Him in the stillness of one's heart? Why all these movements of your body?"

As soon as I had uttered these words, I felt remorse, for I had not intended to injure the old man's religious feelings. But the hajji did not appear in the least offended. He smiled with his toothless mouth and replied, "How else then should we worship God? Did He not create both soul and body together? And this being so, should man not pray with his body as well as with his soul? Listen, I will tell you why we Muslims pray as we do. We turn toward the Kaaba, God's holy temple in Mecca, knowing that the faces of all Muslims, wherever they may be, are turned to it in prayer, and that we are like one body, with Him as the center of our thoughts. First, we stand upright and recite from the Holy Koran, remembering that it is His Word, given to man that he may be upright and steadfast in life. Then we say, 'God is the Greatest,' reminding ourselves that no one deserves to be worshipped but Him; and bow down deeply because we honor Him above all, and praise His power and glory. Thereafter we prostrate ourselves on our foreheads because we feel that we are but dust and nothingness before Him, and that He is our Creator and Sustainer on high. Then we lift our faces from the ground and remain sitting, praying that He forgive us our sins and bestow His grace upon us and guide us aright and give us health and sustenance. Then we again prostrate ourselves on the ground and touch the dust with our foreheads before the might and the glory of the One. After that, we remain sitting and pray that He bless the Prophet Muhammad who brought His message to us, just as He blessed the earlier Prophets; and that He bless us as well and all those who follow the right guidance; and we ask Him to give us of the good of this world and of the good of the world to come. In the end, we turn our heads to the right and to the left, saying, 'Peace and the grace of God be upon you,' and thus greet all who are righteous, wherever they may be. It was thus that our Prophet used to pray and taught his followers to pray for all times, so that they might willingly surrender themselves to God —which is what 'Islam' means— and so be at peace with Him and with their own destiny."

…. Years later I realized that with his simple explanation, the hajji had opened to me the first door to Islam; but even then, long before any thought that Islam might become my own faith entered my mind, I began to feel an unwonted humility whenever I saw, as I often did, a man standing barefoot on his prayer rug, or on a straw mat, or on the bare earth, with his arms folded over his chest and his head lowered, entirely submerged within himself, oblivious of what was going on around him, whether it was in a mosque or on the sidewalk of a busy street: a man at peace with himself.[12]

We can be at peace with ourselves when we are first at peace with God (blessed and exalted is He). Each of us must make a renewed commitment each day to work devotedly for our Heavenly Employer. Beginning the day with prayer just makes sense, and prayers throughout the day —whether salat or du'a— give your soul the energy it needs to persevere. With God's help, we can confront distractions with focused minds with which we can stay on track.

> As I prepare to serve You today, I rededicate my devotion to You.
> May the passion of Prophet Muhammed (peace upon him)
> And of the early followers (may You be pleased with them)
> Cut the pattern for how I live every day as a Muslim.
> With Your help, may I always focus on Your will and purpose,
> And always be in communion with You, my Beloved Savior,
> And totally serve You with my body, mind, and soul.

14. WHY THE NEW FACE?

> The ignorant among the people will ask,
> "What has turned (the believers) from the traditional direction of prayer?"
> Answer, "To Allah belong east and west.
> He guides whom He will to the Straight Way."
> [By giving Muslims a new direction of prayer,]
> We have made you a moderate faith community,
> so that you may be witnesses for the nations,
> The messenger is a witness over all of you.
> We originally appointed the old direction of prayer as a test

>to see who would follow the messenger and who would give up.
>It seemed like a big deal except to those guided by Allah.
>Allah would never allow your faith to be annulled.
>To all people, Allah is the Kindest, the Most Merciful.
>We saw you turning your face toward Heaven,
>so We turned you to a favorable direction.
>Turn your face in the direction of the Holy Mosque.
>Wherever you are, face in that direction.
>The People of the Book realize that this is truth from their Lord,
>Allah is never unaware of what they do.
>(Surah 2: 142-144)

When I was little, I often heard Daddy describing various sites as being either "on this side of town" or "way over on the other side of town." One day, after we had been running errands, I asked him, "Daddy, are we on this side of town or the other side?" I was thirty years old before I figured out why Daddy laughed at my question.

I'm good at a lot of things, but direction is not one of them. I get lost so easily that Daddy used to tell people, "If I took Linda to the end of the driveway and then spun her around a couple times, she wouldn't be able to find her way back home."

When God spun the early Muslims around, many of them became lost. In the beginning of Islam as an organized religion, Muslims faced Jerusalem for the formal prayers, as did the Jews and Christians. After suffering rejection from a great many Jews and Christians as well as pagans, Muhammed (peace and blessings upon him), by God's will, directed the Muslims to face the Ka'bah for these reasons: to symbolize independence from the established religions; to symbolize a renewal of Humanity's relationship with God (congruent with the new Revelations and revitalized zeal for following God's will); to symbolize a return to the original religion of Adam, Noah, Abraham (peace upon them), and all of Humanity; and to symbolize that the true Jerusalem (or Islam), the City of Peace, is the spiritual garden within a believer's soul. Jerusalem remains a sacred city for which all believers should have the hope of restoration and peace, along with Palestine and all the world, but it is the mystic Jerusalem, the spiritual City of Peace, to which believers owe the greater allegiance. Jesus (peace upon him) said that each person must find the Kingdom of God, the eternal City of Peace, within his or her own heart (Luke 17: 20-21).

Abdulla Yusuf Ali explains, "The *Qibla* (direction of prayer) of Jerusalem might itself have seemed strange to the Arabs, and the change from (Jerusalem) to the Ka'bah might have seemed strange (or confusing) after they had become used to the other. In reality one direction or another, or east or west, in itself did not matter, as God is in all places and is independent of Time and Place. What mattered was the sense of discipline on which Islam lays so much stress: which of us is willing to follow the directions of the chosen Apostle of God? Mere quibblers about non-essential matters are tested by this."[13]

The Arabic word *ummah* means 'faith community,' and it is the same as Jesus' Aramaic word, which became the Greek *iklesia* and then 'church' in the New Testament. The same word is in Aramaic portions of the Jewish Bible and is translated to words describing the Jewish nation. There are two global ummahs to which Muslims belong. One is the universal, multifaith Ummah of all worshipers who believe in the One True God. The second is the Islamic Ummah in which Muslims participate in the original religion ordained by God for all of Humanity. Muslims' facing the Ka'bah is a testament to the practical and central Ummah. When the reasons are explained, they make sense to Christians and Jews who truly advocate the universal worship of the One True God (blessed and exalted is He).

"The future religion of the educated, cultured, and enlightened people will be Islam" (George Bernard Shaw).

> May all people praise You, O God; may all people praise You.
> May the nations be glad and sing for joy,
> for You rule all people justly and guide the nations of the earth.
> May all people praise You, O God; may all people praise You.
> *(Psalms 67: 3-5)*

15. THE BIGGER PLAN

If you [Muhammed] were to deliver the completed Qur'an
to the people of the Book,
they would not follow your direction of prayer, so do not follow theirs.
(Jews and Christians) will not follow one another's direction of prayer.
Now that new knowledge has been given to you,
do not follow their self-centered examples,
If you did, you would clearly be wrong.
The people of the Book recognize this
as clearly as they recognize their own children,
Some of them consciously deny the truth.
Truth comes from your Lord, so do not be at all in doubt.
(Surah 2: 145-147)

When Dusty was three years old, I informed him, "Your pants are on backward."

He looked down and saw that I was right, but he was too stubborn to admit his mistake. "I like them this way," he argued.

Adults can be just as stubborn when faced with the truth.

The universality of the true religion, which Muslims call 'Islam', is God's ideal for the Messianic Age. According to prophecies, when Jesus returns as Messiah, he will come with authority from God (blessed and exalted is He). On God's behalf and in accordance with His will, Jesus (peace upon him) will judge the nations and establish peace upon the earth. One avenue of Islamic theory details how Jesus will defeat the anti-Christ, who will come from among the Muslims and will lead the Zionist army in the battle of Armageddon.[14] When the anti-Christ sees Jesus, the anti-Christ will try to flee the country. Theoretically, Jesus will catch up with him at a gate at an airport in Israel and will continue to pursue him until he kills the anti-Christ near the mountain pass of Afiq on the border between Syria and Israel.[15] After that, all people will worship the One True God, and all Earth's inhabitants will enjoy justice, harmony, and goodwill for a time before this world ends.

Jews believe that, if we strive to make the world as much as possible like God's perfect plan for Humanity, He will reward us by sending the Messiah sooner. To Jews this means performing *mitzvot* (good deeds) and creating a world in which the quality of life is improved for all people. Excellent medical care available to all, healthy entertainment, satisfying and productive work situations, free education, and similar benefits are expected in the Messianic Age when the world can invest resources in improving life instead of destroying life through acts of war and oppression.

Christians also believe in following the example of Jesus whose universal message of the Gospel was intended first for the Jews, and then for all people (Matthew 10: 5-6, 18-20). Jesus said, "I am the gateway to salvation. .... I came to bring life in all its fullness. I am as a good shepherd who recognizes his own sheep, and they recognize me. In the same way, the Father [Creator] recognizes me, and I recognize the Father. I would give my life for my sheep. There are other sheep, aside from this flock. I must call them together. They will hear my voice, and they will become one flock with one shepherd" (John 10: 9-10, 14-16).

If Jews and Christians sincerely consider the principles of Islam, they will see that it is in keeping with their own hopes for world peace. It is up to us to live those principles, however. We can't just say that Islam is a religion of peace while some so-called Muslims are wiring their bombs.

> All Your words are true;
> All your righteous laws are eternal.
> Great peace is upon those who love Your law;
> nothing leads them astray.
> I wait for your salvation, O Lord,
> and I follow your commands.
> Too long have I lived among those who hate peace.
> *(Psalms 119: 160, 165-166; 120: 6)*

16. UN-CHRISTIAN AND UN-AMERICAN

> When they are told, "Do not instigate evil across the planet,"
> they say, "We are making things better!"
> Be careful; they really are the ones who cause trouble,
> and they don't even realize it.
> *(Surah 2: 11-12)*

A religious group was predicting the end of the world on a particular Saturday. I was wearing a heart monitor when I had to go to the bank. I was hooked up with multicolored wires hanging from under my shirt and a bulge underneath my shirt. The bank teller exclaimed, "Linda, what did you do?"

I said, "Don't worry; I'm not set to explode until Saturday."

Later that day, Dusty wanted to go to a particular restaurant for his birthday, but he was afraid it was too expensive. I said, "Dusty, I just went to the bank dressed as a suicide bomber. I have plenty of money."

Islam being equated with terrorism is partly the fault of suicide bombers who claim Islam as their motivation; however, Islamophobia is based more on lies than real events. A segment of the American population is determined to undermine and ultimately destroy Islam and the freedom to openly practice the peaceful religion. A verbal bomb was launched when a rural North Carolina pastor posted the church's sign to say, "The Koran needs to be flushed." His action followed a *Newsweek* report alleging that US soldiers had flushed a copy of the Qur'an down the toilet.

At first, the pastor refused to apologize. After much publicity, he finally took down the posting and said, "When I posted the sign in front of the church, it was my intent only to affirm and exalt the Bible and its teachings. It was certainly not my intent to insult any people of faith, but instead to remind the people in this community of the preeminence of God's Word. When I posted the message on the sign, I did not realize how people of the Muslim faith view the Koran –that devoted Muslims view it more highly than many in the US view the Bible. Now I realize how offensive this is to them, and after praying about it, I have chosen to remove the sign. I apologize for posting that message and deeply regret that it has offended so many in the Muslim community."

The pastor's initial action, however, represented the same type of fear, ignorance, and prejudice that has always plagued the world, including the Church. Although there were Ku Klux Klan members in the Southern Baptist church in which I was raised, the white versus black issue was not a theme of Sunday lessons and sermons until the Civil Rights Movement. During that struggle, guest preachers came to the church to spew their poison as they twisted and corrupted Biblical Scriptures in order to "prove" that "Negroes are black because they were cursed by God" and "Black people do not have souls."

Today, my parents would be considered racist, but, in their time, it was considered logical for "whites to stay in their place and blacks to stay in theirs." My daddy, however, allowed true Christianity to overwhelm worldly logic at an emergency deacons' meeting to address the question, "What should we do if 'the Negras' try to enter the church?" Daddy, an usher as well as a deacon, put an immediate end to the discussion: "Well, I'll tell you what I'm going to do; I'm going to escort them down the aisle and find them a place to sit."

"From many, we are one," boasts our nation's motto. Called "the melting pot," the United States gets its beauty from the diversity and plurality of its people. To forbid one of these people the right to exist without denigration is un-American. The crimes against the indigenous tribes, enslaved black Africans, and WW2-era Japanese Americans exemplify the destructive force of bigotry and self-worship.

When Jesus' disciples saw a man using the name of Jesus to drive out demons, they told him to stop because he was not one of their group. But Jesus (peace!) told the disciples that they should not stop that man because "whoever is not against us is for us" (Mark 9: 38-41). Any attempt to stop the practice of Islam as a peaceful religion is un-Christian, because Muslims are also followers of Jesus (peace upon him). Muhammed (peace!) taught that Jesus is "Allah's servant, His messenger, His Word breathed into the Virgin Mary, and a spirit emanating from Allah."[16] Like the Bible, the Qur'an teaches that Jesus lives and that he was taken into Heaven and given a place of honor. True Christians would never "flush" a Book that honors the name of Jesus as the Qur'an does. It would be un-Christian.

The pastor explained that the church's position is that any book differing from the Bible in pointing the way to God is unholy. The consonant theme of the Tanakh (the Jewish Bible), the New Testament, and the Qur'an, however, is the same: the way to God is to submit your whole self to Him.

We all belong to humanity's multifaith and global Ummah. Followers of the three Abrahamic religions look forward to the Messianic Age when justice and peace will be established globally, portending the finale of this world. Certainly if Jews, Christians, and Muslims join forces in creating a world more pleasing to God, God will find favor with us and heal our land. Instead of posting hatemongering and hurtful words that fuel misunderstanding and distrust, people of all religions of Light must work together in a multi-faith jihad against the prevalent evil in our societies.

> Their only words were, "Our Lord,
> forgive us our sins and any excesses in our affairs.
> Establish our feet firmly and grant us victory over the unbelievers."`
> *(Surah 3: 147).*

17. WAKE UP AND SHAKE UP!

> Consider this parable:
> A man passed through a ghost town in ruins. Even the roofs had fallen.
> He said, "Oh, how could Allah ever bring life back to this town?"
> Allah caused him to be dead for a hundred years, and then revived him.
> (Allah) asked [him], "How long have you been here?"
> He answered, "About a day or so."

Then Allah informed [him], "No, you've been here for a hundred years.
Your food and drink show no signs of decay,
but look at your donkey [which is decayed];
of it, We will make a sign for you which will benefit all people.
Watch how we bring the bones together and clothe them with flesh."
When this was shown to him, he said,
"I now realize that Allah is in complete control!"
(Surah 2: 259)

Bam! Bam! Bam! A hard fist pounded the wall over my bed. "Granger! Get outta the sack, Granger!"

I jumped from my bunk. 'Where in tarnation am I?' I stared out the window. I had never seen that place before in my life!

After a long flight from Chanute Air Force Base (Illinois) to Mather Air Force Base (California), I had collapsed into the bunk to which I was pointed. It was dark when I had arrived, and I had been too tired to get acquainted. Waking in a strange place, I had to try to remember where I was and how I got there! Prophet Jeremiah (peace upon him) had an even more confusing experience.

According to Jewish tradition, Jeremiah (peace upon him) knew Nebuchadnezzar as a starving child with scabs and lice on his head. The Prophet foretold the future greatness of Nebuchadnezzar and asked the child for a letter protecting Jeremiah and any of his future friends from disasters wrought by the future king.

Many years later, when the Babylonians were entering Jerusalem, Jeremiah went to the King, presented the letter, and reminded the king of the promised protection. When the Prophet also begged that the city and the Holy Temple be spared, the King refused, claiming that God had commanded destruction. As proof of God's command, the King shot three arrows in different directions. The first arrow, aimed west, turned and struck the roof of the Temple. The second arrow, aimed north, also turned and struck the roof. The third arrow, aimed south, did the same thing. Ultimately, the city and the Temple were destroyed, and Nebuchadnezzar took possession of the articles of gold.

Jeremiah received a promise from God that he would behold the restored Jerusalem. One day, traveling with a basket of figs and a flask of water and riding a donkey, Jeremiah passed the ruins. He asked God how it would be possible for Jerusalem to ever be restored to its former greatness. Jeremiah fell asleep in a cave, later called Jeremiah's Grotto.[17] God caused him to sleep for an entire century. Upon awakening to find his donkey decayed, Jeremiah was told of his long sleep, and, as a sign, God restored the donkey to life.[18] Jeremiah then entered Jerusalem and found the city rebuilt, populous, and prosperous, and he taught the inhabitants according to God's instructions.

Whether this story is based on an authentic account or a fable, the parable is one example of how the Qur'an incorporated Rabbinic teachings, Christian stories, and Arab beliefs familiar to the people contemporary to the time and place of the Qur'anic revelation. In order to present the message of Islam today, we also must use languages, expressions, and cultural traditions familiar to modern people. To rescue an injured person from a ravine, you would not expect the victim to first climb to you, but you would go to him. Spiritually, we must also rescue people from where they are, not from where we are. Muslims must find innovative, impressive, and modern ways in which to thoughtfully respond to the richness of diversity around us. When we conquer cultural, racial, religious, and national prejudices and mental blocks, we are better equipped to witness to people of other faiths and of no faith, and we can show "the People of the Book" that the Qur'an is their Book too.

Sleeping Muslims, wake up and help shake up the world for the sake of Islam!

> We have awakened, and all of creation has awakened for Allah,
> Sustainer of all the Worlds.
> Allah, I ask You for the best the day has to offer
> —opportunity, support, light, blessings, and guidance,
> And I seek refuge in You from any harm in it
> And any harm that may come after it.
> *[Prophet Muhammed (peace and blessings upon him)]*

18. 'NON-ISLAMIC' IS NOT THE SAME AS 'ANTI-ISLAMIC'

> Consider the night as it conceals! Consider the day as it appears in glory!
> Consider the creation of male and female!
> Truly, that for which you strive is diverse.
> [Consider] the one who charitably gives in awe [of Allah]
> and testifies to the best. We will simplify for him/her the path to bliss.
> Truly, We have taken the responsibility to guide.
> Truly, unto Us are the end and the beginning.
> *(Surah 92: 1-7, 12-13)*

One year when Christmas and Eid were in the same week, Gayle the mail-female left a note in my mailbox. The note said, "Linda, I got your Eid stamps. –Scooter."

Scooter the postmaster saw me walking toward the post office, and he dashed over to open the door for me. "Did you get my note?" he asked. I told him I had, and he said, "Well, those Eid stamps got me in trouble." He explained that old lady Biddle had gotten mad because my Eid stamps came before her Madonna-and-Child Christmas stamps. "She got so mad," Scooter said, "that she is writing a letter to the Congressman to complain about the Eid stamp."

"Well, that's just plumb silly," I said.

"Something else that's silly," Scooter continued, "is the government's telling us we can't say 'Merry Christmas'."

"You better say 'Merry Christmas' to me," I told Scooter, "or I'll smack you upside the head."

We laughed, but we agreed that, even though "Happy Holidays" may be more appropriate for a religiously diverse society, we do not need the government or other guardians of political correctness to tell us what words we can use in greetings. Obscene language is protected by the First Amendment while religious speech is often banned as unconstitutional? That kind of silliness makes the USA Constitution seem unconstitutional. Some Christians boycott businesses that use the greeting "Happy Holidays", and some non-Christians boycott businesses that use the greeting "Merry Christmas". According to a brief news blurb, Congress felt the need to pass a bill "to protect

Christmas" (whatever that means). The holidays have become *sillydays*.

During the war in Iraq, Christian, Jewish, and Muslim boys and girls, enrolled in the Baghdad School of Ballet, performed "The Nutcracker" —a Christmas tradition in a predominately Muslim city, with a backdrop of bombed buildings and fire-eaten cars. How silly was that? If they had learned civility from "the land of the free, home of the brave", they would have used all that energy to have ridiculous arguments to suppress free speech, just like freedom-loving Americans do.

Regardless of what one calls it, every day belongs to God, so why should someone be offended by words of blessings for a happy day? If someone says, "Happy Kwanzaa," "Happy Hanukkah" or "Happy Purple People-Eater Day," respond politely and don't worry about political correctness.

Although Christmas is not an Islamic holiday, that doesn't make it anti-Islamic, unless it's observed in an anti-Islamic fashion. Christmas is not only a Christian holy day, but it is also an American holiday during which people of all faiths are invited to focus on peace and goodwill for the whole world. Every family must decide for itself how to approach Christmas in a way that is best for the specific family, and no one should judge another family's decision. With a Christian background and Christian relatives, my Muslim family has created a unique blend of old-time, family traditions and a new, Islamic approach. We offer a halal, Christmas dinner, and every visitor gets a goody bag of gifts and treats. We share the story of Mary and Jesus from the Qur'an, but we also accommodate the Christians by incorporating Biblical texts.

Christmas is the one time a year that inspirational, greeting cards can be given without offending anybody —well, almost anybody. A lady who gave a simple, interfaith, Christmas card to her Muslim coworker told me, "He pitched a fit and tore up the card right in front of me." That was rotten da'wah (witnessing)! He should have just thanked her, and, if he didn't want the card, he could have discarded it when he got home. For the best da'wah, he could have returned the favor by presenting her an Islamic card with an inspirational message.

There are other American holidays that are non-Islamic but are not necessarily anti-Islamic. Like Valentine's Day. What could possibly be wrong with getting —uh, I mean *giving*— chocolate? Aw! I know all about Cupid and Greek mythology, but as long as Cupid is dark chocolate, bring him on!

Nothing is haram unless you do haram things. If you don't want to participate in popular, American traditions, that's fine. You do whatever is comfortable for you as you seek God's guidance. If someone else, however, wants to blend American, family traditions into his or her Muslim lifestyle, it's not your place to judge. Making Islam a natural part of the American scene is not only a collective journey, but also an individual journey. Each person has to feel comfortable where he or she is at any given time along the way. Once a person has submitted his or her whole self to God, truly it is up to God to guide. You can state your differing opinion in a respectable way, but leave the last word for God (blessed and exalted is He).

> O Allah, join our hearts and mend our social relationships
> And guide us to the path of peace;
> Bring us from darkness into light,
> And save us from obscenities, outward or inward;
> And bless our ears, our eyes, our hearts, our spouses, our children;
> And yield towards us; for You are the Forgiving and Merciful One.
> And make us grateful for Your blessing,
> And make us fuller of praise of it while accepting it,
> And give it to us in full.
> [Prophet Muhammed (peace and blessings upon him)]

19. A REALLY BIG SHOW!

> O Believers, when the call is proclaimed to pray on Friday,
> hasten to the remembrance of Allah, leaving business behind.
> That is best for you, if you only knew.
> Then, when prayer is finished, you may disperse across the land
> and seek the gifts of Allah.
> Glorify Allah often so you may prosper.
> (Some), however, when they see some bargain or entertainment,
> they rush off to it and leave you [the Prophet] standing [alone].
> Say, "What is in the presence of Allah is better than any amusement or sale!
> Allah is the best provider."
> *(Surah 62: 9-11)*

"Where were you when the Beatles appeared on the Ed Sullivan show?" That was the question asked by a DJ on an oldies rock 'n' roll radio station. I was a teenager during the days of Beatlemania. On that celebrated night of Ed Sullivan, my parents dragged me to church. Spying the preacher as I went in the door, I went over and whispered in his ear, "Could you please cut the sermon short, so I can get home in time to see the Beatles?"

I was assaulted from the pulpit! "I'm not cutting my sermon short for any kind of entertainment!" the preacher declared, "—especially for some mob in which you can't even tell the boys from the girls." (In case you were born last week, the Beatles were all boys whose earlobe-length hair was considered outrageously long.) He proceeded to preach a suddenly inspired sermon that could have begun with Surah 62: 11, though I'm sure he had never read the Qur'an.

I made it home just in time! I turned on the TV as Ed was introducing "the fabulous four" for the "really big show." According to their song, the Beatles wanted to hold my hand, but God daily offers to hold my soul, and He is the best provider. No entertainer, football game, or wild shopping spree is better than the privilege of standing in the presence of God (blessed and exalted is He). When we enter the Garden of Heaven, we can say, reflecting the words of Ed Sullivan, "Now this really is 'a really big show!'"

One amazing aspect of Heaven will be companions "of equal age" (Surahs 56: 37 and 38: 52). According to scientific hypothesis, an all-encompassing energy field connects everything and everybody. Research has shown that people become healthier and more youthful when in contact with their energetic blueprint, which is specific to each time-space link. Harvard University psychologist Ellen Langer placed a group of seventy-year-old participants in an isolated environment replicating the American scene of 1959. Within just one week, the participants reported that their symptoms of aging had begun to reverse. As they began virtually reliving their time-space link, their joints became more flexible, their eyesight improved, and their minds became sharper.

The total being of God remains a mystery that our scientific studies can never explain. The more we learn of the divine energy field, however, the more we realize that God has put more energy into our eternal rewards than any Earth-bound intellect can imagine.

Prophet Muhammed (peace!) taught, "Allah says, 'For My righteous servants, I have prepared that which has never been seen by the eye, heard by the ear, or been conceived by any human.'"[19]

Rock on!

> You are like a tiger, compelling in Your beauty,
> Yet terrifying in Your strength.
> You are like a honeycomb on the branch of a tree;
> I can see the sweet honey,
> But the branch is too high for me to climb.
> You are like a goldfish swimming in a pond,
> Only an arm's length from the bank;
> Yet if I try to catch You in my hand,
> You slip from my grasp.
> You are like a snake;
> Your skin dazzles in its bright colors,
> Yet, with a single stab,
> Your mouth is able to destroy a person.
> Be merciful to me, O Lord.
> Give me life, not death.
> Reach out to me, and hold me in Your arms.
> Come down to me, and lift me up to Heaven.
> Sustain my feeble soul with Your power.
> *[ManikkaVasahar (8th century), Hindu leader (India)]*

20. IT'S YOUR DAY!

> The Sabbath was designed for those in disagreement.
> Allah will certainly judge among them on the Day of Resurrection
> concerning their differences.
> *(Surah 16: 124)*

As a child, I became accustomed to words of doom for those who did not strictly observe "the day of rest". If someone mowed the yard on

Sunday, "His grass is going to die." If someone painted the house on Sunday, "Her house is going to burn down." If someone washed the car on Sunday, "He's going to wreck that car." If someone had her hair styled on Sunday, "She's going to go bald."

I did not have a clue that Sunday was not even the real Sabbath day. Most Christians worship on Sundays because it is believed that Jesus' resurrection from apparent demise occurred on Sunday.

A poster on the wall of a Sunday School classroom stated, "Jesus was a good Christian boy who went to Sunday School and church every Sunday." How silly! Jesus was a Jew, and according to the Jewish calendar, the Sabbath is Saturday.

Jewish Pharisees elaborated on the Torah's Sabbath Laws and made them difficult to follow, and the Christian denominations appear to fall further and further away from keeping their Sunday Sabbath holy. Churches sponsor car washes and yard sales on Sundays and overindulge at all-you-can-eat buffets.

The Torah, which gives the Sabbath laws, was revealed after the time of Abraham. In modeling Muslims after Abraham, the Qur'an distinguishes Muslims by directing them to the United Day of Prayer rather than the Jewish Sabbath. Instead of celebrating the day in which God observed the world he had created, Muslims congregate on the sixth day, Friday, the day on which Humanity was created. According to Islamic intellectual Shamim Siddiqi, "It was on Friday when Adam was created, and he entered *Jannah* [Paradise] on the same day of the week. Adam was put in this world on Friday, and *Qayamah* (Day of Judgment) will also commence on Friday."

Shamim also explained that during *Jahiliyah* (the Age of Ignorance), Arabs called this day *Yawmul Arooba*. Five hundred and sixty years before the ministry of Muhammed (peace upon him), Kaab bin Loui (an ancestor of Muhammed) renamed the day *Jumu'ah*, and on this day Kaab addressed the Quraysh congregation and told them of the coming of the Prophet of God (peace!). Kaab was so respected by the Quraysh that they started their calendar from the date he died. The importance of Jumu'ah, therefore, was recognized by the Arabs before the advent of Islam (as an organized religion).

Due to long-instilled habit, I still observe Sunday as my weekly day of enjoying God's gift of rest. It's a relaxing day for sitting in the porch swing or by the crackling fireplace to read the Qur'an and sip tea, taking time for long, sincere prayers, writing letters, and taking afternoon naps in the sun.

Whenever I can manage traveling the long distance to the nearest mosque, I can enjoy the *taleem* (education) service, which is similar to Sunday School.

Jesus (peace upon him) introduced a new perspective when he said, "Humanity was not made for the Sabbath, but the Sabbath was made for Humanity" (Mark 2: 27). Jesus did not change the Torah, but his twist of common sense offset the Pharisaic elaborations. Whether previously Jewish or Christian, a convert to Islam may be confused about how to reconcile the Sabbath. The Torah commandments should necessarily remain important to the Jewish Muslim, and I think that Jews should try to continue their beautiful Judaic traditions even as they make Islam their religion. As your Islamic spirit emerges in a natural and relaxed way, you will know when to release the good traditions that once served a purpose in your life but are no longer necessary to your spiritual health. As Jesus implied, it's your Sabbath. Do whatever feels comfortable to you, and don't judge others for their actions. God is to be glorified and exalted every day!

Along your spiritual journey, your life will continue to take on changes, but each change is an important part of the pattern that your life is following. Discard only the parts of your past that are detrimental to your future; hold onto the parts that make you a unique servant of God (blessed and exalted is He). Return to God all that you have been and all that you are, and allow Him to mold your life as He sees fit.

> O Lord, accept and receive all my freedom, my memory,
> My intelligence, my will, and all that I have and possess.
> My Lord, You have given these things to me.
> I now give them back to You. All belongs to You.
> Utilize these gifts according to Your will.
> I ask only for Your love and grace; they are enough for me.
> *[Ignatius of Loyola (1491-1556), founder of the Jesuits (Spain)]*

21. DON'T LET ANYBODY MAKE A MONKEY OUT OF YOU

> You knew those among you who disobeyed [the laws of] the Sabbath.
> We said to them, "Be despised apes."
> We made it an example for their time and later times.
> It was a lesson to those who have reverence.
> *(Surah 2: 65-66)*

"Linda, you better be careful; you're liable to fall off that limb," Saffy Barph called as she took a walk through the woods and past my house.

"Well, if I fall, I'll just get back up," I said as I adjusted myself on a tree limb and prepared to saw off a few low-hanging branches.

She laughed and said, "When you get as old as I am and fall, you won't be able to get up —not by yourself anyway."

I asked, "Exactly how old are you, Saffy?"

She told me her birthday, and I figured out that she was ten days younger than I! She looked ten years older. She drank hard whiskey, smoked cigars, wore a bikini and spent hours in the sun, and chowed down on pork sausage. That kind of stuff ages a person. A person's entire body eventually reflects his or her lifestyle. Our bodies should reflect the lifestyle God has described for us in His Word.

For the Israelites, the Ten Commandments contained the order, "Observe the Sabbath and keep it holy. You have six days in which to do your work, but the seventh day is a day of rest dedicated to Me. On that day, there should be no work performed by you, your children, your employees, your animals [used in labor], or the foreigners living among you. In six days, I the Sovereign Lord created the earth, the sky, the oceans, and everything in them, but on the seventh day, I celebrated."[20] That is why I, the Sovereign Lord, blessed the Sabbath and made it holy" (Exodus 20: 8-11). Further, Jews were warned, "You are to keep the Sabbath holy. Anyone who curses the Sabbath will suffer death. Anyone who performs work on the Sabbath will be separated from his or her people" (Exodus 31: 14).

Remains of some prehistoric, ape-like hominids are thought by some scientists to have been humans affected by rickets caused by a deficiency in Vitamin D. The physical deformities of rickets may have caused victims to be cast from their societal communities. Perhaps rickets affected the fishing village described in the Qur'an: "...they transgressed concerning the Sabbath, for on the Sabbath, the fish [bold due to the traditional lack of fishing activity that day] came right up to them with their heads up [to catch insects]. On days other than the Sabbath, however, the fish [inadvertently trained to hide on fishing days] did not come. Thus We made a trial [through the temptation to fish on the Sabbath when the fish least expected it] of those given to transgression. .... We visited the transgressors with a terrible punishment because of their sin. .... We said to them, 'Be despicable apes!'" (Surah 7: 163-166).

Some Muslims accept this verse as literal in meaning, and others consider it simply a metaphor. Another possibility is that the people suffered from a vitamin or calcium deficiency –like rickets or osteoporosis— and became ape-like in appearance? Whatever is meant by "apes" should not be a point of contention. The verses simply clarify that the Sabbath laws were part of the Torah that Jews should obey, and the Sabbath-breakers' experience is a sign for all believers.

No Muslim is excused from the Jumu'ah congregation "except a sick person, a traveler, a woman [caring for the home and children], a small child, or a slave."[21] In a non-Muslim society, being an employee may feel like slavery to one whose employer will not accommodate the Muslim for the sake of the Friday worship. But don't let your employer make a monkey out of you. You can join the symphony of prayers during a break period, even if you can only stand and pray silently. If you do not get a break, you can have a prayer in your heart and silently ponder the name of God and all the wonders His name implies. Substitute a good deed, because that also is a form of worship. Become more aware and appreciative of your sensory gifts, and remember those who live without some of the capabilities that you have. Through simple acts of kindness and politeness, witness to those around you. Perhaps you can get a recording of the *khutba* (sermon) and listen to it later.

For the sake of our neighbors and friends, Muslims should show respect for the Christian and Jewish Sabbaths. If you live near a church, for example, don't mow your yard on Sunday morning. If your neighbor is a religious Jew, wait until the family has gone to the synagogue before you wash your car on Saturday. When we Muslims show respect for the religious observances of others, we are helping others to take a step toward showing respect for Muslim traditions. May we all be civil to one another and not act like a planet of apes!

I pray that we keep our minds receptive to new perspectives
And avoid extremism so we may grow understanding of
And appreciation for all living beings and
Our connections with the natural world and the universe.
May we become filled with generosity of spirit
And true compassion and love for created things.
I pray that we gain peace and strength from being kind and loving.
May we take nothing for granted in this life.
May we learn acceptance and understanding
In order to rise above mere tolerance.
[inspired by Jane Goodall (zoologist famous for her work with apes)][22]

22. RIDICULOUS DOGMA

Among people are those who, with no knowledge,
purchase frivolous stories,
to mislead from the path of Allah and hurl ridicule.
For them is the humiliating penalty.
(Surah 31: 6)

During the fifties, Mama took me to a traveling, tent revival. It was common then for a preacher and his crew to travel across the country, scouting for a place to set up a huge, carnival-size tent. They would get permission from a farmer with a field laid fallow, from the owner of a vacant, parking lot, or from anyone else with land not in use.

At the revival, the preacher was casting out demons and shouting hallelujahs. People were shaking and rolling in the aisles. Mama explained that the preacher liked for people to fall on the floor and roll around; after the service, he could collect all the loose change that fell from their pockets.

Things were really rocking when Franny Filup stumbled in. She was drunk from whiskey and wanted to relax, out of the cold. She found a chair near the back, and soon she was slouched and snoring, sound asleep.

The preacher uncovered the baptismal pool, an inflated kiddy pool, and began urging people to get saved and be baptized. One woman squealed as she ran up to the preacher. She was shaking and babbling nonsense. Thinking she was possessed, the preacher hit her on the forehead and yelled, "Heal!" She fell backward onto the straw-covered, dirt floor. Her body started writhing and jerking, and suddenly a horrible, bellowing racket rumbled from her belly and roared from her mouth. It was so loud and alarming that it awakened Franny Filup. Franny jumped from her chair and screamed, "O Lordy, Lordy!"

A man near Franny jumped up and announced, "Here's another one! She's got a demon in her too." Several people grabbed Franny and pulled her toward the front. She was cursing and fighting, but they all thought that her fuss was from the demon inside her. The preacher had to smack her in the head several times before that demon would shut up, and then he threw Franny in the pool. When she came up cursing, he dunked her back in and held her head under water. "I'm going to drown this demon in the Living Water," the preacher said with determination. Franny kept struggling until she passed out from exhaustion. "Now she's healed! Hallelujah!" the preacher bellowed as he tossed Franny's wretched body onto a haystack.

An occasional tent revival still hammers its pegs into a local pasture or vacant lot, but today most wild and wooly evangelism is kept indoors. Certain types of church members whoop and holler and enact the holy riot act. They hang from the rafters and roll in the aisles. As a test of faith, one sect carelessly handles deadly rattlesnakes as part of the regular worship service. The antics of "holy rollers" are a stark contrast to the ritualized forms of worship in most churches, however.

Islam is a regulated religion, but it is not free from weird notions and invented ideas. For example, in an Islamic magazine, an article claimed that all gambling is a sin except betting on horse races, because people involved in horseracing have too much money and need to lose some of it anyway. What kind of crazy logic is that?

Unyielding dogma also blemishes Islam. A Christian woman researched Islam in order to learn exactly what Muslims believe. She found so many contradicting dogmas that she decided, "Muslims don't even know what Muslims believe!" Different perspectives and ideas are a normal and attractive part of human diversity, but the religion is misrepresented when multiple individuals each insist that his or her way of thinking is the only correct and acceptable view.

If you believe something only because that's what you've always been taught, or because it's part of your cultural background, or because it's traditional, or because an Islamic leader said so, examine it for yourself to ensure that it is consistent with God's majesty. Although God's ordinances are absolutes that cannot change, they must necessarily be interpreted and appropriately applied with a proper balance of Revelation and reason for the best advantage for our modern world. Let us not be a religion of hardheads.

> O God, with your guidance may we ponder and evaluate ideas,
> cast away false teachings, and guide others to truth.
> Help us to recognize those who want to be teachers of God's law
> but do not know about what they are talking,
> even though they speak with confidence.
> May we forsake false traditions and foolish discussions
> that only start arguments.
> May we each have the love that comes
> from a pure heart, a clear conscience, and genuine faith.
> *(Adapted from 1 Timothy 1: 3-7)*

23. SOME DOCTRINE IS JUST CHICKEN POOP

> Here you are!
> You are those who argue about things of which you have some knowledge,
> Why would you argue about something unknown to you?
> Allah knows, and you do not know.
> *(Surah 3: 66)*

When I was growing up, my family always had chickens. It was a normal part of our life, but, as far as chickens were concerned, I thought abnormal was better. I hated the brown, icky, chicken poop that squished between my toes when I ran outside. I hated having to clean it off the floor when it was tracked inside the house.

I hated watching a chicken flop around the yard after Daddy chopped its head off with an axe. When the cut was made above the voice box, the chicken continued its distressful cackling for several minutes before its body fell silent. I hated the smell of the feathers after the chicken was scalded to expand the skin for easier plucking. Some people eat chickens' feet, but Daddy cut them off and tied them to a string necklace. Like a crazed, chicken warrior, I wore the symbol of the hunt around my neck as I plucked the stinking feathers. I hated seeing Mama clean out the guts and cut up the chicken for Sunday dinner. Once, I told her, "When I grow up, I'm never going to cut up a chicken."

She answered, "When you get married, you have to do a lot of things you don't like. That's why, when a woman gets married, her name is changed from Miss to Miz'res" (a country way of pronouncing 'Mrs.' so that it sounds like 'miseries').

I liked the chicken and dumplings and southern fried chicken that Mama made, but I hated all that blood-and-guts stuff. Even today, I can't eat chicken if I have to skin and cut the raw chicken myself.

I figured on having NO chickens whenever I had a place of my own. Tom, on the other hand, had always wanted to raise chickens. I hauled him to North Carolina from a foreign country called California and tried to civilize him, but I could never get him to realize how messy chickens were. He often mentioned that he would like to get some chickens, but I always had something grumpy to say. God, however, took Tom's side.

One day, a pair of stunning chickens mysteriously appeared in our front yard. We thought maybe they had been released by our county, which had recently repopulated wild turkeys to the area. The chickens were embellished with lavish colors of navy blue, turquoise, vermillion, yellow, and burnt sienna. The hen and rooster had never had their wings clipped, and the rooster's spurs and comb were intact. They could fly over the house and into the trees. Tana named them "Lillian and Buster," and they learned to come when called by name. They had distinct personalities and were a joy to have around. They didn't even poop everywhere! After they hatched a family, I would often sit with a chicken on my lap or walk around with one on my shoulder or on top of my head. Few people have ever seen a truly happy chicken, so they don't know that contented chickens purr like cats and sing like sparrows. I never knew it myself till then!

Only later did we learn that Lillian and Buster had been acquired by a family way over on the other side of the woods. The father in the family heard that the chickens came to us when called by name, but he did not believe it. He came over to see for himself. The chickens were in the yard. I called them, and they walked right into the house. The wife said, "Bubba was real impressed with them chickens coming to you. He can't even git his dawg to come when he calls him."

When the owners saw how happy the chickens were here, they decided to let the hen and rooster stay with us. I was delighted! I loved those chickens! Who knew that chickens could make such wonderful pets? God knew, and I didn't.

Floundering like chickens with their heads chopped off, some people cackle incessantly about religion. Just as a chicken-feet necklace falsely proclaims the hunt of a chicken warrior, pious clothing and rehearsed arguments may make a person appear to be a spiritual warrior while he or she may be just another birdbrain. Always search for truth, without taking someone else's religious instruction for granted. God wants you to use your own brain. Don't be stubborn about religious doctrine; God (blessed!) may surprise you with a new perspective. That's what happened to me when Islam found me!

> I know, O Lord, that a person's life is not his or her own;
> It is not intended for a person to direct his or her steps.
> Correct me, O Lord, but only in justice, not in anger,
> or You would reduce me to nothing.
> Pour out Your wrath on nations that do not acknowledge You,
> on people who do not call on Your name.
> (Jeremiah 10: 23-25)

24. IN YOUR WILDEST DREAMS

> Remember that you said, "O Moses, we shall not believe in you
> until Allah shows Himself to us."
> You were seized as you beheld the lightning [of the Divine Presence].

> We revived you from your death
> and gave you the opportunity to be grateful.
> *(Surah 2: 55-56)*

Lillian the hen began disappearing for days at a time. Buster became frantic whenever she was missing. Coming in like a fighter jet, she would drop by for a brief visit from time to time; Buster would make a fuss, and then she'd be gone again. Finally, in the dead of winter, she came strolling home with fourteen little chicks (we call them peep-peeps). At that time, we did not have a safe, warm place for them, so we brought them all (babies and parents) inside the house. Have you ever spent an entire winter with a house full of chickens?

On nice days, I let the chickens outside. Whenever I was ready for them to come in, all I had to do was call them, and they all came running. They would walk right into the house and settle down into the cardboard box I had lined with pine straw.

One day, after the chickens had been out for a while, Tana came running inside with a wet, cold, dead, baby chick in her hand. She had found it upside down in the dog's water bowl. Although it appeared hopeless, I tried to revive the peep-peep. I gently rubbed its chest as I dried its stiff, cold body with the warm air from a hair dryer. I was amazed when the little blob of fluff began kicking its legs. All life belongs to God (blessed and exalted is He), and, even when He uses people as instruments, all praises belong to Him.

The Divine Presence of God appeared in the form of terrifying thunder and lightning (see Exodus 19: 10-19; 20: 18; 33: 20). The consequence of beholding God face-to-face was death (Exodus 33: 20). According to quantum physics, time –past, present, and future— exists together all at once so that whatever is going to happen has already happened. Only God (blessed!) has the power to change what is. I suggest that the Children of Israel, terrified by the awesome Divine Presence, actually died in a future that never came about –that God reached into their future and changed it. In this way, they were revived from a death they never actually experienced.

Perhaps there is the possibility that, after the creation of the new earth, God will reach into our past and rewrite history. He will resurrect, not only life, but also the potentials that lives may have experienced if things had been different. Imagine what personal and universal horrors you might erase if it were possible. Well, anything is possible for God, no matter how wild the dream.

> Gracious God, at times my days run together
> Into weeks, into months, into years
> Without any conscious thought on my part.
> Then suddenly I come to myself
> In the space of a moment and realize
> How unaware and without purpose I have been.
> Yet, when I try to define my purpose,
> It seems strangely elusive.
> What did You have in mind
> When You breathed the breath of life into me?
> I ask that You will give me clarity of purpose;
> That You will reveal to me my own reason for existence;
> That You will give me the sure and certain assurance
> That, even when I have lost track of myself and my life,
> Your purpose, though unknown to me or forgotten by me,
> Is still being lived out through me.
> I ask this for the sake of Your love.
> Gracious God, I ask You to plant
> A seed of stillness in my soul.
> Everything in my life moves evermore quickly,
> And I am continually expected to fit more things
> Into time that is already brimful with activity.
> Even when I have movements that require nothing of me,
> My mind races, and I seem unable to locate a switch to turn it off.
> Give me, each day, the desire and capacity
> To breathe in the wonder of air,
> To envision a still lake on a windless dawn,
> To drop deeply into the well of my own being
> And to find there the peace of Your presence.
> I ask this for the sake of Your love.
> *[Renée Miller (USA)]*[23]

25. CHALK IT UP TO TRUTH

> They say, "In order to be guided,
> you must become Jews," or "... Christians."
> Say, "No, [I choose] the faith of Abraham the upright.
> He was not of those who idolized [false] gods."
> Say, "We believe in Allah and the revelation given to us [in the Qur'an],
> and we believe in the revelations given to
> Abraham, Ishmael, Isaac, Jacob and his descendants, Moses, Jesus,
> and the other prophets, from their Lord.
> We do not elevate one above another, and we submit to Allah."
> If (the people of the Bible) believe as you believe
> [that there is One God and that
> one must submit his/her whole self to God],
> then they are on the right track.
> If they decline, however, then they are only in opposition.
> Allah is enough for you against them. He is the Listener and the Intellect.
> *(Surah 2: 135-137)*

"I need to speak with General Bud McHazzerd immediately," my commander's voice boomed into the phone.

'Oh, gee whiz,' I thought.

My air national guard unit was involved in an intense exercise in which we were practicing war plans in the event that the United States was attacked by submarine from the Gulf of Mexico. General Bud McHazzerd was a *fictitious* marine commander, whose role could have been played by any of the men in my unit. All the men had abandoned me, however. It was up to me to man the station, and that included being Bud McHazzerd.

I replied, "Yes, Sir; just a minute, Sir." I beat the phone over my head while I tried to figure out what to do. I have a squeaky, little voice and could never be a marine commander named Bud —well, 'except in the cartoons,' I thought. I remembered a cartoon in which one of the characters ate chalk in order to have a sweet voice.

I spoke back into the phone, "Hello, Commander; this is Bud. You'll have to excuse my voice; I've been eating chalk, and it made my voice a little squeaky."

Besides having something about which to joke, my commander also had praises of "attagal" (slang for "that's the way, girl") for my being able to think quickly and respond to an awkward situation.

Muslims must also be able to respond quickly and appropriately to situations in which our beliefs are challenged. The argument for Islam is that it is the original religion. It was the religion of Adam and of Abraham (peace upon them) who lived before the existence of the Jewish nation and before the message of the Gospel. Although the Scriptures of the Torah, the Prophets, the Writings, the Gospel, and the Qur'an are components of God's Word to humanity, God's Word as a living, fluid, spiritual fire within Humanity existed from the beginning and inspired the true religion, the worship of the One True God and complete submission to Him. Islam as an organized religion began with the Revelations that formed the Qur'an, but Islam as a personal spiritual walk with God was ordained at the time of humanity's creation.

I suggest three definitions for Islam: (1) Complete submission to God; the original religion ordained by God for Adam and Eve and all creation. (2) The organized religion based on the Qur'an and the Sunnah and Hadeeth of Muhammed (peace and blessings upon him). (3) The term used by Muslims to describe the peace a believer feels when he or she submits his or her whole self to God.

In order to define Islam for non-Muslims, Muslims must reflect the selected passage in words and deeds. It is not enough to say that you (a Muslim) believe in the original Books of the Bible, but you must acquaint yourself with Biblical teachings and be able to focus on the things that make the Bible and Qur'an alike –not, as many do, what makes them different. All truth is God's truth regardless from where it comes.

The American Muslim leader Imam Warith Deen Mohammed said:

> When we read the Qur'an and Bible with proper understanding, we can clearly see that these great religious leaders were not divided one against the other. Jesus not only supported the Scripture that Moses taught, but he interpreted it and explained it so that the people could get more light on what Moses had taught them. When Prophet Muhammad of Arabia came behind Jesus, he did the same thing. He spoke from the Scriptures that Jesus had left, and he explained and interpreted what Jesus left. If our great heroes in religion

have not divided themselves one against the other, and if they have shown us that they belonged to one unified family, why are we divided?

You don't have to eat chalk to sound sweet when you have the voice of truth to speak for you. Be sure of what you believe and be able to respond to critics with intelligent, honest words that express your beliefs in a simple manner without denigrating another's religion.

Lord, teach me to love our enemies.
Make me an instrument of Your love,
For all people regardless of race, religion, nation of origin, gender,
Or any other aspect of pluralism.
Teach me to hate divisiveness and to speak and act against it.
Encourage me to stand up for those things that are righteous,
No matter what the consequences may be.
Help me this day to do some good deed in Your name,
Even though it may be for one whom I consider an enemy.
[inspired by "Teach Me to Hate Division" by Alan Paton (South Africa)][24]

26. THE SPICE OF LIFE

Among His signs are the creation of the skies and Earth
and of the variations in your languages and your colors.
Truly, in these are signs for those of knowledge.
(Surah 30: 22)

Persimmons grow wild on small trees and bask in the sun for many summer days before turning from green to orange. Until ripened by the first frost, persimmons are bitter to the human tongue. Sweet potatoes (and yams) grow within the unlit embrace of soil. Even raw, the taste is mild, and many acres are dedicated to growing sweet potatoes as a valued food product. Although sweet potatoes and persimmons are quite different, with the right ingredients, they can be combined to make a yummy, autumn pudding. I have a persimmon tree in my orchard. As soon as the frost bites them, I collect the persimmons and process the pulp to integrate with sweet potatoes for the traditional, autumn dessert.

As in a recipe, different people can come together in a healthy union. God has given us the right ingredients for combining our diversities into a peaceful and productive society without prejudice and strife. Political correctness encourages tolerance, but tolerance, like intolerance, is based on a negative value judgment. Instead of tolerance, we need to acquire sincere understanding and appreciation for one another. We must realize that spiritually there are really only two races: the righteous and the unrighteous. The righteous are responsible for living examples of kindness for those lost in sin. There will be peace and respect in America and throughout the world when every person truly believes that all people were created equally, with liberty and justice for all.

When I was in training for my black belt, several other kick boxers and I were having so much fun beating each other up that I forgot the time. I glanced at the clock; it was almost midnight. "Flying catfish!" I said out loud. "I better get home before my husband calls out the national guard!"

While I was taking off my boxing gloves, one of the men sat on the floor beside me and asked, "What does your husband think of your being here so late at night with all us black men?"

I looked around the gym. It was the first time that I realized that I was the only female there and the only white person. I was surprised. We fighters treated one another with so much respect and dignity –aside from beating the snot out of each another— that neither race nor gender was a factor. When I got my black belt, I was an even closer member of the fighting family.

In the same way, Muslims should be in spiritual training, and, by the time they get their black belts, honor and respect will have replaced any prejudices stemming from our diversity.

In the Name of God, the Most Gracious, the Most Merciful.
We appeal to You, O Lord, to have us all recognize
What you have stated repeatedly in the Holy Scriptures,
That we are all created from the same blessed pair, a male and a female,
That we are of different races and cultures,
Certainly not to despise each other,
But to be of comfort to one another.

O Allah, guide us all as Americans,
Through these difficult times.
Help us not to confuse evil acts of misguided individuals,
Of any denomination,
As emanating from the dictates of any divinely inspired faith,
Most certainly not coming from Islam,
The name that translates as peace.
Help us, O Merciful God,
To overcome our negative sense of fear
And our resulting attitudes of prejudice.
Help us rediscover the feeling
Of security, peace, and inner comfort,
Under Your protective will.
We beseech You, O Lord, Creator of the Universe,
To enlighten our hearts with a sense of
Greater forbearance and willingness to forgive,
And guide our leaders onto the right path, not to return evil for evil.
O Lord, strengthen our nation and protect us from evil,
Elevate our society and enrich the fabric of our country.
Enable us to help Humanity to overcome
Aggression, poverty, and disease.
We plead to You, O Lord,
As Prophet Muhammed did before us,
Grant that our present day be better than our yesterday,
That our tomorrow be better than today,
And, best of all,
That our ultimately blessed day be the day we stand before You.
Amen.
[Imam Fawaz Damra (Islamic Center of Cleveland, Ohio)][25]

27. THANKFUL FOR AN AWL AND ALL

Who can provide you with sustenance
if He were to withhold His provision?

> Bunk! They persist in pride and rebellion.
> *(Surah 67: 21)*

How often do you thank God (blessed and exalted is He) for the most mundane things? I even thank Him for toilet paper. My family used corncobs and crumpled newspapers until I was nearly grown.

Each day of mine is either hilarious or tragic. Sometimes it's hilariously tragic or tragically hilarious. This particular day was no different. With half a dozen cats sleeping on top of me, it's always a struggle for me to get out of bed in the morning. I wrestled my way out from under the covers. Munchkin latched onto my nightgown with her claws and her teeth, trying to keep me in bed so we could all snuggle.

I got free and wobbled to the kitchen. The cats began begging for fish food. All the animals here had food oddities. The dog preferred the cats' food, and the rabbits liked the goats' food. Raccoons ate the dog's food, and the goats ate the chickens' food. The chickens liked macaroni and cheese, and the ducks' favorite food was fried chicken.

The fish struggled to suck down some flakes. He had been having a hard time swallowing since he had gotten a flake of food stuck sideways in his throat. That was the first time I ever saw a fish do the shimmy-shimmy shakes!

I grabbed a little grub myself as I loaded a box with tools to take to my sister's house to do some repairs. I put the box into the back seat of a cramped, old clunker so small that the back seat was almost in the front seat. I got into the car and pulled the seatbelt. I felt resistance, so I just yanked till the belt was free. I buckled it, and the belt lay limp across my lap. I picked it up and studied it. It was ripped apart! I looked behind me and saw my hacksaw sticking up out of the box. It was grinning with pieces of seatbelt stuck in its teeth. Some people would have been upset, but I was thankful. I have a car. With a seatbelt! I have a hacksaw. And I have an awl and thread with which to repair the seatbelt. I'm grateful for all those things.

I'm grateful that Tana cared enough to buy me some plastic, scented cherries to hang in the car, but I was allergic to the deodorant on them. Heading down the road, I started sneezing. Each time I sneezed, I inadvertently accelerated, and I sneezed in rapid succession. "Aaachooo!" went I. "Vrrrmmm!" went the car. "Aaachooo!" "Vrrrmmm!" "Aaachooo!" "Vrrrmmm!" I was just grateful there was not a highway patrolman to stop me and question my sporadic driving.

By the time I neared my sister's house, my breakfast of Slim-Fast and M & M's was wearing thin. I stopped at a greasy food joint for a bowl of watered-down chili. Another customer began a conversation with me as she waited for her grease-burger. She was complaining about the bitter wind and clouds.

"I thought it was supposed to be a nice day," she said.

"It *is* a nice day," I insisted. "We aren't having a tsunami or a flood or an earthquake or a tornado. With all the crazy weather around the world, I'm just thankful to wake up and find that my bed is still in my house and that my house is not in the creek."

I finally got to work repairing my sister's floor. My sister Toy reminded me, "When you get my age, you won't feel like crawling around on the floor and up ladders and stuff like that." I was already older than she was when she first started telling me that.

I worked for several hours and then stretched my aching neck and shoulders. "Ohhhh, pus and spit," I softly moaned.

Toy was in her bedroom while I was in the kitchen. Toy, who couldn't hear an avalanche falling on a landmine field, said, "Linda, you sound tired."

I yelled back to her, "How can you hear me moaning when you can't hear a word I say when I'm talking straight at you?"

She said, "What?"

I muttered, "Huh? What did you say? Is somebody talking? What? Are you saying something?"

Toy came out of her bedroom. "Are you talking to me?"

I said, "No, I'm just making fun of you."

She said, "What?"

I came to a stopping point and loaded everything back into the car. I got home just in time to see the crazy raccoons fighting over the last piece of cherry pie somebody had left me. I chased away the raccoons and stared longingly at the miserable remains of what I could only imagine to have been a scrumptious pie. I went into the house and stared out the window at what was left of the pie. That was the first time in my life that somebody, besides Mama, had ever baked me a cherry pie. And I missed it! Smoke puffed from my ears. Suddenly a raccoon ran out of the woods, snatched up the remnant of pie –pan and all— and dashed back into the woods.

I tried to be thankful about that cherry pie. The raccoons were thankful.

They were grinning with pieces of cherries stuck in their teeth. I was thankful that somebody loved me enough to bake me a cherry pie, but I wanted to have my pie and eat it too.

Of course, I didn't *need* a cherry pie; I just wanted it. Prophet Muhammed (peace and blessings upon him) told a funny story about Job (peace upon him) and how he wanted all the little blessings he could get. "When Prophet Job was taking a bath, golden locusts started falling on him. Job collected them [to eat] and wrapped them in his clothes [that he had laid aside for his bath]. The Lord asked Job, 'O Job, haven't I given you enough stuff that you don't need locusts?' Job answered, "Yes, by Your power! Still I cannot forego any of Your blessings.""[26]

Later that evening, my brother Ron called to ask how I liked the cherry pie he had baked and left for me on the picnic table. I told him what had happened to the pie, and he said, "Well, raccoons gotta eat too." But, Ron, I feed them plenty of dog food!

When Tom learned of the cherry pie disaster, he came home and baked me a cherry pie himself. Finally, it was I grinning with pieces of cherries stuck in my teeth.

> Now that the sun has set,
> I sit and rest and think of You.
> Make peace sink into my weary body.
> Make my legs and arms stop aching.
> Make my nose stop sneezing.
> Make my head stop thinking.
> Grant me sleep in Your arms.
> *[Dinka evening prayer (Sudan)]*

28. I'M BACK!

> The servants of the Most Gracious
> are those who walk upon the earth in humility,
> and who, when addressed by the ignorant, say, "Peace!"
> [They are] those who spend the night in adoration of their Lord
> as they prostrate and stand.

> [They are] those who say,
> "Our Sovereign Lord, avert us from the wrath of Hell
> for its wrath is indeed inescapable.
> It is indeed a wretched residence and place for retirement."
> [They are] those who, in spending, are neither extravagant nor miserly,
> but maintain moderation.
> [They are] those who call upon no god other than Allah.
> They do not end life, which Allah has made sacred,
> except in matters of justice.
> They do not commit acts of sexual immorality.
> Anyone guilty [of any of these crimes] reaps punishment.
> The penalty on the Day of Resurrection will be doubled,
> and he/she will exist with shame continuously.
> [That is] unless he/she repents, believes, and lives righteously.
> And performs deeds of goodness.
> Allah will exchange the evil of such a person for goodness.
> Allah is Most Forgiving, Most Merciful.
> Whoever repents and lives righteously
> has truly turned to Allah with true conviction.
> *(Surah 25: 63-71)*

My first, true love was a '65 Chevrolet Corvair Monza Sports Coupe. I worked in the furniture shop for a year and saved my money until I had $1000, the exact price of the Corvair. It was used and a bit beat up. There was a big hole in the floorboard just behind the driver's seat. If I hit something, I could turn around and look through the floor to see what I had run over. I loved that old car, and I became known as "that crazy blond in the purple Corvair." When I joined the air force, Daddy made me sell my car. He didn't want it junking up the yard while I was gone. I sadly watched it being driven away by some stupid boy who wrecked it a couple weeks later.

I never expected to have another cool, sports car in this life. I figured one would be waiting for me in Heaven. But guess what Tom bought me for our thirtieth wedding anniversary. Uh-huh. A red one! In excellent condition. A classic '66 Corvair. With no hole in the floorboard! When my neighbor Saffy Barph asked about my car, I explained how cool I was when, as a teenager, I wore bell-bottoms, tiny red sunglasses, love beads, flowers in my hair, and raced around in my purple Corvair.

Saffy laughed and said, "I'm afraid those days are long gone for you and me both."

I said, "Speak for yourself. I'm back!"

Muslims (as well as Jews) do not believe in the concept of original sin. The Church teaches that everyone is a sinner from the time he or she is born. When I was a school kid, a friend told me how distraught and depressed her mother was because she had a baby that died before the infant could be baptized. The father was a Lutheran minister, and the family believed that the innocent baby would spend an eternity in Hell because she didn't get sprinkled. I was raised Southern Baptist, and I had never heard such a ridiculous idea. Later I learned that Catholic hospitals used to have baptismal founts in the birthing rooms so that every baby could be immediately "saved" through baptism.

One of the Scriptures that the Church uses to justify the concept of original sin is one of the Psalms of David: "Surely I was sinful at birth. I was sinful from the time my mother conceived me" [Psalms 51: 7 (51: 5, Christian Bible)]. David (peace upon him) wrote this hyperbole to express how rotten he felt after Nathan (peace upon him) had confronted him about David's hanky-panky with Bathsheba.[27] In another place, David said, "You [O God] drew me from the womb, made me secure at my mother's breast. From birth, I belonged to You. Even as I was in my mother's womb, You were my God" [Psalms 22: 10-11 (22: 9-10, Christian Bible)]. At no place does the Bible say that a baby will go to Hell if he or she dies before being baptized. Muslims whisper the shahada into the ears of newborn babies, but we don't believe that a baby will go to Hell if it dies without that blessing.

As soon as an infant is born, Satan begins to tease him or her and whisper suggestions of mischief. Muslims believe that everyone is born pure and with the fire of God's wisdom. Every person, however, has the freedom to choose whether to allow the fuel of God's guidance to build the fire into the full measure of God's grace or to allow the fire to die until the soul is left to wander in miserable darkness.

There are many reasons for a person's not developing a life pleasing to God (blessed and exalted is He). Some are innocent victims of their family environments or of lives emerging from tragic situations. Others are rebellious and stubborn. But when a lost sinner pokes at the dead embers that only God can reignite, and then gives him- or herself in complete submission to God (blessed!), he or she can happily say, "I'm back! AlhamdulAllah! I'm back!"

> Lord, tend Your fire within my heart.
> Awaken my soul not as a frightened lark
> That flits about confused and distressed.
> Awaken me as a baby content with rest,
> Eager to begin another blessed day,
> Learning and loving Your precious way.

29. SPARE THE SPIT AND FUMES

> They invest, whether in times of prosperity or adversity.
> They restrain anger and forgive people.
> Allah loves those who perform goodwill.
> *(Surah 3: 134)*

I had a rotten day. A driver in a parking lot smacked into the side of my '66 Corvair. I saved the spit and tears for later even though the other driver, completely at fault, was upset only because she was going to be late for "an important appointment." I had to keep her car blocked so she wouldn't take off without waiting for the police report.

When I learned that she was just going to a bridge party, I said, "Oh, I thought it was something *really* important, like a doctor's visit."

She snapped, "Well, it may not seem like much to you, but it's important to me! I just lost my husband, and I'm trying to get on the best I can." Tana, who was with me, thought that, when the woman said she had "lost" her husband, she had gambled him away at one of her bridge parties.

Despite the other driver's being obnoxious, I remained calm, gracious, and forgiving. This was a wonderful example for Tana. She had wanted to cuss the old bat –uh, I mean, elderly lady— but I quickly clamped my hand over Tana's mouth. Finally, the old lady simmered down to an apologetic attitude. Tana remarked on how much she had learned about how to properly handle a tentatively explosive situation.

The Jewish book of Proverbs has advice worth remembering: "A gentle response calms anger, but a harsh one stirs it up. When wise people speak, they make knowledge attractive, but silly people spout nonsense. The Lord sees what happens everywhere. Whether we are kind or angry, He is watching. Kind words bring assurance, but cruel words crush a person's spirit. Hot tempers elevate arguments, but patience brings about peaceful solutions. Kind people think before they respond. Arrogant people are quick to respond, but their words stir up trouble. A smiling face will make a person happy, and good words will make everyone feel better" (Proverbs 15: 1-4, 18, 28, 30).

As Muslims, we should concentrate on being calm and courteous and live an example of souls at peace with God and the universe. Spit and fumes only breed bacteria and germs. The soil of patience and kindness is a flowerbed of delight and tranquility for the whole world to enjoy.

> O Lord, put courage into my heart,
> And take away all that may hinder me from serving You.
> Free my tongue to proclaim Your goodness,
> So that all may understand me.
> Give me friends to advise and help me,
> So that, by working together, our efforts may bear abundant fruit.
> Above all, let me constantly remember
> That my actions are worthless
> Unless they are guided by Your hand.
> *[Prophet Muhammed (peace and blessings upon him)]*

30. A FACE FULL OF UNBELIEF

> One day some faces will brighten, and some faces will darken.
> To those whose faces are dark:
> "Did you reject faith after having accepted it?
> Now suffer the torment for your disbelief."

> Those whose faces are bright, however,
> will live within Allah's mercy eternally.
> *(Surah 3: 106-107)*

I got my damaged Corvair repaired and repainted by someone who specialized in vintage vehicles. It looked so good that maybe I should have *paid* that woman for hitting me.

Tom's car, on the other hand.... Well, I was beating up my punching bag when I heard Rip the dog whimpering. I looked out the window and saw smoke. Rip loved to play with fire, and he often pulled things from the burn pit. Tom had burned trash earlier, and Rip had pulled some still-smoldering, junk mail from the hole. He had dragged it into the woods where the heat kindled dry leaves.

A ring of fire was creeping through the leaves and undergrowth. I hung up my boxing gloves, got a bucket of water and a shovel, and proceeded to work on the crawling flames. My daddy was practically an arsonist —always burning piles of stuff in the yard— so I had a lot of experience in firefighting. I did not realize, however, that Rip's fire had already cut a path through the woods, circled back, and was creeping to the back of the car shed.

When the tiny flames hit the dry vines tenaciously clinging to the wooden supports of the shed, the fire exploded into an ecstasy of newly found energy. The fire quickly zapped up to the fiberglass roof. Tom returned from an errand just as tremendous flames surged across the entire roof of the shed. He called 911 for backup, but there would be no salvation for his 1930 Model A Ford and 1952 Ford truck or for our lawnmower, bicycles (including a rare two-seater), and all the other stuff that gets thrown into a car shed. The windows popped in the beautiful, restored vehicles, gasoline cans exploded, and a fiery rage consumed everything. (My Corvair was safely parked under a shade tree.)

I went further into the woods to control the flames still creeping through the leaves toward other people's land. Fire trucks arrived, and the spectacle became surrounded by firefighters and most of the local population. One of the firefighters shot a hard blast of water through the woods. The blast hit the ground in front of me and bounced ashes and dirt all over my face. When I came walking out of the woods, everyone's mouth dropped open, and eyes bulged in horror. My face was black from the ashes, and everyone thought that I was burned. I had to fend off the firefighters trying to give me first aid.

The black on my face went away with soap and water, but, unless a backslider repents and allows God to wash away the grime of sin during this life, he or she will have to live with it continuously. Horrifying looks will testify to the gloom and despair of being deprived of the light and grace of God (blessed and exalted is He).

For the fire chief's report, we had to explain how the fire started. The fire chief shook his head and said, "I've heard a lot of wild tales, but this is the first time anybody has tried to put it off on the dog."

On the Day of Judgment, people will likely have plenty of excuses; they might even try to put it off on the dog. But the true tale, however wild, will come to light, and there won't be an emergency number to call to get out of that hot spot!

The burned fiberglass turned into something that looked like silky threads. Birds used those threads to build nests. What a wonderful way for God to give us the message that, no matter what doom and gloom this world gives us, He is always able to help us make good use of it.

> [They are] those who say,
> "Our Lord, we have indeed believed,
> so forgive us our sins and save us from the agonizing fire."
> *(Surah 3: 16)*

31. HE CHOSE ME

> Say, "O Allah, Master of Sovereignty,
> You empower those You choose, and You demote those You choose.
> You honor whom You please, and You debase whom You please.
> In Your hand is all goodness. Truly, you have power over all things.
> You cause the night to overcome the day, and the day to fade into night.
> You bring the living from the dead, and You bring the dead from the living.
> You give sustenance to whom You please, without measure."
> *(Surah 3: 26-27)*

Despite his wild acts of pyromania, Rip was the best dog I ever had. After a long, happy life, he died peacefully in his sleep. I sure miss him! Rip was so gentle that he would not even harm the rabbits that spotted our yard, but he had a ferocious bark. He kept away prowlers; wild, carnivorous animals; and dangerous, stray dogs and wolves. We were safe with Rip as our security guard and burglar alarm, and, as long as I kept a dog, I never had trouble with the deer eating my garden.

Rip was one of two puppies abandoned by an irresponsible idiot who had shoved the dogs from his car and onto the road. I was working in my art studio one day with the door propped open. A sad-eyed dog walked into my studio, plopped down at my feet, and stayed. When a neighbor told me about the other dog, I found the pup, and cared for him until I could find a permanent home for him. I named the pups "Rip" and "Tore" because they left a mess of ripped and torn debris all over the yard. I gave Tore to a man who immediately fell in love with the beautiful, all-white, longhaired dog that was a mix of collie and miscellaneous mutt. I kept Rip who was white with brown splotches. I adopted Rip because he first adopted me. He found me and made me his friend.[28]

God (blessed and exalted is He) chose me, unworthy as I am, to understand the truth of the Qur'an. Sometimes I wonder why He did not choose someone with more influence and prestige. I can only dabble in attempts to try to share His truth while someone with greater talents, fame, and wealth could do so much more. His choice is a mystery to me, but I chose to follow the path of Islam because God first chose me.

The Qur'an says that Christians who accept the Light of Islam in addition to the Gospel receive "a double portion of His mercy" (Surah 57: 28). Who could turn down an offer like that?

> Supreme God, Your light is brighter than the sun.
> Your purity is whiter than mountain snow.
> You are present wherever I go.
> All people of wisdom praise You, so I too put faith in all Your words.
> I know that everything You teach is true.
> Neither the angels in Heaven nor the demons in Hell
> Can know the perfection of Your wisdom,
> For it is beyond all understanding.
> Only Your Spirit knows You; only You can know Your true self.

You are the source of all being,
The power of all power, the ruler of all creatures.
You alone understand everything You are.
In Your mercy, reveal to me all that I need to know
In order to find peace and joy.
Tell me the truths that are necessary for the world in which I live.
Show me how I can meditate upon You.
Help me learn from You the wisdom that I need.
I never tire of hearing You, because Your words bring life.
[Prince Arjuna (8th century BCE), warrior (India)][29]

32. HELL IN A FLASH!

Truly, as for those who do not believe in Our signs,
We will burn them in a fire. Every time their skins are roasted,
We will give them new skins to keep them enduring the punishment.
Truly, Allah is Victorious, Perfectly Wise.
(Surah 4: 56)

Hot flashes —big deal. That's what I used to think, but menopause is a lot worse than it sounds. The intensity of a hot flash is comparable to stepping from an icy cold, air-conditioned office and directly into the full blast of a hot, summer day on blacktop pavement in Alabama. The difference is that the heat comes from within. A hot flash begins in the center of the body and builds like a billowing ocean wave. Suddenly, with the force of a tidal wave crashing on the beach, a flash of hell surges through the pores of the skin as the body screams, "Wipe out!"

I wondered if global warming was my fault. I think I may have been the main ingredient in a few, perfect storms. I felt like a walking fire hazard. Flowers wilted whenever I passed a garden, and my name was added to the list of things banned while pumping gas.

As suddenly as it came, a hot flash dissipates. The hairs of the body tingle as the sweat leaves them, and the skin cools like coastal sand under a setting sun. Finally, the skin feels refreshed and ready for the next big wave!

If the Qur'an were written only for women in their post-prime, metaphors of Hell would likely be in terms of menopause. Whatever descriptions are used, however, the horror of Hell cannot be fully comprehended. The Qur'an says that in Hell a person will "neither die nor live" (Surah 20: 74). What the hell kind of existence is that!

Those who reject God will enter a spiritual existence where they are forced to accept God's reality by having to continuously accept His rejection of them. Just when the unbelievers feel that their senses, or "skins," are adjusting to the inferno of existence without the grace of God, their full awareness will be restored so that they will experience the full-shock trauma they got when they first entered continuous damnation. No metaphor in any human language can adequately prepare a person for that! Global warming is nothing compared to eternal menopause!

> O Sovereign Lord, my Defender, I call to You. Listen to my plea.
> If you do not respond,
> I will be among those condemned to the world of the dead.
> Hear me when I cry to You for help,
> When I lift my hands toward Your holy place.
> Do not condemn me with the wicked, with those who do evil,
> with those whose words are friendly, but who have hatred in their hearts.
> *(Psalms 28: 1-3)*

33. TAKE THE STAIRS

> As for those who believe and perform righteous deeds,
> We will admit them to an eternal home
> of gardens nourished by underground rivers.
> They will have pure, holy companions.
> We will admit them to deep, cool shade.
> *(Surah 4: 57)*

Given a choice, I usually prefer the stairs to the elevator; it helps keep me in shape. After all, people should be able to tackle the stairs in case the building catches fire and the elevators are off limits. Life often offers choices in which one choice is the easy way out while the more difficult choice will lead to greater reward. If you always take the easy way out, you won't be in shape for taking on the difficult challenge when there is no choice.

Iggy McGooey took an easy way out. He had sown his wild oats all over the county, and, as a result, had about a dozen illegitimate children. He refused to get a job because he knew that all his earnings would have to go for child support. Iggy's wife then had to work two jobs to support their legitimate family.

One day Iggy's wife came home from working all day, exhausted as usual. Iggy was relaxing with a can of beer, and Mrs. McGooey dutifully started making supper. Mrs. McGooey opened the cabinet and got a can of beans. Suddenly, she had a hot flash! With an accompanying, inspirational, mood swing, she hit Iggy over the head with the beans and knocked him out.

If bad women were condemned to spend an eternity in menopause, bad men would be condemned to have to live with them. Everyone will add to each other's misery.

Whether it's a spouse who is a cowardly jerk, the loud-mouthed idiot next door, or the backstabbing villain at the work place, each of us knows someone who strives to make everyone else's life as miserable as possible in order to make his or her own way easier. Such people may think they are on their way up, but they may be surprised to find that the elevators are down due to eternal fire.

Like taking the stairs instead of the elevator, earning salvation is more difficult than pursuing self-interests. The companionship we will enjoy, however, is one of the things that will make Heaven worth the extra effort.

In his description of Heaven, Abdulla Yusuf Ali wrote, "Dress of most artistic taste will add dignity to social (interaction), and there will be thrones and symbols of honour. There will be companionship —individual companionship, companionship of equal age, as well as general companionship. And those whom we loved in this life —mothers [and fathers], wives [and husbands], sisters [and brothers], relatives, children, friends— will add to our joy by their company in a transformed Love as superior to earthly Love as...the Garden of Heaven [is] to an earthly Garden. The condition of Faith and good Life is of course attached, for no disharmony can enter to mar the dignity of Heaven. .... Perfected Love will not be content with Self, but like a note of music will find its melody in communion with others."[30]

Paradise, I think, is the original creation from which our souls have descended. In this world of struggle, we are given the opportunity to perform the righteous deeds that will earn God's favor so we may be forgiven of any faults. When a person of faith validates that faith by a righteous lifestyle, God's reward is grace. A shade tree in Paradise awaits each faithful believer, and we can all look forward to picnicking in deep, cool shade with pure and holy companions.

> ...Our Lord, we believe, so record us among the witnesses.
> What reason do we have not to believe in Allah
> and the truth that has come to us?
> We long for our Lord to include us in the company of the righteous.
> *(Surah 5: 83-84)*

34. A LEAGUE OF HYPOCRITES

> The hypocrites, both men and women, are in cahoots with each other.
> They compel evil and forbid what is right,
> and they close their hands [from doing good deeds].
> They have forgotten Allah, so He has forgotten them.
> Truly, the hypocrites are defiantly disobedient.
> *(Surah 9: 67)*

In the military, I looked pretty darn good in my dress blues. One day I was walking down a sidewalk beside which some noisy, male airmen had congregated. I heard one of them say, "Quit cussing, guys; there's a lady coming." The men became quiet, and all eyes turned to study me as I walked toward them.

I kept my military stride in perfect balance, with shoulders back, gut sucked in, eyes straight ahead, and no expression. Just as I got to the group of soldiers, I turned to the one that had hushed the others. I gave a charming smile and said, "Thank you, sweetie."

His mouth spread into a smile that almost wrapped around his head, and all the other men went, "Ooooo-ahhhh."

I enlisted in the WAF when the men's and women's services were separate. Male and female members were encouraged to maintain an honorable amount of decorum and respect between the genders. In order to allow the military to integrate the unique qualities of women throughout the armed services, the women's branches were discontinued, and women and men began training and serving more closely together. Later, when I enlisted in the North Carolina Air National Guard, the two gender categories were combined, so I can testify to the difference before and after the combination.

Previously, men's and women's boot camps were separate, and the all-female classes included instruction on proper attire and behavior for ladies, and men were taught to keep a respectable distance from female members. The chaplain's office offered occasional, mandatory, gender-separate meetings to discuss such things as sexual responsibility and sexual harassment.

As women benefited from equal opportunities (with some exceptions) of a combined military, their right to their own boot camp was lost. The men also lost the unique camaraderie of a male-only boot camp. Women are now thrust into the awkward situation of having to physically perform alongside men who sometimes joke and snicker whenever a woman struggles to toe the mark. In the field, men and women often do not have the privacy of separate latrines and sleeping facilities. If exposed to chemicals, men and women have to strip naked to be decontaminated in the same tent.

With the feminist movement, many women got the idea that, in order to be equal to men, they had to take up the same bad habits as immoral men who engaged in cursing, drinking, and sexual immorality. The barrier, or metaphorical veil, between men and women in the armed forces has been destroyed. As a result, the military has become rancid with immoral degeneration. There are many moral, religious men and women in the services, but they are surrounded by more vulgarity, more temptations, and more disrespect than ever before. Women are not safe from many of the men with whom they serve as rape statistics rise.

The solution is, not to take a step back to inequality, but to take a step forward to different but equal branches that inculcate values and morals in a manner respectful to both men and women. Women join the military for the same reasons as men. The most common reasons are to honorably serve one's country and to defend rights and freedoms, for educational opportunities and to learn valuable skills, and for expanding one's knowledge of the world outside one's own hometown. There are a wide variety of jobs in the military; for examples, slots in medical fields, chaplain services, communications, aircraft maintenance, food services, and logistics. Women have proven to be valuable assets in the overall performance of the military, but they (and men) should not have to suffer humiliating and embarrassing situations simply for the sake of a mixed-gender military.

Most of the femi-ninnies who pushed for gender-combined services never even served in the military. They had their own agenda and had no sincere interest in what was best for service women. There are alternatives for achieving equality without sacrificing dignity, but the hypocrites aren't interested in sensible solutions. For example, women's service aboard submarines has already been established with some controversy, but no one even has the guts to suggest an all-female crew.

During Desert Storm, Colin Powell reportedly said that female recruits knew what they were getting into when they joined, so they don't deserve any special consideration. My opinion is that, because women knew what they were getting into *and joined anyway,* they do deserve special consideration. Both men and women serving in the armed forces deserve living and working conditions that are as dignified and comfortable as possible. The hypocrites did not help women take a step forward, but a plunge downward.

> May all Your enemies perish, O Lord,
> but may those who love you be like the sun rising in its strength.
> *[Judges 5: 31, from the song of Deborah
> (judge, army commander, and prophet) (peace upon her)]*

35. FOR A MIGHTIER UMMAH

> The believers, both men and women, are protectors of one another.
> They enforce what is just and forbid what is evil.
> They observe routine prayers, practice the required charity,
> and obey Allah and His messenger.
> On them, Allah will pour His mercy.
> Indeed, Allah is Victorious, Perfectly Wise.
> *(Surah 9: 71)*

When I was building a rock chimney onto the house, a redneck strolling through the woods stopped and remarked, "That must be awfully hard work for a woman." Did he think it would be an easy task for a man?

The director of an Islamic women's shelter for victims of domestic abuse sought a Muslima to perform the duties of an imam for the women at the shelter. Dozens of calls were in vain as Muslim leaders insisted that women could not fill the role of imams. Finally, the director called a church, and three, female, church leaders were immediately dispatched to the shelter. Christian women then counseled Muslim women and led them in Christian prayers –all because much of our Islamic leadership has no vision. Yes, we do need female imams –not to lead mixed-gender, congregational prayers, or anything else that violates Qur'anic injunctions or the Prophet's practices and directives— but to minister to girls and women and to insure that Muslimas' concerns are addressed. Women must be trained in the duties of an imam, not to assume the responsibilities of the male imams, but to fill an existing void. As the Islamic community progresses toward addressing the genuine ills of society –eg, teen pregnancy, domestic abuse, homelessness, drug and alcohol abuse— trained Muslimas are needed to serve in shelters, group homes, and rehab centers housing girls and women needing specialized group and individual attention, and to witness and minister to women in prisons and hospitals. Female counselors should be available at all Islamic centers to talk with girls and women about personal and feminine issues. Female leadership is also needed to help bring about solutions to the specific problems women encounter; eg, negative and demeaning experiences with the male leadership, being denied the right of access to and participation in lectures and discussions, dirty and inferior accommodations for women, and unfairly restrictive segregation that prevents women's participation in opportunities for education and spiritual growth.

The Prophet (peace upon him) did not forbid women from the mosque, and he permitted women to lead prayers in their homes and for groups of women. In Turkey, women trained as imams are called *murshidat,* which means 'guardians of the mosque'. In the USA, we now have female Muslim chaplains. Placing Muslimas in leadership positions is both traditional and modernly progressive.

Leadership in the mosque is not a right; it is a duty of those called into such service. It is not about equal rights or equal opportunities. Roles in leadership should be for the glory of God (blessed and exalted is He), not personal glory and certainly not for the glory of the femi-ninnies. Those who vehemently discourage female leadership, however, apparently have no vision for the future of Islam; if they did, they would realize that changes are needed in order to accommodate the specific and diverse needs of an evolving Ummah. Change is a good thing; the Living Word is revealed in variety and change. Insh'Allah, believing men and women will eventually elect more women to effectively and appropriately protect the interests of girls and women, to assist the male imams whenever the feminine perspective is needed, and to motivate and teach the female segment of the Ummah. Both masculine and feminine attributes are needed in order to create and maintain balanced and effective leadership.

> Lord, show us where there is loneliness,
> That we may take friendship.
> Show us where individuals are not seen as persons,
> That we may acknowledge their identity.
> Show us where there is alienation,
> That we may take reconciliation.
> *(Prayer for Women's World Day of Prayer)*

36. WILL THE REAL GUARDIANS PLEASE STAND UP?

> What chance do they have against Allah's punishment
> while they obstruct from the Sacred Mosque?
> They are not its guardians. Its guardians are only the righteous.
> Most of them do not understand.
> Their worship at the house [of worship] is nothing
> but whistling and clapping.
> Taste the penalty of your unbelief.
> *(Surah 8: 34-35)*

On a sultry, hot day, I was tending my garden while sweat stung my eyes and the tiller was rattling my bones. One of the McGooey brothers plopped his bony butt on a grassy mound beside my garden and watched me plow while he drank a Sundrop (a soft drink made in North Carolina). It's a good thing I had to stop the tiller to fill it with gas because I was about to work myself into a heat stroke. After the tiller was quiet, the boy said, "I sure am tired!"

"Why are you tired?" I asked.

"I've been swimming all morning at the park," he whined.

I huffed. It aggravated me that a healthy, stout seventeen-year-old boy was complaining about being tired from playing at the kiddie pool. He continued to complain while he relaxed and drank a Sundrop and watched a woman over half a century old grind her bones to dust as she worked like a mule. If he had any dignity, he would have given me the Sundrop and taken over the tilling while I sat on the grassy mound. But he had no gumption. His parents didn't teach him how to act, and he didn't have enough sense to figure it out on his own.

I've been to Islamic centers where the participants didn't know how to act. In hillbilly English, "They just ain't got no raisin's." They were never taught how to act in a dignified and courteous manner, and they didn't have enough sense to refine themselves. I'm sure God gave them brains; I guess they just never turned them on.

On an online news media,[31] Dr. Waheeduddin Ahme described the experience of attending a mosque where nobody knows how to act:

> If you walk into a typical masjid in Cairo or Karachi as a tourist, you will find their internal décor stupefying. Their imposing structures, the magnificence of their calligraphy, their arches and the niches will hold you spellbound. If you look at the worshippers, you will find that they are mostly old men, non-elite and sub-affluent, who have rushed in, ten minutes after the *adhan* and will soon rush out, to find their shoes near the doors, and just as quickly disappear into the melee of the city streets. There will be no women among the worshippers, as traditions forbid them from being a part of the communal religiosity. You will be told that the upkeep of the masjids is the responsibility of the ministry of religious affairs or the *waqf* boards and the public should have no part in it.

Unfriendly, hypocritical, and hurtful experiences are often reported of mosques and Islamic centers in the USA. My family and I went to an Islamic center where Tana and I were the only females. The imam got up, looked straight at Tom, and said, "Men are supposed to go to the mosque to pray; women are supposed to stay home!" After that, we *all* stayed home; we never went back.

Dr. Ahme, however, is encouraged as Islam in America progresses from its pioneering stage. About the Milwaukee Islamic Da'wa Center, he says:

> .... If you are a visitor from the Old World arriving at the Friday prayer, it will not be the building that will overawe you but the awesome diversity of the people. You will see both men and women praying in the respective sections of the masjid. You will find in its milieu, a cross-section of all the races in the world. You will receive a lesson in anthropology with which to go home. You will hear a *khutba* in English, which you will be able to understand, unlike those in Karachi or Jakarta, which will essentially be in Arabic and fall on deaf ears. Here the *khateeb* will be explaining a verse or two from the Qur'an or exposing a moralizing exhortation or lamenting about the social ills and the general misfortunes, which have befallen the Islamic *Ummah*. The exposition will enlighten you and the experience will touch your heart.
>
> In reality, our masjids in America are closer to the archetypical example of *Masjid-a-Nabuwwi*, the first and the foremost and the pristine. The first masjid is described in the *seerah* [the Prophet's biography] books to have been built with palm trees as pillars, with mud walls, dusty floor, and leaves as its roof. It neither protected the worshippers from the scorching desert sun nor from the rain when it poured in. It is also stated that there was an old woman, who used to clean the floor with her bare hands, and when she died, the Prophet (peace upon him) went to her grave and prayed for her. Here is clear evidence, which proves that women were not barred from the masjid in the Prophet's time. A room inside the masjid, which was separated by a curtain, served as the living quarter for the Prophet (peace upon him) and was exposed to the same hazards as the rest of the masjid. This archetype, with mud walls, dusty floor and leafy roof was the capital of the Islamic dominions, the seat of

the government and the residence of the head of state. It was also a temple of learning, the high court of justice, and the assembly point for the armies as they marched out to battles.

The masjids in America have played and will continue to play a vital role in the lives of our children and adults. They house our schools and our social clubs. They house our discussion forums. They provide us with our friends, acquaintances, brotherhoods and sisterhoods. It is here that we formulate our political and social strategies. They are also the information outlets for non-Muslims and prospective Muslims. It is fair to say that without our masjids, Islam will have a hard time surviving in this country.

At a fundraiser for an Islamic community center, a visiting speaker said, "We don't need any more mosques in the United States. We have plenty of mosques! What we need are community centers!"

I had a notion to jump up and pick a fight with that city slicker! There's no mosque where I live. I have to drive an hour through horrible traffic in order to hear a sensible khutba in English. Within a five-mile radius of my house, however, there are at least a dozen churches. Every neighborhood has two or three churches. Until there is a mosque in every neighborhood, there are not enough mosques. I suggest that the large, city mosques establish satellite *mosquettes* in small communities. The large mosques could sponsor the mosquettes until the mosquettes can become financially independent.

Dr. Ahme explained that an Islamic center "has a vitally important role to play in the lives of our people. It must provide basic religious services...and be an outlet for Islamic information in the neighborhood, where people are deemed to be more receptive to Islam. It must receive people into Islam and provide them with post-*Shahada* support. In addition, the center has the responsibility to provide basic Islamic education to the children. .... The responsibility [for these functions] must be shouldered by the community as a whole in accordance with the universal principle of civic governance. If we are one community, united in our goals, as our doctrine proclaims and our rhetoric vociferously professes, then we cannot shower all our communal wealth on one project and leave the others dilapidated, depleted, and destitute."

Insh'Allah, as in a hadeeth, the sun will rise in the West,[32] and Islam will be revived in all its glorious splendor. Until then, we will cringe when we hear of the poor performance of Islam in so-called Islamic countries. We will be saddened and discouraged when we hear of someone's hurtful experience in an American mosque or Islamic center. When will the new, true adventure begin? God has a plan, and He is the best planner.

> O God, make the door of this house wide enough
> To receive all who need human love and friendship,
> But narrow enough to shut out all envy, pride, and malice.
> Make its threshold smooth enough to be no stumbling block
> To children or to straying feet,
> But strong enough to turn away the power of evil.
> O God, make the door of this house
> A gateway to Your eternal kingdom.
> [Thomas Ken (1637-1711) (England)][33]

37. DID YOU THINK GOD WAS JOKING?

> O Believers, believe in Allah and His messenger
> and in the Book sent to His messenger,
> and in the (Scriptures) sent previously.
> Anyone who denies Allah, His angels, His Books, His messengers,
> and the Day of Judgment has surely lost the way, straying afar.
> Say, "We believe in Allah and in what has been bestowed upon us
> and in what was bestowed upon Abraham, Ishmael,
> Isaac, Jacob, and the [twelve Judaic] tribes.
> We believe in what was given to Moses, Jesus,
> and the prophets, from their Sovereign Lord.
> We do not prefer any above the others. To Allah we submit our will."
> *(Surah 4: 136 and Surah 3: 84)*

With the thrill of adventure bubbling in my brain, I hiked deep into a wild gorge where the river beat itself to a froth in the high Sierra Nevada Mountains. In my backpack was a candy bar, a bottle of grape soda, and a gold pan. There was something magical about reaching into a pool of cold, surging water, scooping up a pan of dirt, and then swirling and washing away the sand and pebbles. Such delight when the sun finally excited bits of yellow flakes! I felt the surge of ecstasy that fueled the 1849 gold rush.

What would you think of someone who foolishly threw out the gold flakes along with the sand and left the pan empty? Many Muslims do just that when they consider the Bible.

God (blessed and exalted is He) revealed perfect Scriptures that partially make up what is now called the Bible (whether Christian or Jewish). Gradually, these Scriptures became diluted, either by scribal additions and changes or inadvertently through the oral traditions.

The Tanakh (Jewish Bible) makes its own case to show that manipulation of the Scriptures did indeed occur: "The Sovereign Lord spoke to (Ezekiel). 'O mortal man,' He said, 'denounce the prophets of Israel who invent their own oracles. Tell them to listen for the Word of their Sovereign Lord.' The Lord God said, 'These foolish prophets are doomed. They build their own inspiration and fabricate their own visions'" (Ezekiel 13: 1-3). "How can you say that you are wise in the knowledge of My commandments? The Scriptures have been changed by the pen of dishonest scribes!" (Jeremiah 8: 8).

Unlike the Qur'an, which was revealed to one messenger during the expanse of one stretch of years, the verses of the Bible were recorded by a variety of messengers at different times. The Jewish Scriptures include commandments, prophecies, visions, and historical accounts revealed by God; inspired poems, prayers, and praises; and historical accounts recorded by the scribes. The New Testament consists of a retelling of the Gospel message as recorded in the journal of one of Jesus' disciples, four accounts of Jesus' life and ministry, and letters and other documents by early Christians. Because the Bible is not comparable to the pristine quality of the Qur'an, the word 'Scripture' has an entirely different meaning in reference to the Bible. Still, God (blessed!) has commanded us to believe in the truth remaining in these Scriptures. "Truth is clearly contrasted against fabrication" (Surah 2: 256). If you read the Bible and prayerfully trust God to help you discover truth, He will help you pan out the sand to find the golden nuggets of His sincere message. Wherever it is found, all truth is God's truth, and we shouldn't discard any of it.

> O Lord, lead me to the true faith as You have guided others.
> Forgive me as You have forgiven others.

Protect me as You have protected others.
Bless me with what you have provided.
Keep me safe from the evil you have allowed,
For You decree for others,
But no one can pass decrees upon You.
No one in Your care is defeated,
And no one is rewarded
When You have declared opposition.
O Lord, You are the most praised and the most awesome.
[Prophet Muhammed (peace and blessings upon him)]

38. CAN YOU SEE OVER THE DASHBOARD?

Such [hypocrites] are the people whom Allah has condemned.
He has made them unhearing and unseeing.
Will they not ponder the Qur'an, or have they locked their minds?
(Surah 47: 23-24)

Tana was too little to see over the dashboard when I stopped the car at the end of a country road. I looked across at a neighbor's yard. For Halloween, Miss Tubby had fashioned a homemade ghost in her front yard. I commented, "I think Miss Tubby's ghost is funny."

Unable to see the specter to which I referred, Tana said, "Mama, Miss Tubby ain't even dead."

In religion, many people are unable to see over the dashboard. They argue, "The Bible tells us everything we need to know about how to live and be saved. We don't need the Qur'an or any other such book." They can't see over the religious dashboard, a mental block of preconceived ideas. They find no sense to the idea that God revealed a Book after the Books of the Bible had already been recorded and religious beliefs founded on them.

One of the world's most knowledgeable experts in the area of Christian literature, Professor Bart Ehrman (University of North Carolina, Chapel Hill), explains that the New Testament is a very "human book" that emerged out of conflicts over understanding God and religion. In his book *Misquoting Jesus: The Story Behind Who Changed the Bible and Why*, Dr. Ehrman wrote:

> During the second and third centuries...there was a wide range of diversity: diverse groups asserting diverse theologies based on diverse written texts, all claiming to be written by apostles of Jesus. Some of these Christian groups insisted that God had created the world; others maintained that the true God had not created this world (which is, after all, an evil place), but that it was the result of a cosmic disaster. Some of these groups insisted that the Jewish scriptures belong to the inferior God of the Jews, who was not the one true God. Some of these groups insisted that Jesus Christ was the one Son of God who was both completely human and completely divine; other groups insisted that Christ was completely human and not at all divine; others maintained that he was completely divine and not at all human; and yet others asserted that Jesus Christ was two things —a divine being (Christ) and a human being (Jesus). Some of these groups believed that Christ's death brought about the salvation of the world; others maintained that Christ's death had nothing to do with the salvation of this world; yet other groups insisted that Christ had never actually died.
>
> Each and every one of these viewpoints —and many others besides— were topics of constant discussion, dialogue, and debate in the early centuries of the church, while Christians of various persuasions tried to convince others of the truth of their own claims. Only one group eventually 'won out' in these debates. It was this group that decided what the Christian creeds would be: the creeds would affirm that there is only one God, the Creator; that Jesus his Son is both human and divine; and that salvation came by his death and resurrection. This was also the group that decided which books would be included in the canon of scripture [the New Testament].[34]

Ehrman states that whether or not the New Testament texts were indeed inspired by God doesn't really matter, because we do not have them. All we have are copies of copies which, in addition to containing human errors in copying, were purposely altered by scribes making sure that the winner's view of Christianity was reflected.

Dr. Ehrman applied a very personal touch as he described his own spiritual journey. He began the journey as a "born-again Christian" believing that "the Bible is the inerrant word of God." As a scholar, he learned "the basics of the field known as textual criticism —a technical term for the science of restoring the 'original' words of a text from manuscripts that have altered them." As he investigated and learned how the New Testament manuscripts had evolved, Ehrman had to face the reality that the Christian Bible is not, in totality, "the inerrant word of God," and he had to reconcile his faith based on this knowledge.

I wondered if a person does not feel a void when he or she discovers that the New Testament is not the perfection of God's Word but is, as Ehrman describes, "a very human book." Such a void can be filled by the Universal Qur'an, but are we Muslims adequately prepared to present this reality to disillusioned church members?

Our society is filled with confusion, pain, and turmoil, and people are seeking answers to overwhelming problems as they struggle to find purpose in their lives. We Muslims have the answers in a truly inerrant Book, which we are failing to proclaim because we are not living the Qur'an. We read it, recite it, write about it, explain it, ponder it, discuss it, refer to it, depend on it, display it, calligraphy it, frame it, illustrate it, engrave it, and publish it. But until we live the Qur'an in such a way that others see less of us and more of God, the vibrancy of the Qur'an is like an unlit lantern.

Muslims too must grow up enough to be able to see over the dash-board. Arrogance and hypocrisy exists among Muslims who are fluent in Qur'anic Arabic; knowledgeable about such things as Sunnah, Shariah, and Tafseer; and excellent in the performance of rituals. I would rather never learn any Arabic at all or obtain any Islamic theology if the knowledge would make me so arrogant that I could not be a good witness. Of course, we can be both knowledgeable and spiritual, but the Islamic world needs a spiritual revival. As born-again Muslims, we will have the fire of Islam burning in our hearts and souls so that the warmth of love and compassion can be felt by all those around us. We must live the Qur'an so vibrantly that others will want to know the secret of our joy and will want to partake of the security of Muslim companionship. First, each of us must have a closer walk with God (blessed and exalted is He) and develop such a relationship with Him that the voids in our own lives overflow with His grace and mercy. It is that overflow that will attract and rescue others floundering in emptiness.

As a true believer, a Muslim, and not one of the polytheists,
I turn my face to Him who has created Heaven and Earth.
My prayer and my devotion belong to Allah, Lord of the Worlds,
He who has no partner.
Thus am I commanded, and thus do I submit.
O Lord, You are kind. There is no god but You.
You are my Master, and I am Your servant.
Where I have erred, I acknowledge my sin.
You alone can forgive sin.
Guide me to the finest moral character.
Only You can guide me to perfection.
Dispel my evil nature; only You can drive out evil.
I obey You and rejoice in You.
All prosperity is in Your hands, and there is no evil in You.
I am Yours; I belong to You.
You are blessed and exalted.
I turn to You in repentance and seek Your forgiveness.
[Prophet Muhammed (peace and blessings upon him)]

Jana & Snuggles

God so loved the animals that He sent human arms.

Linda Tham

39. GOD DID NOT PUT OUT A "HELP WANTED" SIGN

Allah will say, "O Jesus son of Mary, did you tell people,
'Worship me and my mother as divinities, detracting from Allah'?"
[Jesus] will say, "Glory to You! I would never say such a thing!
If I had said anything like that, You surely would have known it.
You know what is in my heart, though I do not know all that is in Yours.
Truly, You know fully all that is hidden.
I never said anything to them except what You commanded me to say:
'Worship Allah, my Lord and your Lord.'
I was a witness for them while I lived among them.
After You raised me [to Heaven], Your were the Watchful One over them.
You are a witness over everything.
If You decide to punish them, they are still *Your* servants.
If You decide to forgive them, You are the Victorious, the Perfectly Wise."
(Surah 5: 116-118)

A family friend announced that her daughter and son-in-law were finally expecting their first child. The friend's visitor leapt for joy and exclaimed, "Oh, if I only had a picture of the Virgin Mary, I would offer a prayer of thanks!" Several times the Catholic visitor mentioned that she wanted to pray but needed a picture of Mary. Finally, the friend got a picture of her own daughter and told the Catholic, "Here's a picture of Mary." The visitor set the picture up against the back of a chair, knelt, and prayed to the high school picture of a young, Mexican girl.

People can become so familiar with giving a holier-than-human status to other people, they may fall folly to praying to anything. The Qur'an refers to this as "associating partners with God." The overwhelming sovereignty of God is never compromised in Islam.

The Qur'an emphasizes the same thing that Jesus taught when he said, "Do not call anyone on earth your Father, for you only have one Father, and He is in Heaven" (Matthew 23: 9). Catholics pray to Mary (peace upon her) as an intercessor, but there is nothing in the Bible that orders such a thing. Catholics also call the Pope and their priests "Father." The Qur'an, like Jesus, says not to put anyone on such a pedestal as Catholics have done with Mary and the Pope. Catholics have also put saints and Jesus' disciples in such a position even though Jesus told the disciples not to assume the responsibilities of being masters and lords (Matthew 23: 8, 10).

When unbelievers associate partners with God and then die in their unbelief, their demise will be in the fire of Hell (ie, Surah 3: 151). Christians, however, are not unbelievers or polytheists. The Christian perception of God is different from the Muslim perception, and we Muslims believe that the Christian perception has been compromised with the invention of the Trinity. The Qur'an warns Christians of such blasphemy (ie, Surah 5: 73), but this warning is given so they may take heed; it is not given so that we Muslims may pass judgment. In the featured passage above, Jesus refers to the Christians as God's "servants," and Jesus leaves it up to God to decide whether to punish them or forgive them. If Jesus (peace upon him and may he bring peace) is not going to make that decision, then certainly Muslims have no right to make the judgment that someone is going to spend an eternity in Hell for associating partners with God.

The Qur'an gives admonition so that we may look inside ourselves and judge our own character and make adjustments to better glorify God (blessed and exalted is He). Of course, we can use Scriptural criterion for discerning who among us has true spiritual quality, but discerning is different from judging. We can see the error of someone's doctrine without making a negative judgment about the person or the person's religion.

God did not put out a "Help Wanted" sign. Jesus is leaving the judgment job to God, and I suggest you do the same.

O Lord, forgive us when we disregard the needs of others.
O Lord, forgive our prejudices that prevent us from loving.
O Lord, forgive us for not having a great enough vision for unity.
O Lord, forgive us for not including all people in the family of humanity.
O Lord, forgive us for debasing the belief systems o others
O Lord, forgive us for not appreciating those who differ from us
O Lord, forgive us for being impatient and dismissive of others' views.
O Lord, forgive us for packaging our faith in such a way
That Your love and grace are not part of the package.
O Lord, forgive.
[inspired by "O Lord, Forgive" (Canada)][35]

40. I THINK I NEED A BIGGER CAMERA

> No vision can grasp Him, but His grasp encompasses all visions.
> He is beyond our comprehension, but He comprehends all.
> *(Surah 6: 103)*

The fifty-two millimeter lens on my camera had been the instrument of many wonderful photographs across the United States, but when I got to the Grand Canyon, the lens simply could not grasp a complete picture. The majesty, splendor, and intensity of the sculpted rocks and ravines just wouldn't fit! I got a wide-angle lens and was able to get more into a picture, but then everything seemed miniscule compared to the overwhelming grandeur. I got some good shots, but none adequately portrayed the experience of actually being there.

Like a camera lens, our view is limited. The awesomeness of God is beyond our comprehension, and, even with a wide-angle view, a believer is unable to grasp a whole picture. God, on the other hand, has greater than 360-degree vision. He not only sees all things in the present, but He also sees the past, the future, and the possible. Because He has all knowledge, God is perfectly capable to help us overcome existing problems and prepare for future situations. God (blessed and exalted is He) has all the facts, and He can create solutions that we cannot even imagine. Nothing is beyond His sight or His reach.

While a Christian, I heard a radio preacher trying to explain why God had to sacrifice His son to pay for our sins. The preacher told a story about a railroad operations manager who took his small son to work with him. The little boy was playing and fell into gears that, at that moment, were at rest. The gears, when in motion, switched the tracks. The operations manager was about to help his son out of the gears when an emergency call came over the radio. A train was approaching an impassable track suspended over a ravine. The operator needed to switch the tracks immediately. If the operator switched the tracks with his son in the gears, the little boy would be crushed to death. If the operator took time to pull his son out of the gears, hundreds of people on the train would plunge to their deaths. The operator made the painful decision to switch the tracks immediately, thereby sacrificing his son for the salvation of the train's passengers. The preacher equated God with the operations manager and the little boy with Jesus. The story bothered me. It made God appear to be as helpless as a human being.

Later that day, I was driving down the highway and noticed a billboard sign. Big letters exclaimed, "God loves you this much." Below the statement was a humiliating picture of a crucified Jesus with his arms stretched out. I thought of a similar T-shirt that stated, "God said, 'I love you this much,' and then He stretched out His arms and died."

I thought, 'I need a bigger God.'

Not long after that, God (blessed!) began to speak to me of Islam. I thought He was joking at first, but finally it clicked. The Islamic perspective of God does not limit Him to the point that the only way He can forgive is through a sacrifice. The Jewish sin sacrifice, through the animal's suffering and death, reminds Jews of the horror of sin. The sacrifice, however, does not enable God. He simply says, "Be!" and it is. He forgives and then grants New Life.

God can, not only forgive sins, but also blot them from the eternal record. When too much light hits film, the negative's image is burned away, and the print will just be white. In the same way, God's light flashes away our negatives and gives us white moments that we do not have to explain on the Day of Judgment.

Our God really is an awesome God!

> Wheresoever I turn my eyes,
> Around on earth or toward the skies,
> I see You in the starry field;
> I see You in the harvest's yield.
> In every breath, in every sound,
> An echo of Your name is found.
> The blade of grass, the simple flower
> Bear witness to Your matchless power.
> My every thought, Eternal God of Heaven,
> Ascends to You, to whom all praise is given.
> *(Abraham ibn Ezra (1092-1167), Judaic scholar (Spain)]*

41. UNSOLVED MYSTERY

Allah said, "O Jesus, I am taking you and then raising you to Me.
I will vindicate you [of the false accusations] from the blasphemers.
On the Day of Resurrection,
I will declare your followers superior over the unbelievers.
On that day, you [all humanity] will return to Me.
I will judge among you concerning the matters about which you dispute."
They also said that they killed Jesus the Messiah,
son of Mary, Allah's messenger.
But they did not kill him or crucify him,
although such was made apparent to them.
Those who differ about this are full of doubts about it
with no authentic knowledge, but only conjecture to follow.
Rather, Allah raised him to Himself.
And Allah is Victorious, Perfectly Wise.
(Surah 3: 55 and Surah 4: 157-158)

When Tana was very little, our family went to an outdoor drama of the life of Jesus (peace upon him). When the mob beat and crucified the character playing Jesus, Tana cried. "They're hurting my Jesus." She did not understand that the play was an enactment; to her it appeared real.

Different theories have been offered to explain how it was "made to appear" as if Jesus (peace!) had been executed. A few of the theories are that Jesus' face was superimposed over that of another man who was crucified instead; Jesus was taken from the cross alive, but in a catatonic state to later recover in the tomb; a phantom image of Jesus was crucified; and the crucifixion scene itself was an apparition. I suggest that it is an injustice to Islam if we settle on any one theory, and then close discussion of this unsolved mystery. Abdulla Yusuf Ali observed, "The end of the life of Jesus on earth is as much involved in mystery as his birth...."[36]

In 1945, a band of Muslim camel drivers in Egypt unearthed ancient, clay urns sealed with bitumen. The urns contained manuscripts, which became known as the Nag Hammadi Codices. They have been dated to the fourth century, and some of them claim to be the testimonies of Jesus' disciples. They were obviously not actually penned by the disciples, but no one can say whether these are forgeries or were derived from earlier writings and/or *agrapha* (oral traditions). Among the manuscripts were records that bear an uncanny resemblance to some ideas drawn from the Qur'anic passage about the crucifixion. In a document called the "Coptic Apocalypse of Peter," Jesus tells Peter that false teachers of the Gospel hold onto the image of a dead man because of their thinking that Jesus' death is what brings salvation.

Confused, Peter says, "I saw him apparently being seized by them, and I said, 'What am I seeing, Master? Are they taking you, or are you still holding onto me? Who is that one above the cross, who is happy and laughing? Is it another person whose feet and hands are being nailed?:

In the report, Jesus told Peter, "The one you see above the cross, happy and laughing, is the living Jesus. The one into whose hands and feet they are driving the nails is his physical part, which is the substitute. They are putting to shame that which is his likeness. But look at him and me. …. The son of their glory is the one they have put to shame rather than the servant [of God]. …. He [the servant] stands joyfully looking at those who persecuted him. They are divided among themselves; therefore, he laughs at their lack of perception, and he knows that they are [spiritually] blind. Indeed, therefore, the suffering one must remain, since the body is the substitute. That which was released was my incorporeal body, and I am an intellectual spirit filled with radiant light."

Jesus prophesied, "These things which you [Peter] experienced, will be presented to another race of people in another century." Muhammed Ali, the Muslim camel driver who figured prominently in the discovery of the Nag Hammadi Codices, had no idea of the verbal dynamite he had pulled from the time-space capsule we call 'the past'.

The document, which bombs the idea of a *literal* death on the cross, suggests that Peter had miraculously seen into the spiritual dimension while still viewing the temporal world: "After (Jesus) had said these things, (Peter) came to his senses."

According to the New Testament (NT), Jesus pointed to "the sign of Jonah": "Just as Jonah was three days and three nights in the belly of a huge fish, so the Son of Man will be three days and three nights in the heart of the earth" (Matthew 12: 40). People have struggled to interpret this because, if "in the heart of the earth" means 'dead,' then it doesn't make sense. From the time Jesus' body reportedly expired until the body's resurrection was only about a day and a half. The word translated to "heart" doesn't mean 'core' or 'center,' however; it means 'mind'. The mind of the world does not perceive the true reality of God; what we experience here is an imitation existence in which we prepare for the true reality. We may conclude that Jesus' prayer was granted after, in the Garden of Gethsemane, he asked to be spared from the suffering of the cross. From the time of his prayer to the day recognized as the day of Jesus' resurrection would have been three nights and roughly three days. Isn't it possible that for those three days Jesus' physical body or a phantom image of it was given over to the illusion of this world while his true self was laughing at the confusion? The more important connection to Jonah, however, is that, although Jonah seemed like a goner in the belly of the whale, he was still alive, just as Jesus was.

In another document among the Nag Hammadi Codices, an account attributed to John claims that Jesus said, "I have suffered none of the things that they say of me; that suffering that you and the others saw was just a dance [in other words, it was all choreographed]. I want it to be called a mystery. .... You hear that I suffered, yet I did not suffer; that I did not suffer, yet I did suffer; that I was pierced, yet I was not wounded; that I was crucified, and I was not crucified; that blood flowed from me, yet it did not flow. Simply put, those things that they say about me, I did not endure, and the things that they say I did not suffer, I did endure."

Such mystic writings speak of two different worlds. Perhaps this dual-world existence is the secret to understanding the Qur'anic passage. Whether the codices contain any measure of authenticity, the fact remains that there were early Christians whose perspectives of the crucifixion were similar to that presented by the Qur'an. We should explore the possibilities about how these perspectives came to be and try to find connections to increase our understanding.

The NT itself describes a dual-world existence. When a person dies, he awakens to face the judgment. He doesn't get to run around raising hell, but that's exactly what Jesus purportedly did. "His body was put to death, but his spirit was kept alive, and he went to the souls that had been kept imprisoned since the flood of Noah, and he preached to them. ….. The Gospel was preached even to those who are now dead, so that, although they will be judged according to their physical lives, in their spiritual existence they may choose to serve God" (1 Peter 3: 19; 4: 6).

Legends among various peoples claim that a bearded spirit-man visited them from the spiritual world. The Algonkin indigenous tribe called him *Cheezoos*. He talked to them of the Great Spirit and told them that he would someday return. We can only theorize that Cheezoos was Jesus in his unencumbered, spiritual body.

The apparent but unreal crucifixion/resurrection mystery may be directly linked to the elusive secrets of the dual particle/wave concept of quantum theory. Prophet Muhammed (peace and blessings upon him) transcended the spiritual dimension in his Mi'raj experience. Perhaps, like Jesus, he also experienced a dual-world existence, only to return wholly to the physical realm. Aishah, a wife of Prophet Muhammed, explained, "The apostle's body stayed where it was, but God removed his spirit by night."

According to the Bible, Jesus said, "The reason the Father [Creator] loves me is because I am willing to commit my life only to receive it again. No one can take my life, but I give it willingly. I have been given the power to give my life and to take it back. This is in accordance with a command from the Father" (John 10: 17-18). By God's will, both Jesus and Muhammed (peace upon them) connected to the spiritual dimension in a way that we have not understood.

If we continue investigating the theories and physics of quantum mechanics as well as the revelations of history and archaeology and other sciences, new discoveries may help explain the mystery of the crucifixion episode. Too many people, including some Muslim intellectuals, seem willing to set their rocking chairs on the path of knowledge and roll with canned theories. As for me, I intend to continue my journey, so please don't throw your rusty cans on my path.

> Lord of Mysteries Seen and Unseen,
> Heal our blindness so we may see
> Beyond the temporal world
> And into Your numinous reality.

42. TAKE MY ADVICE: CHECK THE MANUAL

> (Many people of the Book) say, "No one will enter Paradise
> unless he/she is a Jew," or "…a Christian."
> That is based on their own desires.
> Say to them, "So, prove it! If it's true!"
> Indeed! Whoever submits his/her whole self to Allah and does good deeds
> will be rewarded with his/her Lord. No fear or grief will be there.
> *(Surah 2: 111-112)*

Every time my husband is on a trip, things break. Within the first week that Tom was on a overseas assignment, the lawnmower quit working, the fancy, new sink stopper fell apart, the kitchen stove went berserk, the front bumper fell off the family car, a sliding door fell off the track, and the truck quit running. And that was a good week.

I crawled under the sink and fixed the stopper. I got new hardware and rehung the door. When the stove had gotten stuck in the 'on' position and started shooting sparks and belching smoke, I had immediately shut off the circuit breaker, and later I huffed and puffed and got the dead thing out of the house by myself. I fiddled with the truck and got it running again. And a car doesn't have to have a bumper, does it? I still had to fix the mower, but I couldn't find the manual that came with it. Tom doesn't believe in manuals. When he gets a manual, he simply opens a door or drawer and throws the manual like a Frisbee; it lands where it will, and Tom wrestles everything down and fixes it by sheer will. Some people can figure things out for themselves, but other people (like me) have to have a manual.

I think people are like that with religion too. Some American indigenous tribes, for example, never received a Book of Scriptures, but they were able to find the inner wisdom needed to maintain good, honorable lives, walk peacefully with God (blessed and exalted is He), and live in harmony with nature. In 1811, Red Jacket of the Seneca Indians told Christian missionaries, "We do not worship the Great Spirit as the white people do, but we believe that the forms of worship are not important to the Great Spirit. It is the homage of sincere hearts that pleases Him, and we worship Him in that manner." Other people, however, cannot maintain or fix their souls without written instructions. The Bible and Qur'an and other books of world religions are valuable sources of maintenance and repair information. Even independent thinkers find that, from time to time, they need a little help. When Tom has tried in vain every way he can think to put a new gadget together, I drag out those annoying instructions. He grimaces when I start reading the instructions out loud, and he would never admit that they actually help, but, all of a sudden, he figures out the magic formula.

The indigenous tribes were wise and independent, but even they had problems among their tribes —problems the Qur'an could have solved. No matter how good you are at keeping your life on track, life is always easier when you follow the manual. Get every day off to a good start: read your Book!

> Our Lord, You comprehend all things in mercy and knowledge.
> Forgive, then, those who repent and follow Your path.
> Save them from the penalty of Hell.
> Our Lord, grant that they enter the gardens of eternity,
> which You have promised to them and to the righteous
> among their parents, spouses, and children.
> You are the Victorious, the Perfectly Wise.
> Save them from harm. For any whom You save from harm that day,
> You will have bestowed on them mercy indeed.
> That will truly be the highest achievement."
> *(from Surah 40: 7-9, the prayer of those surrounding God's throne)*

43. DIG IN AND BE SURPRISED

> Those for whom We have sent the Book study it as it should be studied.
> They believe in it. Those who reject it are the losers.
> *(Surah 2: 121)*

I had been out riding my motorcycle one day when I stopped by to visit a friend. While I was there, his neighbor came over and asked to borrow a "plug-gaper." My friend did not have one.

As the neighbor started to leave, I asked, "What is it that you need?"

"Nothing you'd have," he scoffed.

"Is it the same as a filler gauge?" I prodded.

He looked a bit surprised. "Yeah."

"I have one in my pocketbook," I said as I began to dig.

With a questioning look, the neighbor turned to my friend who simply shrugged his shoulders. With a preconceived notion of what women keep in their pocketbooks, my friend and his neighbor were surprised when I produced the filler gauge used for measuring the gap on spark plugs. Later, the neighbor, still a bit puzzled, returned to borrow my socket wrench.

Many people have equally inaccurate, preconceived notions of what is within the Qur'an. They believe what they've read and heard, but they've never dug into the Qur'an for themselves.

A man was shocked by my T-shirt as I walked down a sidewalk. He read my shirt but changed the statement to a question: "Muslims love Jesus too?" He became angry and insisted, "Muslims don't have the right to love Jesus!" He began following me and demanding responses to his ridiculous questions and comments.

"The Koran says, 'All Jews must die!'" he announced.

"It does not!" I insisted.

"Well, that's what I heard," he said.

"Well, you need to read it for yourself," I told him.

Instead of gullibly accepting slanderous reports of what the Qur'an says, misguided smut-seekers need to read and try to understand the Qur'an for themselves. If they did, they may be surprised to find exactly what they need to spark their souls and get a grip on their lives. Even many Muslims have memorized the Arabic ayats (verses) without really pondering their meanings. When you open your Qur'an, open your mind and your heart also; you may be in for a unique surprise.

> Our Lord, we have heard the call of one calling us to faith:
> "Believe in your Lord," and we have believed.
> Our Lord, forgive us our sins, blot out our iniquities,
> And allow us to die among the righteous.
> *(from Surah 3: 193)*

44. ADD LIVING WATER

When you read the Qur'an,
seek Allah's protection from Satan, the rejected one,
He has no authority over those who believe and put their trust in the Lord.
(Allah) grants wisdom to those He has chosen.
The one who receives wisdom has received an abundant goodness.
None remembers [God's graciousness] except those of pure minds.
(Surah 16: 98-99 and Surah 2: 269)

To earn a little extra money, I grew plants and sold them from the back of an old, pickup truck. I got permission to park the truck at the edge of a car wash.

I had started some seeds in Jiffy-7 pots, which are peat wrapped in mesh and condensed to about one-fourth-inch wafers. Soaked in water, the peat wafers swell to about three inches. One day a customer asked if I would sell her some of the little pots for starting seeds. I bought them by the case, but I had packaged some for small purchases, and I told her the price. She gave me the money, and I handed her a small, brown bag.

Surprised that the bag was not bigger, the customer opened it and peered inside. She was shocked. "I asked for little pots!" she complained. "Why did you give me cookies?"

The customer was amazed when I explained that the "cookies" would turn into "little pots" when she soaked them in water.

To many people the Scriptures are just cookies, because the readers have not added the Living Water of God's wisdom. Before reading the Qur'an or the Bible, you must first take refuge in God from Satan's deceptions, and ask for God's guidance in understanding and applying God's true Word.

The term *ijtihad* means logic, and it identifies the practice of studying Scriptures, seeking various meanings, and applying those meanings to today's lifestyle and situations. The beauty of God's Word is in its fluidity –its ability to remain as constant as the level surface of still waters, while at the same time adapting to societal and personal diversities just as water fills the various depressions in the floor beneath the water's surface. The Scriptures are as true today as they were in the times in which they were given, and they speak to today's societies and individuals just as they did to those who first heard them. People and cultures vary and change with time, however, and the meanings and applications of God's Word must remain flexible to meet contemporary needs.

The next time you read Scriptures, don't forget to ask God (blessed and exalted is He) to add the Living Water necessary for the planting of the Word within your soul.

> I am, O my God,
> But a tiny seed, which You have sown in the soil of Your love
> And caused to spring forth by the hand of Your bounty.
> This seed craves, therefore, in its inmost being,
> The waters of Your mercy and the living fountain of Your grace.
> Send down upon it, from the Heaven of Your loving kindness,
> That which will enable it to flourish beneath Your shadow
> And within the borders of Your court.
> You are He who waters the hearts of all
> Who have recognized You from Your plenteous stream
> And the fountain of Your living waters.
> Praise be to God, the Lord of All the Worlds!
> *[Baha'u'llah (1817-1892), founder of the Bahai faith (Persia)]*

45. WHEN CATS RULED THE WORLD

> Allah has created every living creature from water.
> Among them are those that slide on their bellies,
> those that can each walk on two legs, and those that each walk on all fours.
> Allah creates whatever He will. Truly, Allah has power over all things.
> *(Surah 24: 45)*

Some of the animals that achieve balance on their two hind legs are kangaroos, apes, lemurs, meercats, bears, and my cat Munchkin. You would have laughed if you had seen her prancing sideways across the carpet, swinging her paws like boxing gloves. She was acrobatic in chasing the reflections rehearsed by the morning sun brushing past the treetops.

I let the cats raise a chicken I hatched in the incubator, and that turned out to be the weirdest chicken that ever lived! Munchkin taught the chicken Nugget to box. Munchkin stood on her hind legs and held her paws up like a boxing coach holding pads. Nugget, doing a slide-shuffle-slide like Mohammed Ali (the boxer), pecked one paw and then the other, over and over. When Nugget got old enough to defend himself, he was fearless. He would pick fights with stray dogs and have them yelping in terror. He even got into head-butting matches with Baby Boy the billy goat.

The cats taught Nugget to play. Even when he was grown, Nugget still played with balls, a squeaky rubber bone, and other toys. His favorite game was untying shoe laces. Every time he saw a pair of shoes, he would run to them, untie them, and then run away with a chicken's version of laughter. When Tom came home from Iraq, wearing sandals, Nugget was confused at first because there were no shoestrings; but then he got angry and chased Tom into the woods. After that, Tom could not step outside without that crazy rooster chasing him. I finally had to chain Nugget up with the dog.

Like Munchkin and Nugget, every creature has its own unique personality. Zoologists studying animals in the wild often give names to their subjects and describe their peculiarities. When they closely share life with humans, animals acquire more human-like characteristics. The Qur'an urges us to observe the animals, to ponder their amazing designs, and to see them as part of our own world. We should respect them as partners glorifying God and sharing the breath that God gave us. Animals, wild and domestic, should be remembered in our prayers as we express our concern for their welfare, safety, and happiness. When animals suffer and struggle, we humans must reflect God's mercy as we try to solve problems facing the animal kingdoms. When one link of the circle of life is threatened, the entire planet is at risk. Part of our God-given responsibility is to maintain and improve the natural features of our planet. The struggle for survival is something humans share with the plants and animals. The struggle affects all of creation indiscriminately with blights, diseases, and disasters.

Understanding the animals as individual creatures loved by their Creator helps us avoid anthropocentric notions and envision the awesome God –the One who was God of Earth's plants and animals before human beings rose from the mix of water and dust. In God's reality –where the past is still as real as the present— God (blessed and exalted is He) is still the God of nature in a time before our physical creation. In linear time, cats and chickens were praising God on this planet while we were still mud pies.

On a mass e-mailing, I received daily discussions about whether or not cats would go to Heaven. I deleted all those e-mails without wasting my time reading them. I don't know what kind of hell-cats other people raise, but I know my kitties are all going to Heaven. Every time I unfurl my prayer rug, the kitties vie for a spot. I prostrate over a huddle of cats as they purr their praises along with my praises. They are not exactly sure what we're doing, but they know it's something special that all good kitties and their cat-people should do.

Allah, make us as wonderful as our cats think we are, and make our brats as wonderful as our cats.

> O Great Spirit, You are Lord of all Worlds.
> As I travel over mountains and through valleys, I am beneath Your feet.
> You surround me with every kind of creature.
> Majestic deer, pheasants, and bears cross my path.
> Open my eyes to see their beauty
> So that I may perceive them as the work of Your hands.
> By Your power, by Your thought, all things are abundant.
> Tonight I will sleep beneath Your feet,
> O Lord of Mountains and Valleys, Ruler of Trees and Vines.
> I will rest in Your love, and You will protect me
> As a father protects his children.
> You will watch over me as a mother watches over her children.
> Tomorrow the sun may rise, by Your word.
> I cannot be certain where my path will lead,
> But I know that You will guide my footsteps.
> *(A prayer of the Sioux)*

The cat taught the chicken to fight.

46. BE BURGER AND FRIES!

> [In Heaven]
> We shall bestow upon them fruits and meats as they desire.
> ...and any poultry they want.
> *(Surah 52: 22 and Surah 56: 21)*

In rural North Carolina where halal food is not available, we eat mostly vegetables at home, but, on the road, there are few options for avoiding meat. On a short trip to the mountains one day, Tana and I stopped for lunch at a fast-food joint. Tana is a junk food queen. Even if we go to a fine restaurant, she orders a not-very-halal hamburger and fries and a gallon of ketchup. She was chowing down on her grease-burger while I picked the brown-and-slimy from my salad.

"Do you think there will be hamburgers in Heaven?" I asked her.

"Absolutely!" she guaranteed.

"Do you think there is death in Heaven?"

"No." She seemed sure of that too.

"If there's no death in Heaven," I asked, "how is it that you're going to be able to eat a cow?"

She did not even have to ponder the predicament. She quickly responded. "God just says, 'Be!' and it is."

"Exactly!" I was pleased that she was able to answer so confidently, without my having to give any hints.

The agony and finality of death are dreadful to contemplate. Death brings grief to people and even to animals left behind when relationships are split apart by death. Heaven is a blissful existence untouched by fear or grief. If we take the Scriptures literally, my theory is that food will be created as food —not processed from a once-living creature. We will be able to enjoy the beauty of creation and interact as friends with all God's creatures. In other words, we'll be able to have our cow and eat it too!

When we enter the purely spiritual realm of existence, our bodies will be changed to immortal bodies. Perhaps animals too will be new creatures; perhaps the savage, bloodthirsty carnivores of this world will suddenly crave veggie burgers. I think that even nasty, little, blood-sucking ticks and leeches will be transformed into different creatures —ones that won't give us the creeps.

In addition to the symbolism of world peace, perhaps there is literal truth to the promise, "The wolf will live with the lamb; the leopard will rest with the goat; the calf and the lion and the yearling will walk together, and a little child will lead them. The cow will eat with the bear, their babies will sleep together, and the lion will munch grass like the ox. The infant will play near the hole of the cobra, and the child will stick his hand into the viper's nest without harm. No destruction will be on my holy mountains, for the earth will be as full of the knowledge of the Lord as the sea is full of water" (Isaiah 11: 6-9).

I think the "fruits," "meats," and "poultry" of Heaven, however, imply much more than just-say-"Be" burger and fries. *Spiritual fruits* include love, honesty, charity, kindness, compassion, and good deeds. In our spiritual existence, our acts of praise, worship, and honor will have a depth that is now beyond our understanding. We will be able to attain a perfection that is not possible within these feet of clay. In Heaven, we can really put some meat on our bones, spiritually.

> Our food comes from the sacrifice of earth and sky.
> It is the gift of the entire universe and the result of human labor.
> I vow to live a life worthy to receive the gift of food.
> All praises belong to You, Great Provider of Sustenance.
> *(Adapted from a Buddhist prayer)*

47. PIGS ARE FOR PETS

> Partake of the lawful and good sustenance that Allah has provided for you.
> Be grateful for the blessings of Allah if you truly serve Him.
> He has forbidden for you only carrion, blood, pork,
> and anything over which a name other than Allah has been said.
> Someone may be forced by necessity [to eat forbidden foods].
> If he/she eats without any desire to disobey and without indulging,
> then Allah is Most Forgiving, Most Merciful.
> *(Surah 16: 114-115)*

My brother Billy owned some undeveloped land at the coast. A land developer, wanting to build houses, was buying up as much land as possible. He wanted Billy's land to add to the neighboring land the developer had purchased for the housing project. Billy refused to sell for what the developer was offering. To get a better price, Billy put up a sign: "Future Home of Granger's Pig Farm." The developer was shocked and significantly increased his offer. Thanks to nasty, smelly pigs, Billy got the money he wanted.

Pigs don't have to be nasty and smelly however. A pet like Arnold in the old TV show "Green Acres" exhibits the best of pork –without barbeque sauce. A South Carolina woman suffering from depression got an Arnold-like pet to live in the house with her. She claimed to keep her support hog clean and healthy –free of parasites. As the pig responded to the woman's kindness, the plump pig consoled the woman and helped heal her depression. The city in which the woman resided made her get rid of the pig, however, calling it an industrial food product and not a pet. Too much government!

Both the Torah and the Qur'an forbid the eating of pork, but that doesn't mean that pigs are vile, disgusting creatures. I thought it was silly when a Muslim parent pitched a fit at the public school for letting her child read the story of "The Three Little Pigs." The pig industry is a filthy business, but cute little pigs are not offensive. Wild boars and sows are part of the circle of life. Everything has a purpose.

Raising a hog to slaughter each fall was considered part of survival for my family when I was growing up. After the pig was killed with a shot to the head, we spent weeks processing the meat. Mama rendered the lard, used for frying, and saved it in a wooden barrel. The cracklings (what remained of the fat) were added to dough to make crackling biscuits. Daddy salted the hams and bacon and hung them in the milk house. Mama made souse meat by pickling the diced snout, ears, and feet. The intestines became chitlins, and the stomach and lungs were eaten as tripe. We kids took turns grinding fatty pork for sausages. The ground liver, spleen, kidneys, and pancreas were added to cornmeal to make livermush. We crispy fried the skin for breakfast. Daddy liked the brains scrambled with eggs; he thought the brains would make him smart. I guess he was at least as smart as the pig.

To one of Jesus' teachings, a scribe added, "In saying this, Jesus declared all foods clean" (Mark 7: 19). The scribe's explanation, however, should be understood to mean all foods *except what God has forbidden*. Jesus objected to the Pharisaic elaborations of the Torah, but his teachings did not conflict with God's commandments. Jesus confirmed the Torah laws and approved things previously forbidden (Surah 3: 50) by Pharisaic amendments.

Dr. John Kellogg, developer of cornflakes and other cereals, was a Seventh-Day Adventist who took seriously the Torah's command not to eat pork. In his 1897 dissertation "The Dangers of Pork-Eating Exposed,"[37] he observed, "In the case of no other animal is so large a portion of the dead carcass utilized as food. It seems to be considered that pork is such a delicacy that not a particle should be wasted."

Breeding pigs are kept in stalls too small for the pigs to even turn around. The pig can do nothing but stand or sit in her own filth. Pig farms wash away wastes into open lagoons breeding protozoan, bacteria, viruses, and parasites. This industrial waste poisons the surrounding water supply by seeping into underground springs and rivers and by spilling into lakes and rivers during heavy rains. A PBS report claimed that, in North Carolina, there are "more hogs than people," and that the state's pig industry annually produces 9½ million tons of hog manure. Critics refuse to use the term 'pig farming' for the inhumane pig industry in which some pigs never see the sun or breathe fresh air. Raising animals, edible or not, in such a way is anti-Islamic, anti-Judaic, and anti-Christ.

In Biblical and Qur'anic times, there was no humane way in which to kill a pig. A pig does not have a neck with arteries close to the skin for a quick kill with a knife. A knife has to be used in a painful sawing motion. Shooting a pig in the head is quick and relatively painless, but it does not allow for the blood to drain properly. In some countries, pigs are clubbed to death as the terrified pigs squeal from pain, confusion, and horror. So cruel!

Dr. Kellogg explained that the abnormal amount of fat under the skin of the ill kept pig is due to unhealthy liver, lungs, kidneys, skin, and intestines which are unable to carry away the impurities accumulating in the pig's body. "Lard, then, obtained from the flesh of the hog by heating," Dr. Kellogg wrote, "is nothing more than extract of a diseased carcass!" The pieces of fat added to pinto beans, collard greens, and other such southern delicacies are, as described by Dr. Kellogg, "concentrated, consolidated filth!"

The problem with pork fat, as compared to other meat fats, is that pork contains huge amounts of intra-cellular fat (particles of fat inside the meat cells) while, in other animals, the fat is contained in fat cells, which are outside the meat cells. Intra-cellular fat creates numerous problems for the human body, which is not equipped to process it. Health problems range from obesity to cancer.

Professor Hans-Heinrich Reckeweg, in his article "The Adverse Influence of Pork Consumption on Health,"[38] stated, "The fact that pork causes stress and gives rise to poisoning is known. It is obvious that this does not only apply to preparations of fresh pork such as cold cuts, knuckles, feet, ribs, and cutlets, etc., but also to cured meats (ham, bacon, etc.) and to smoked meats prepared for sausages.

"Consumption of freshly killed pork products causes acute responses, such as inflammations of the appendix and gall bladder, biliary colics, acute intestinal catarrh, gastroenteritis with typhoid and paratyphoid symptoms, as well as acute eczema, carbuncles, sudoriparous abscesses, and others. These symptoms can be observed after consuming sausage meats (including salami which contains pieces of bacon in the form of fat)."

I don't know what most of those ailments are, but I'm glad I grew up to be an herbivore!

Dr. Reckeweg recognizes both Moses and Muhammed (peace upon them) for their contributions in promoting God's prohibition of eating pork. "These fundamental, time-honored principles based on the laws of nature call for a strict ban on eating pork by all people. These laws have been firmly established in the Jewish and Islamic religions and are necessary in the civilized Western world, not least to avoid enormous healthcare expenses."

Professor Reckeweg advises not to even feed pork to your dog! Pork-fed pets, he says, can develop mange, itching sores, and severe internal diseases. Circus animals that are fed pork become lazy and obese, suffer from severe bloody noses (attributed to high blood pressure), and have short lives. Minced pork has been known to kill a pond's entire stock of trout within a matter of days.

High cholesterol and its subsequent health problems are other concerns of pork as a homotoxin (a poison affecting humans). Typical to pork-eaters are fatty folds in the skin and irregular deformation in the buttocks and hip areas. People who regularly consume large amounts of pork begin to look like pigs themselves! The Piggersons, a real family near where I live, have no necks because they eat so much pork. They have two pig statues on the porch banisters. The statues are very fitting since the Piggersons look more like pigs every day! This "disease" is called *scrophula*.

Professor Reckeweg stressed that the commercially grown pig "is a very sick animal having few muscles and small bones, but with an abundance of mucous and fatty connective tissue, suffering from fatty degeneration of the cardiac muscle and liver with possible dropsy." When the pig is eaten, "all its connective tissue and lymph material, including the irritants and toxic hormone factors are consumed." In the current hog industry, a cute, pink piglet weighing only a few pounds is gorged with food and given growth hormones to fatten it to several hundred pounds within one to two years. "The human system is unable," stated Professor Reckeweg, "to deal with the excess fat, cholesterol, growth hormones, mucous-swelling substances, and other toxic factors." The only way the body has to detoxify from pork consumption is to concentrate the toxins into inflammations. For examples: Gall stones form and then must painfully pass through the body; and, the appendix becomes inflamed and must be removed, although surgical removal of the organ does not eliminate the increasing toxic layer.

Tapeworms and trichinae are among the threats of pork. As for those who defend pork eating with the claim that sufficient cooking will kill parasites, Kellogg muses that "it must be delightful for the pork-eater to contemplate his ham or sausage with the reflection that he is partaking a diet of worms." In order for the parasites to be killed, the entire piece of meat must be subjected to at least 212 degrees. Even then, Kellogg says, one must "swallow a million monsters at a meal," satisfied that "they are cooked and so cannot bite." When parasites have survived, entire families and communities have died from eating pork. People have died even from eating other meats processed with the same equipment with which pork was processed. After pork has been processed commercially, the equipment must be taken completely apart and sterilized, along with all utensils and the work area, before processing any other kind of food.

<blockquote>
Beloved Lord, Almighty God,
Through the rays of the sun, through the waves of the air,
Through the all-pervading life in space, detoxify and revitalize us,
And, we pray, heal our bodies, hearts, and souls.
(Sufi prayer)
</blockquote>

48. WHO'S ENDANGERED NOW?

> There is not a mobile creature on the earth
> that does not depend on Allah for its sustenance.
> (Allah) knows (each creature's) residence and its final destiny.
> Everything is perfectly recorded.
> *(Surah 11: 6)*

A crisp, autumn morning barely revealed the sleek and stealthy bodies of deer gliding through fog painted yellow by the brush strokes of a rising sun. I stood at the window, blew the clouds from my steaming coffee, and enjoyed the beauty of the deer family. A long-legged, spotted fawn stayed near the graceful doe as the buck carried high his six-pointed crown. They were indeed a royal family surrounded by a guard of golden mist.

During the day, I sat on the front porch swing to read my Qur'an. Glancing up, I saw that the deer had returned to steal a few apples from the orchard. They saw me too, but felt no fear in the quiet, Qur'an-soaked atmosphere. The fawn strolled into the yard, and I walked over to it to rub its head. Its parents calmly but cautiously watched from a distance. It was a moment of rare blessing. That deer family represented hope within our small enclave of natural environment, daily succumbing to ever-encroaching pavement and progress.

One wintry day, the solitude of our country existence was shattered by gunshots in our surrounding woods. It was not hunting season, and, besides, the shots were fired on private property. I grabbed the shotgun, fired a couple times over the sheltering trees, and yelled, "You idiots get off my property!" A red pickup truck sprayed the air with red dirt as the cowardly goons sped away.

It was too late, however, to save the doe and fawn murdered in their beds as they slept. The buck barely escaped, but he too was killed just days later. He had ventured outside the edge of the woods where my neighbor Naulty Pyne lived. Spying the buck from the Pynes' kitchen window, Naulty fetched his high-powered rifle. From the safety of his own back porch, Naulty fired upon and killed the king of the royal family. What great sportsmanship, Naulty! What an excellent example of "thrill of the hunt"!

My heart was broken, and I will always miss that beautiful deer family. I hold onto my hope of someday attaining Paradise and strolling through Heaven's orchards with the three deer that blessed my life for such a short span on Earth. I also have hope that justice will be served on the Day of Judgment when all the records will be made known. I plan on standing beside the deer when this story is told. People like Naulty Pyne may be surprised to find their names on Heaven's list of endangered species.

May there be peace on Earth, peace in the skies and peace in Heaven.
May there be peace within the waters and peace for plants and animals.
Divine Being, bestow upon us peace for all.
Accept the holy prayers and invocations for peace
So that universal tranquility and joy may be known.
Empower us in our meditations so that we may
Resolve and dissolve harm, violence, and conflicts,
And change whatever is terrible, sinful, cruel, and violent.
May Earth become filled with positive energies.
May Earth be beneficial for all creatures.
(Adapted from the Hindu Atharva Veda 19: 9)

49. KILLING IS NOT A SPORT

Allah made cattle for you so you may use some for riding
and some for food.
They ask you what is lawful for them.
Say, "All humane/ethical things are lawful for you.
Trainers have trained hunting animals by teaching them
from what Allah has taught you.
Eat what they catch for you, but say Allah's name over it.
Be reverent of Allah. Truly, Allah is quick to take account.
O Children of Adam,
wear your beautiful apparel at every place of prayer.
Eat and drink but do not waste by excesses.

> Allah does not love wasteful people.
> *(Surah 40: 79, Surah 5: 4, and Surah 7: 31)*

With drunken, crazy hunters wandering through our woods, shooting at anything that moves, I went to the sheriff's department and filled out the necessary paperwork to allow deputies to come onto our property at any time and make arrests. On the form, I had to agree to put up a sign with a specific size and specific words, including the number of the state statute. Nobody sells signs like that! I had to make my own. I cut a piece of plywood larger than what is required, painted it, and then lettered it. At the bottom, I added a few words of my own: "Killing God's creatures for fun is not a sport; it's a sin."

Of course, there are responsible hunters who hunt as a means of survival. I know a few people who kill a deer or two every year, and that is all the meat their families use until the next year. There is nothing wrong with that as long as the families give thanks to God and are conscientious of the fact that life was sacrificed for their benefit.

Theodore "Teddy" Roosevelt experienced a disappointing hunt on one of his many ventures. Not wanting to let the President end his trip without success, companions of the hunt brought a restrained bear into the camp so that Roosevelt could take a shot and take home his prize. President Roosevelt, however, would not kill an animal captured simply for his pleasure. The story inspired the creation of the renowned Teddy Bear. The captured bear escaped the fate of the many animals killed for the sheer pleasure of killing.

My neighbor Rhed Grissel was an avid hunter. His house was decorated with stuffed heads and carcasses of animals sacrificed on the altar of Rhed's wanton ego. He boasted of the zebra skin hanging on the wall, and he had a gorilla paw ashtray, a monkey head candy dish, and pillows covered in leopard skin. For target practice, he shot birds out of the sky and left their bodies in the field where they fell. Scripture has never given people permission to destroy life for such frivolous purposes. Something is spiritually and mentally wrong with people who think killing is a recreational activity.

God allowed people to kill and eat, but His permit does not come without restraints. In "Train them according to Allah's instructions to you," Scripture implies that animals used for hunting are to be trained to kill swiftly and without unnecessary torture and wantonness. Hunting dogs should be released in the name of God with the beneficiary's acknowledgement of God's sacrifice of His creatures for our benefit. Our understanding of this verse should be applied to today's hunting tools. Whether using a bow and arrow or a rifle, a hunter should be sure of a certain shot in order to bring a mercifully swift end to an animal's life. Never should life be taken frivolously without solemn gratitude to the animal and to God (blessed and exalted is He).

Most of us, however, get our food from the grocery stores. Meat not only has to be *halal* (permissible), but it also has to be *tayyib* (humane, ethical, pure, natural, cruelty-free). If we cannot be sure that meat was processed from an animal experiencing humane conditions in being raised and slaughtered, we may have to be satisfied with vegetables and plant-based meat substitutes. I sure am!

Even eggs and dairy products may have a history of cruelty behind them. We don't always know if food is tayyib. We just have to do the best we can as we pray and work for a better future for all creation.

We must be responsible citizens of this awesome planet on which we live. Resources are exhaustible, and we must not waste what God (blessed!) has given us. History and current events are replete with grotesque acts of rampant wildlife destruction and carnage. Many plants and animals have become extinct or endangered due to the carelessness, greed, and vanity of people.

Excess, however, is not limited to the over-killing of species. One news report stated that 64.5% of Americans, including children, suffer from obesity. Our government keeps coming up with new regulations over food and restaurants to try to resolve the problem, but there will not be a solution until people become moral and responsible citizens who realize that gluttony is not only a health hazard, it's also a sin.

O Allah Almighty,
Bless us and fill our hearts with contentment
For the countless blessings on this earth.
Bless us with a sense of justice
So that we may do justice among ourselves.
Bless us, O Allah Almighty,
With thankfulness and appreciation
For Your bounties in the flora and fauna.
Bless us with faith, unity, and discipline
So we may not be among the trespassers.

> O Allah, we cannot deny Your favors
> Bestowed upon us in mind, body, and soul.
> Accept our thanksgiving.
> Guide us with Your wisdom, and do not allow us to stray.
> *[Humeyra Kazmi (Pakistan)]*[39]

50. WITHOUT A CLUE

> Now a messenger from among yourselves has come to you.
> It distresses him that you should perish [unsaved],
> so passionately concerned is he over you.
> To the believers, he is most kind and merciful.
> *(Surah 9: 128)*

While waiting in line at a lunch counter, Duston began a conversation with the man behind him. On learning that the man was a poultry farmer, Dusty asked, "What does it mean when hens crow?"

"Hens don't crow," the man insisted.

"Well, okay," Dusty patronized. "What does it mean when hens go, 'AaaaackaagaaaaAwwwwwk.'" The astonished man stared as the horrible sound was emitted from Dusty's mouth.

"I've never heard a sound like that in my life!" the man exclaimed.

"Mama says that the hens are just trying to fill-in when the roosters don't feel well," Dusty told him.

"But hens don't care," the baffled man said. "Hens just don't care!"

"Hmmph; ours do," Dusty said. "Do you have trouble getting your chickens to drink plain water after they've gotten used to iced tea?"

Confused, the man asked, "How would chickens get iced tea?"

"Well, they just hop on Mama's shoulder and drink from her glass."

While the man stood there with a look of befuddlement on his face, Dusty continued. "Do your chickens like plain macaroni? Our chickens only eat macaroni with cheese."

"B—bu—but how would chickens get macaroni?" the man whined.

Dusty gave the man a discerning look and said, "You don't have any business raising chickens; you don't know anything about them."

Dusty decided to change the subject and get some advice on using an incubator. He had been thinking about buying some fertile hummingbird eggs.

"Do you know anything about using an incubator?" he asked.

"Sure," the man replied. "Take fresh eggs from the chickens' nests, put the eggs in the incubator, and turn them once a day for twenty-one days."

"But what if they're not chicken eggs; what if they're hummingbird eggs?"

Almost in tears, the man cried, "B—bu—but how would chickens get hummingbird eggs?"

The poultry farmer did not have a clue about chickens as anything but food. He didn't know how affectionate and responsive a chicken can be. He didn't realize that each one has a unique personality. You can learn a lot from a birdbrain, but I doubt that poultry farmer learned much from his feathered crew.

Many people do not have a clue about spiritual matters. If you try to discuss such things, they prefer to change the subject.

I am fortunate that my parents took me to church where I learned about moral responsibility, God's love and grace, and how to live in order to be saved. Some people grow up in homes where God's name is never mentioned except in vain, and they learn moral values from television. B—bu—but how can such birdbrains ever taste the truth? We believers must live so that our lives are sermons without words. We must pray that our witness will win some lost soul back to the sheltering wing of God's Divine Presence and away from the heat of an eternal broiler.

> O God, O God, unite the hearts of Your servants,
> and reveal unto them Your great purpose.
> May they follow Your commandments and abide in Your law.
> Help them, O God, in their endeavors,
> and grant them strength to serve You.
> O God, do not leave them to themselves,
> but guide their steps by the light of Your knowledge,
> and cheer their hearts by Your love.

Truly, You are their Helper and their Lord.
[Baha'u'llah (1817-1892) founder of the Bahai faith (Persia)]

51. GOD'S INVESTMENT

Alas for the servants!
A messenger never comes to them without their mocking him.
We gave Moses the Book [the Torah]. We sent messengers after him.
We gave Jesus, the son of Mary, evidence [miracles]
and strengthened him with the Holy Spirit.
When a messenger comes to you with (a message) that you do not want,
do you become arrogant? You call some imposters, and you kill others.
(Surah 36: 30 and Surah 2: 87)

The chickens had never had their wings clipped, so they could fly. It looked funny to see big, colorful chickens roosting way up in the tops of tall, oak trees, but the chickens enjoyed their freedom in the woods. The hens laid their eggs in different places, so every day we got to go on an egg hunt.

That all changed one brisk, morning. I looked out the window and was horrified to see both roosters bloodied all over and nearly dead. Freddy had come to the front door for help, and he stood there swaying on one leg; Buster was collapsed in the driveway and barely conscious. I was still in my flannel pajamas, the night's drool was dried on my face, and my hair reflected the shock of my being eaten by nightmares. I thought nothing of my appearance, however, as I snatched up my car keys, bundled the roosters, and headed for the vet several miles away. I nearly ran off the road several times, as I had to keep shaking the roosters to keep them awake. They were in shock, and I was afraid that if they slipped into unconsciousness, they would die.

When I entered the veterinarian hospital, mouths dropped open, and everyone stared in silence. Standing there with a bloody chicken under each arm, blood smeared all over my pajamas, my face washed in tears, I must have looked like a mental patient's artistic rendering of his worst headache.

There were deep, bite marks in Freddy's and Buster's backs and necks, and the doctor had little hope of their survival. But –surprise— they recovered. At a cost of four hundred dollars. Four hundred dollars! That's four, zero, zero. $400! How many chicken dinners would that buy? Of course, I could never eat one of my chickens. I'll just stick to veggie chik'n..

It turned out that the chickens had been attacked by a roaming bobcat. Our neighbor got a picture of it on his security camera. After several hens were killed that year by the bobcat, we invested in expensive pens to keep the chickens safe during the night and whenever we are away from home. I turned the chickens' radio to a rock 'n' roll station and hung a disco light. The chickens were grooving, and the wildlife was confused.

I was willing to sacrifice hard-earned money to save the lives of my chickens, but that's nothing compared to the sacrifices the prophets made to proclaim the message of God (blessed and exalted is He). The prophets were part of one huge sacrifice that God (blessed!) made for our salvation. He took the best of His people and put them in the worst of conditions to suffer physical hardship and emotional abuse so that we might have the message of God's grace and mercy. Noah (peace!) was the butt of jokes; Moses (peace!) had to constantly tolerate ingratitude and suspicion; Jeremiah (peace!) was placed in a log and sawn in half; John the Baptist (peace!) was beheaded; and, if you walk into any Catholic church, you'll see that Jesus (peace!), through images, daily suffers the shame and humiliation of the cross. There are many such examples including that of Muhammed (peace!) who was called from a relatively safe and prosperous lifestyle to enter a life of demeaning hardship and struggle. We should thank God every day because He loved us enough to sacrifice the welfare of the people He had the most reason to love. We can thank Him by keeping our souls lively with divine music and lights that confuse the evil prowlers of darkness.

> We praise You, Almighty God,
> For the prophets and martyrs
> Who gave their thoughts and prayers and agonies
> For the truth of God and the freedom of the people.
> We praise You that, amid loneliness and the contempt of men,
> In poverty and imprisonment,
> When they were condemned by the laws of the mighty
> And buffeted on the scaffold,

You upheld them by Your Spirit, in loyalty to Your holy cause.
Grant that we too may be counted in the chosen band
Of those who gave their lives in ransom for many.
Send us forth with the pathfinders of Humanity
To lead Your people in another day's march
Toward the land of promise.
[*Walter Rauschenbusch (1861-1918), Baptist minister (USA)*][40]

52. SWEEPING AWAY THE DARKNESS

Don't they travel throughout the land so that their minds may learn wisdom
and their ears may learn to listen?
Truly, their eyes are not blind, but their hearts within their breasts.
[Remember] the man of the fish [Jonah]!
When he left angrily, he thought that We had no power over him.
In the depths of darkness, he cried,
"No god is there but You! Glory to You! I was wrong."
Those who reject Our signs cannot hear or speak and are in the dark.
Allah leaves whom He will to wander.
He places whom He will on the Straight Way.
(*Surah 22: 46, Surah 21: 87, and Surah 6: 39*)

As I headed into a store, I noticed a man standing beside a batch of brooms with their handles stuck down into a barrel. "Would you like to buy a broom and help out the blind?" he asked.

"I can tell these brooms were made by the blind," I said. "They're upside down."

"What?" He was bewildered

I picked up a broom and pointed to the bundled straw end. "This part is supposed to be on the bottom. The handle goes at the top."

The man's head jerked nervously a few times before he took the broom from me. "No. Look. You just have to turn it this way, and it's okay," he said as he turned the broom right side up.

"Well, I don't want to buy a broom that I have to fix as soon as I get it home," I said.

I headed into the store as the man stood there, jerking his head from side to side and staring at the upside-down brooms.

Even though I was jerking that man's brain around, I really think that the broom is a good symbol for the blind. God (blessed!) provides tools so that physically handicapped people can sweep the darkness out of their lives. Other senses are intensified to make up for the sense that is missing. The United States Air Force prefers to hire the blind to build jet engines. The sense of touch is so sharpened for the blind that they can feel slight imperfections that would be overlooked by sighted people. The blind workers have swept away their darkness by seeing with their fingers.

By God's will, Jonah (peace!) discovered God's light wrapped in the darkness of the whale's belly, and the darkness released him to safety. God could have easily let Jonah slide on down where the sun never shines. To some people, it seems unfair that God chooses whom to guide and whom to lead astray. Perhaps God's mercy is hidden in that which seems unfair. There is a saying, "What you don't know can't hurt you." I always thought that was a stupid saying, but maybe sometimes it is true when it comes to God's guidance. God knows that certain people will put on blindfolds if He gave them sight, and then He would have to judge them accordingly. If He leaves them sightless, however, perhaps He will take that into consideration on the Day of Judgment.

Occasionally I like to sleep outdoors alone and contemplate. I had a phenomenal experience during one of my backyard escapades. The moon snuck behind the partly cloudy ceiling. Where normally there should have been yellow moonbeams, there were beams of darkness. It was strange and surreal. As I studied the anomaly, unspoken words wafted into my mind: "He wraps His light in darkness and speaks in a voice of silence. His hand guides behind us, and His footsteps lead ahead, but He allows us to choose our own paths. His Spirit moves without shadow, but He protects us in the shadow of His wing. How mysterious is our God! Who can pretend to understand Him? He proves Himself over and over, and still we doubt. He promises eternal life; yet we fear death. We ask for favors and rationalize the miracles. How mysterious we are! Only God can understand us."

> Help us to be immune from doubts, notions, and illusions
> That shroud our hearts and prevent us
> From exploring the hidden mysteries.
> *(Sufi prayer)*

53. THE LONE MUSLIM

> Who is worse than those who invent a lie about Allah?
> They will return to the presence of their Lord.
> Witnesses will say, "These are they who lied about their Lord."
> Undoubtedly, the condemnation of Allah is on those who sin.
> Those who create a hindrance from the path of Allah and
> look for something faulty in it are the same ones who deny life after death.
> *(Surah 11: 18-19)*

When a young man has a sporty car that girls like, he calls it a "chick magnet." Well, I drive an old-man magnet —not that I want to attract old men, but every time I drive my '66 Corvair —with its lipstick red color that matches my blond hair— crazy, old men want to run away with me. I guess if I ever decide to run away, I'll have to get me a newer car —a young-stud magnet.

In a parking lot, as I was getting out of my old-man magnet, a crazy, old man approached me. "Well, that's a fine looking car you got there! I ain't seen one of them in a long time. I need me a woman with a fine car like that. Let's me and you run off together."

"Well, I wasn't figuring on running away today," I said.

He tried another angle. "Well, just come home with me and let me bake you a cake. I can make any kind of cake you like." He proceeded to describe various, tempting cakes with all their luscious ingredients.

"If I ever need a sugar daddy, I'll look you up," I said. "But I already got a crazy, old man at home, so I reckon I'll just stick with him for a while longer."

"Well, alright," he resigned. "I reckon I'll stick with the crazy, old woman I got at home then."

We laughed and chatted awhile. Here in the Bible Belt, part of polite conversation is to ask one about his or her religion, so the old man asked me, "Where do you go to church?"

"I don't worship in a church anymore. I worship in a mosque."

His mouth dropped open, and his eyes bugged out. "You mean you're a Muslim!?"

"Yeah, but don't say it so loudly; I don't want to get my car spray-painted with misspelled words."

"But you're a nice lady," he said, as if being Muslim and nice weren't supposed to go together.

"Well, I don't strap on my bombs when I drive my Corvair," I told him. "I have another car for that."

He was a bit stunned, so I finally had to grin so that he'd know I was joking.

He chuckled, and then he said, "Well, I sure am glad I met you. I never met a Muslim before in my life, and you're a whole lot different from what I thought you'd be."

I realized that at that moment I represented every Muslim in the world.

If you are Muslim, YOU also represent every Muslim in the world. When people know you are Muslim, you have to be careful to paint the proper image of all Muslims. If anything in your life –your lack of a smile or friendly word, for example— reflects poorly on you, it reflects poorly on all of us. If you are rude or arrogant or devious or greedy, you're telling a lie about me. Worse yet, you're telling a lie about the Prophet (peace and blessings upon him). You are also living a lie about God (blessed and exalted is He). And that's a real bombshell!

The true Muslims have a difficult task of overwhelming the poor image of Islam that has been our legacy. None of us can do it alone. We must be ambassadors for one another as well as ambassadors for the Prophet (peace and blessings upon him) and for God (blessed and exalted is He). We must also pray for the recovery of the renegade Muslims who have created a false Islam of havoc and terror. How can we successfully witness to nonbelievers until we have some success in witnessing to our own renegades?

Not only Muslims, but also Christians, Jews, and other believers owe it to God to be kind, generous, and courteous when interacting with others. Christians use the measuring tool, "What would Jesus do?" Judging by the way some churchgoers act, one could think that Jesus (peace upon him) was an arrogant, condescending, hatemongering hypocrite. Likewise, the message of the Israeli wall confronting Palestine is not the message of the Divine Father of us all. Regardless of our diverse religions, people of faith should cooperate in advancing the peace and goodwill consonant in all religions of light. May we respond to criticism, hostility, prejudice, and arrogance with graceful words of serenity and noble acts of kindness. We must pray for opportunities to effectively express our faith and for enough patience to tackle any situation and enough humor to tickle any situation.

> For all that we ought to have thought and have not thought,
> For all that we ought to have spoken and have not spoken,
> For all that we ought to have done and have not done,
> For all that we ought not to have thought and yet have thought,
> For all that we ought not to have spoken and yet have spoken,
> For all that we ought not to have done and yet have done;
> For misguided thoughts, words, and works,
> O God, we pray for forgiveness, and we repent with sincere penance.
> *(Sixth century BCE Zoroastrian prayer)*

Me & my old man magnet

Linda Pham

"Oooo! I got keys!"

I'm cool, and I still get to dress like Mary.
(peace upon her)

54. THE RACE IS ON

> Hasten to forgiveness from your Lord.
> A garden whose expanse is that of the skies and Earth
> is prepared for the righteous.
> *(Surah 3: 133)*

My backyard garden was a paradise for my chickens. When I let them out in the morning, they raced to the garden and looked for caterpillars. They picked the Japanese beetles from the okra leaves, and then scratched under the huge squash plants for an assortment of creepy, crawly goodies. My chickens were always eager to leave their coop and seek the rewards of the lively summer garden.

Humanity should be even more eager to escape the walls of sin and race along the Straight Way to our final goal. My chickens were vulnerable to hidden snakes in the grass, sly foxes in the bushes, and wild bobcats ready to pounce from the trees. In the same way, we are prey for evils and temptations in the world around us. We must keep focused and run swiftly. Otherwise, we may become ensnared by the trappings to which we fall when we dawdle and stray from the path onto which God has directed us.

A New Testament writer urges, "We are encouraged by a heritage of witnesses [the prophets and other servants of God]; therefore, may we abandon everything that hinders, dispel all sins that so easily entangle, and run with perseverance the race marked for us" (Hebrews 12: 1). The writer advises us to "fix our eyes on Jesus" (peace upon him) (12: 2), but now we also have the example of Prophet Muhammed (peace upon him). We should accept this double blessing as a double challenge to outperform our Christian friends in the race to achieve lives of righteousness.

One time, when I was in the military, the soldiers were assembled for the chapel service. The commander and his wife entered in a side door. All the seats were taken. I got up from my seat, walked over to the commander's wife, and offered her my seat. She said, "That's okay, honey; somebody is bringing us some extra chairs."

When I sat back down, the man beside me said, "Do you realize that you just put every man here to shame?"

I said, "Well, maybe every man here needed to be put to shame."

Likewise, Muslims should be first to recognize a need and rush to fulfill the need. When disaster strikes, Muslims should be first on the scene with supplies, medical care, emergency housing, and counseling. More Muslims should become actively involved in projects involving environmental concerns and wildlife preservation. Muslim involvement is needed to innovate ways to reduce crime and rehabilitate criminals, beautify neighborhoods, and improve education and community services. The global community needs Islamic initiative to improve the world at large and end oppression and injustice everywhere.

Our reward will be the Garden spanning Heaven and Earth. The faithful believers will inherit the Earth —not this ruined Earth, but the recreated Earth already prepared for us in the future past. We will return to the future Garden of our past, for which we were originally created. We believers will have the opportunity to live on this planet as it was meant to be. Let's all vow to get it right the next time and keep the planet clean and healthy for all inhabitants, including the wildlife. In the meantime, let's do what we can to contribute to the welfare of this present world.

> O Allah, grant me the eye to appreciate Your greatness
> And the beauty and wonder of Your creation.
> O Allah, grant me the humility to walk humbly on this earth,
> As I remember that I am of earth's clay and Your divine breath.
> O Allah, grant me the heart and mind to fully submit to You.
> *[Humeyra Kazmi (Pakistan)]*[41]

55. SPIRITUAL SUSTENANCE

> Give good news to those who believe and work righteousness.
> Their portion is gardens beneath which rivers flow.
> Every time they are fed with fruits from it, they will say,
> "This is like what we used to have."
> They will be given similar things.
> They will have decent companions with whom they will abide eternally.
> *(Surah 2: 25)*

A scientific mystery exists for which I think the government should fund research. Why is it that when I eat only one pound of chocolate, I gain five pounds of me? That just doesn't make any sense. I have noticed, however, a spiritual parallel to that mystery. When God (blessed and exalted is He) gives me one pound of grace, I gain five pounds of faith. And the chocolate and grace we get in Heaven will be many times better than what we get here.

From humorous greeting cards to Hollywood fantasy, Heaven is often depicted as a sterile, unfamiliar place with bumbling angels and heavy, foreboding gates. We are promised, however, a place familiar to us with things we enjoy and people we love. After having been declared clinically dead, many revived patients describe beautiful fields of flowers through which they wade to meet friends and relatives running towards them. They are overwhelmed with feelings of calm and peace.

The Qur'an explains that each successful believer will be given four gardens and that each garden will have two springs of water (Surah 55: 46, 50, 62). I imagine my gardens will be: (1) a mountain garden, (2) a tropical garden, (3) a plains garden, and (4) an arid garden. Each garden will have orchards, rows of vegetables, and flowers unique to each garden's climate. I'm also hoping for a chocolate tree.

The meaning of "fruits" in Surah 2: 25 may include literal food, and when the roll is called up yonder, I'll be in chocolate heaven, insh'Allah. I think the primary meaning of "fruits," however, is sustenance for every aspect of our lives. The enjoyment of dining involves all our senses —smell (fresh-baked bread), sight (glistening, red strawberries), sound (the snap and crunch of carrots), taste (vine-ripened tomatoes), and feel (the texture of smooth, creamy pudding). Also, we benefit from physical nourishment and the fellowship of friends and family who share our meals. Food is an excellent metaphor to use in reference to art, literature, nature, music, and anything else that sustains us and yanks us from the clutches of depression, despair, and hopelessness. Such things are only a taste of the goodness God has in store for us in all the wonderful flavors of Heaven, and our favorite food should always be the Word of God and the time we spend before Him in worship.

"Taste and know that the Lord is good..." (Psalms 8: 34).

God, we thank You for all Your gifts:
Day and night, fruits and flowers, trees and water,

All the treasures with which You have blessed us.
The heat of the sun, the light of the moon, the songs of the birds,
The coolness of the breeze, the green grass like a mattress of velvet
—all owe their existence to Your grace.
Dear God, may we forever breathe the breath of Your love
And every moment be aware of Your presence above.
(Adapted from a Pakistani prayer)

56. THE GOODLIEST LAND

Humanity should consider his/her food.
[He/she should consider] how We pour water in abundance.
We fragment the earth in cracks.
From it are produced grain, grapes, nutritious herbs, olives, date palms.
[Also produced are luxurious, enclosed gardens,
and fruits and fodder as provision for you and your cattle.
(Surah 80: 24-32)

The school bus returned little Dusty to the edge of the woods after school. He slowly ambled home. He took time to skip, throw rocks, chase rabbits, talk to terrapins, trade songs with birds, and snack on "survival food." He hunted under rocks and behind tree bark and ate grubs, herbs, and berries. The pickings were slim, but he was communing with the haunts of long-past indigenous tribes who first traversed this land and found it then to be generously stocked.

Early explorers used the phrase "the goodliest land" to describe the forests, fields, and plains of North America. It was said that a squirrel could travel from Wilmington, North Carolina, to the Mississippi River without ever leaving the treetops. Native Amer-Indians cultivated orchards of muscadines, plums, persimmons, pawpaws, and various nuts. Enclosed by the dense forests, vast prairies of wild grasses were home to healthy herds of buffalo, long since slaughtered by European settlers.

According to the Tanakh (Jewish Bible), God's original plan was that plants would suffice for food: "I have provided multiple grains and fruits for

Humanity to eat, but for all wild animals and birds, I have provided grass and leaves" (Genesis 1: 29-30). The sages teach that God, in His full knowledge of impending evil, destined the world to use meat for food because, after the flood of Noah, the earth would not be able to sustain the lush gardens, bountiful orchards, and grassy plains of the original creation. Our Garden of Eden has perished from this dimension, and "the goodliest land" is only a vision from our sweetest dreams and our hopes for the new creation.

God has made lawful the eating of meat except carrion, blood, pork, and animals killed in any inhumane manner (Surah 5: 3). God (blessed and exalted is He) has given us permission to kill and eat, but, as this was not part of His original plan, we should be ever mindful of the sacrifice He has made in order to sustain us. With that in mind, I think we should want to slaughter fewer living creatures to satisfy our carnivorous appetites and increase our appreciation for the wonderful and diverse flavors and textures of fruits, vegetables, and grains. We must meet the global food crisis with a plan to retain and rejuvenate more farmlands instead of covering too much good soil with housing developments, condominiums and mansions, and tourists' traps. Farmland should not be wasted on tobacco and opium poppies.

When we do enjoy good meat, we should have the attitude of grateful American indigenous tribes. After killing an animal, indigenous tribes paid tribute, saying, "I am sorry I had to kill you, Little Brother, but I had need of your flesh. My children are hungry and crying for food. Forgive me, Little Brother. I will honor your courage, strength, and beauty. I will place your bones on a mighty tree and decorate them with streamers of red beads. Each time I pass this way, I will remember you and honor your spirit. Forgive me, Little Brother."[42]

O Great Spirit,
You have given us fruits and grains
For all people's happiness so our bodies will become strong.
You blessed us with food growing from the good earth.
We give thanks because You have given us food
To sustain us upon the earth.
Help us to always remember that these gifts are from You.
(Adapted from a prayer of the Seneca American indigenous tribe)

57. CREATION GONE HAYWIRE!

> Corruption has invaded land and sea
> Because of (the evil) earned by the hands of Humanity.
> Allah allows people a taste of what [sins] they committed
> So perhaps they may return [to Allah].
> *(Surah 30: 41)*

I held Dottie in the palm of my hand when the tips of her miniature wings were still damp from the egg. Lillian sat on the remaining eggs as she and I greeted the first hatchling of the batch. Like the mother hen, Dottie was calm and unafraid.

All the chickens felt safe within their little houses enclosed with chicken wire. The chicken coop was designed to keep out bobcats, foxes, owls, and other wildlife partial to chicken dinners.

One day I let the chickens out to freely roam around the yard. In the evening, the chickens went back into their coop, but ran back out nervously. I couldn't figure out what was wrong with them until I went in to gather the eggs. A giant, mutant, alien snake was curled in the nest; he was swallowing all the eggs. I dashed back to the house and yelled for Tom to bring his pistol.

We had never killed snakes as they serve an important part in the balance of nature, but the snake I found in the henhouse was a monster, and I wanted its head shot off.

Tom wrestled the snake much like someone would wrestle an alligator. He finally got a good grip around its neck. Tom is five-foot, nine-inches tall. He held the snake above his own head as far as he could reach, and the snake's tail was still draping on the ground. Its belly was about seven inches thick. Tom made me get a burlap sack in which to put the snake, and I had to carry it as Tom drove the pickup truck. When we came to a wild creek, Tom opened the sack and let the snake go.

We watched that strange, hideous snake slither through the tall grass and find its way to the creek. Tom said, "Something just doesn't look right about that snake."

I said, "It's getting away without having its head blowed off. That's what's wrong with it." I always regretted releasing that snake to terrorize all the unsuspecting critters living around that creek. Also, I learned that snakes hunt within a fifty-mile radius, so that same snake could come back.

When I went out another morning, Lillian was dead. Her body was stretched and distorted –the effects of snake venom. Buster the rooster was traumatized, and all the peep-peeps were gone. When I began trying to comfort Buster, Dottie heard my voice, came running from the woods, and flew into my hands. She had survived! Somehow, she had managed to squeeze through the chicken wire and hide in the woods.

I buried Lillian. The next morning I had to bury Busty, Lillian's devoted, lifelong mate. Buster had died of a broken heart. My heart also was broken.

I was devastated again when, days later, a different monster, mutant, alien snake killed and swallowed four, beautiful, pullets (half grown chickens). Fortunately, I discovered the snake still in the chicken coop. I ran as fast as I could to get the rifle and make it back before the snake escaped. I had to put four bullets into the back of his head before he finally stopped striking at me. Of course, the snake was not evil; he was only trying to survive, but I had to insure that my remaining chickens survived.

The earth was created pure and good, but knowing the evil that humanity would commit, God preordained that land and sea would become corrupt with death and disaster. That is the struggle into which He has put us to give us opportunities to earn our way back to Paradise. The region in which I live had been experiencing a drought for several years. According to farm and wildlife officials, the drought had caused wildlife to become desperate, aggressive, and even unnatural.

In seasons of rain and drought, blessings and curses fall on everyone, good or bad. King Solomon received the offer of a great bargain: God said, "If I withhold rain from the sky, if I send locusts to ravage the crops, or if I release pestilence; when my people who profess my name humble themselves, pray, seek my favor, and reject evil, I will hear in my Heavenly abode. I will forgive their sins and heal their land" (2 Chronicles 7: 13-14). Unfortunately, the world prefers spiritual darkness, and we all must suffer. And so, I keep my spiritual rifle loaded, as well as the tangible one, with a round in the chamber.[43]

> I call on You, and I trust that You will answer me,
> O God, listen to me and hear my prayer.
> Display your faithfulness in wondrous deeds.

You are the one who rescues those who seek refuge from predators.
Protect me as You would a favored child.
Hide me in the shadow of Your wings.
(Psalms 17: 6-8)

58. A BETTER HOPE

Abraham said, "My Lord, explain how You would exchange life for death."
"Do you not believe?" (Allah) asked.
"Yes, but fulfill my understanding," (Abraham) pled.
[Allah instructed,] "Raise four birds and train them to come to you.
Place a piece of (their dead bodies) on each hill, and then call to them.
They will swiftly return to you.
Know that Allah is Victorious, Perfectly Wise."
(Surah 2: 260)

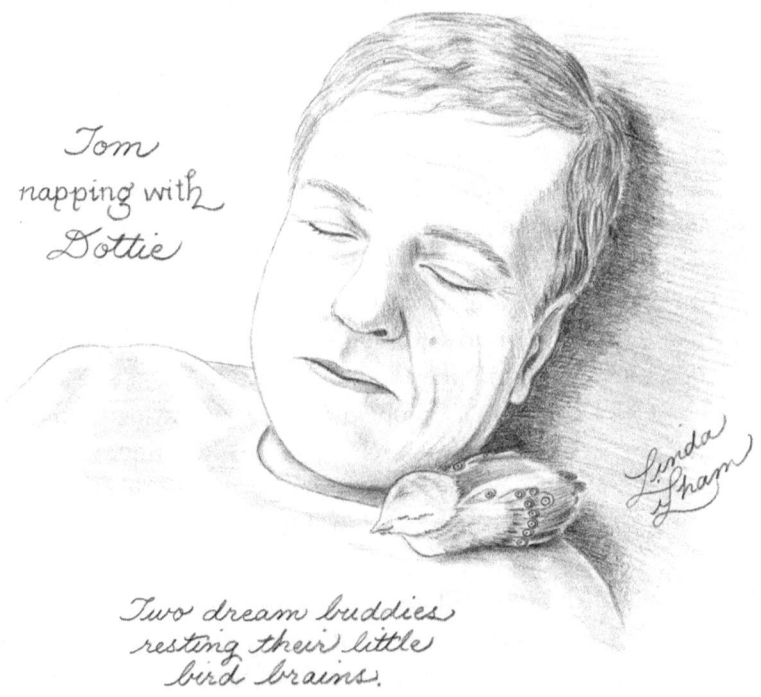

Tom napping with Dottie

Two dream buddies resting their little bird brains.

Dottie was a beautiful, little chicken. Her feathers were multiple, tortoiseshell colors, and she had white, racing stripes on her wings. After surviving a snake attack, she was glad to stay in the people-house. Dottie nested on my pillow, and gently pecked my eyelids to wake me in the mornings. She had a happy song and spent most of her time sitting on my shoulder and singing more like a songbird than a chicken. Everyone in the family loved Dottie, and she loved us. She snuggled under chins, nestled in hair, and traveled in apron pockets and overall bibs. She shared iced tea from our glasses and pecked the cream filling from our cookies. Dottie took bubble baths with me and preened my wet hair. She taught me a lullaby for soothing her to sleep, and she felt safe. She was happy, and she made me happy. When I was sad, Dottie brought me joy. Her happy song was a healing balm.

One day Dottie hopped a ride on my shoulder when I went to the bank. I think the bank teller's hair reminded Dottie of her mama hen. When Dottie saw that long, curly, light brown hair, she flew straight for it and snuggled under it. The other tellers and I had quite a time getting Dottie untangled from all that hair!

Another time, she traveled under my baseball cap to the grocery store. She sat on my head and sang. Other shoppers kept looking around, wondering from where that noise was coming. Whenever someone looked at me, I just wrinkled my forehead and innocently looked around too.

Whenever I was working in my art studio, I propped my screen door open so that Dottie could go outside and enjoy her favorite pastime, chasing bugs. She could come and go as she pleased, and I felt that she was safe near the house with the dog, cats, and adult chickens surrounding her.

I was working at my drawing table when I heard Dottie's distress cries. I ran outside, but I was helpless to save Dottie from the hawk flying away with her. I screamed, and cried, and prayed. But Dottie was gone, and I couldn't get her back. I hurt so much that I thought my heart would just stop beating. I couldn't smile for weeks. Even months later, when something would make me start to laugh, I would remember Dottie, and then I would cry instead. I still miss Dottie, and I will for the rest of my life. She was such a treasure to me!

All the family cried for little Dottie, but we have hope that Dottie will be restored to life and we will see her again in our eternal home. My broken heart will be restored when I reach my final goal back to the future where God's original creation is safe and beautiful.

Surah 2: 260 doesn't say that Abraham actually carried out God's suggestion. Perhaps the idea was enough as our hope must be enough to sustain us in this life. When Tana expressed this hope to her Christian friends, they laughed at her and scoffed, "Heaven is for people, not animals; chickens don't have souls." I told Tana that she should take their scoffing as an opportunity to witness for Islam by saying that our religion offers a better hope because we believe that God has a plan for all His creatures.

The number of birds, four, in the verse suggest the four corners of the world —north, south, east, west. I don't know where the hawk took Dottie before ripping her tiny, fragile body into bite-sized pieces, but God knows, and He is able to restore her and keep her as one of the treasures of Heaven. I was blessed that God let me borrow her to comfort me for a little while on this earth.

>Most worshipful God,
>You created humans to walk the earth with its abundance.
>We ask You to bless our family with success and prosperity.
>Make our farms yield an abundant harvest,
>And allow our animals and chickens to be healthy.
>Ask and demand from us whatever You will,
>But protect us from danger, illness, and evil prowling the earth.
>We will remember and honor You always.
>This is our hearts' desire and what our words express.
>*(Adapted from a prayer of the Igorot tribe of the Philippines)*

59. THE QUANTUM LEAP

>We have decreed that death be your shared fate.
>We will not be frustrated from changing your life form
>into something new to you.
>The great terror will bring them no grief. The angels will meet them:
>"This is your day that you were promised."
>On that day We will roll up the skies like a scroll rolled up for manuscripts.
>As We produced the first creation, We will produce a new one.

> This is a promise that We have undertaken. Truly, We shall fulfill it.
> *(Surah 56: 60-61 and Surah 21: 103-104)*

What a great promise! I can hardly wait!

I often relax in the woods surrounding our house. I plop down into the fern- and moss-studded natural humus, lean against a sheltering tree, and ponder: What was creation like when it was fresh and new? I imagine vast fields of wild strawberries and muscadines; lush forests of sassafras, chinquapin, wild azaleas, and lady slippers; pools of pristine water bubbling from underground springs; herds of handsome deer; friendly chipmunks and skunks; and a gentle bear. Then I lament how things have become spoiled by the introduction of humanity's evil, including pollution and rape of the land. Suddenly my imagined bear tries to eat me, and I run back into the house and get my relaxation from bubble bath.

The Qur'an explains that people pray for evil as fervently as they pray for goodness (Surah 17: 11). Everything, even inanimate objects, has a kind of awareness with which God alone can communicate. When people radiate negative energies –through actions, words, or thoughts— every thing and being around us absorb that negativity. They don't want it, so negative energy is reflected back onto humanity. That is why there are so many natural disasters, humanitarian crises, and personal struggles. To improve the world, people need to concentrate on radiating positive energies so that the world will, in return, gratify us with complementary positive energies.

I look forward to the way things ought to be. But that world, the new creation, already exists in a different dimension. Time and space are only relative to the world as we know it. We think of time and space as in a straight line; eg, the nearest star (after the sun), Proxima Centauri, is 4.26 light-years or 25.05 trillion miles away. According to quantum physics, however, time and space are rolled up like a scroll, so, to get from one point to another, one has only to pass through the wall of the time-space continuum. At the end of the world as we know it, the metaphysics of the scroll concept will be revealed when the sky is curled like a rolled manuscript.

In our physical bodies, we are incapable of taking the quantum leap, but when we are unencumbered, our souls will not be confined to time and space. We will enter God's reality where "a day is comparable to fifty thousand years" (Surah 70: 4). In the spiritual realm, there are no histories, current events, and possibilities. Past, present, and future are one total existence rolled up together as completed manuscripts. God (blessed and exalted is He) is able to transform us into a spiritual existence in which we will be able, in this world's future, to relive the best of times past.

Anyone who has lost a loved one to death can take comfort in knowing that, although you can no longer be with your loved one in this life, it is possible for your loved one to be with you. My theory is that a loved one can take the quantum leap and visit our past to relive precious moments. Perhaps he or she can travel beyond our future to a time when we are able to seek God unencumbered. You'll find out for sure when you take the quantum leap beyond the great terror and into the great reward.

> The garden is rich with diversity.
> Hundreds of kinds of plants grow underneath the trees
> And have a multitude of colors and fragrances.
> Basil. Mint. Lavender.
> Great Spirit, keep my remembrance pure.
> Raspberry. Apple. Rose.
> Great Spirit, fill my heart with love.
> Dill. Anise. Tansy.
> Great Spirit, blow Your wind into me.
> Rhododendron. Zinnia. Poppy.
> May my prayer be beautiful.
> May my remembrance, O Great Spirit,
> Be as incense to You in the sacred Garden of eternity
> As I remember the ancient gardens of your creation.
> *(Adapted from a prayer of the Chinook American indigenous tribe)*

60. HEAVENLY ROCK 'N' ROLL

> When the sun folds! When the stars fade away!
> When the mountains vanish!
> When the full-term, pregnant camels are abandoned!
> When the wild beasts herd together!
> When the oceans are swollen!
> When the souls are paired [with their bodies]!

> When the scrolls are laid open! When the sky is stripped!
> When Hell is ignited! When Paradise is presented!
> Each soul will then know what it has forwarded.
> *(Surah 81: 1-14)*

One morning I picked up my hand mirror so I could put on my makeup. The mirror had fallen out, and I stared into the slate gray backing. It scared me to death! I thought someone had stolen my face!

That same day, I had another scare. I took the trash to the burn pit and set fire to it on a slightly breezy day. Hours later, I looked out the window and saw the woods full of smoke. "Oh, creeping crud!" I ran out the door, expecting to have to start beating out a forest fire. I didn't see any smoke anywhere. I went back into the house. I looked out the window, and the woods were full of smoke. I went back outside. No smoke. Back inside the house, I finally realized that the windows were steamed from the air humidifier trying to soothe my allergies. What a joke! I was just happy that the reality was good news even though the world through steamed windows had given me a real scare.

Although our eyes have never directly peered into God's reality, our souls know the face of God (blessed and exalted is He). This dim and confusing existence is a frightening disappointment to our souls. This life is uncertain and filled with nightmarish possibilities, including how our lives will end. God created diseases and disasters as a veil for death so that we might focus our fears and anger on the things that lead to death rather than death itself, which is a natural part of living. Someday that veil will disappear, along with all the veils covering God's reality. Our world will rock and convulse, and, like a scroll, our perception of time and space will roll up to reveal the reality that angels see —where fifty thousand years are like one day.

Someday our universe will hit the Omega Point —the point at which our continually expanding universe will stop expanding and will begin collapsing on itself. That will be a great day of rock 'n' roll! Everything that has ever lived will be resurrected. All past deeds will be reviewed, except those that, by God's grace, have been blotted out by His amazing forgiveness. The mountains will shatter, and the sky will roll up like a scroll. For the unforgiven sinners, it will be a day of "great terror."

Some sinners will be as surprised as Scrappy Rumpwilder was the day he got a hot seat while hunkering in the car shed. (Hunkering is the fine art of squatting with a huddle of yarn-spinners.) Some of Daddy's buddies came over, and he took them into the car shed where he had a bottle of whiskey stashed. I hunkered behind the shed and spied through the slits between the boards of the walls. The men hunkered, smoked cigarettes, passed the bottle of whiskey, and listened to one of Daddy's stories. Scrappy Rumpwilder must have been a plumber, because when he hunkered, he exposed an embarrassing amount of his personality. Scrappy bumped against a shelf on which was a can of lighter fluid missing its cap. The can fell over on its side, and lighter fluid dribbled into the gap between his pants and exposed backside. The fellow beside Scrappy held his cigarette out to the side and flicked off the ash. A few lively, mischievous embers bounced off too, and they jumped right into Scrappy's britches.

Daddy was nearing the end of his tale when Scrappy jumped up with a yelp. Everybody thought he was laughing. Daddy said, "Scrappy, I ain't got to the good part yet."

Scrappy yelped again. Somebody insisted, "Hunker back down here, Scrappy, and let Bill finish his story."

Scrappy's britches suddenly brightened with ignition. Daddy, with a calm drawl, said, "Well, Scrappy, your hind end's on fire."

A lot of hind ends will be on fire when "Boogy Oogy Woogy" is a hit in Heaven. The faithful believers, however, can look forward to their great inheritance of the fresh, clean, new, old creation.

At that time, we will experience life as a New Testament writer explained it: "Now we see only a vague reflection [of reality] as in a mirror, but then we shall see face to face. Now I only partially understand, but then I will know fully, just as I am fully known [by God]" (1 Corinthians 13: 12).

> One day my soul must depart from its body.
> When will it be? In winter or summer?
> In town or country? During the day or night?
> Suddenly or with warning? Due to illness or an accident?
> Will I have a chance to confess my sins?
> Will there be a cleric to assist me?
> I know none of these things.
> One thing only is certain —that I may die,
> And sooner than I would like.

Dear God,
Take me into Your arms on that most important day.
May all other days be sad, if only that day may be happy.
I tremble with fear at the prospect,
Yet I know that You, and You alone, can save me.
Set my whole heart on Your promise of Heaven.
Guide my feet in Your ways, O Lord,
That I may walk the Straight Path towards eternal life.
Let me cast off everything that holds me back on my journey there,
So that all my strength may be directed towards that goal.
[Francis of Sales (1567-1622), Bishop of Geneva]

61. EXTRA LOVIN'

Whatever you are given is a convenience of this life,
but that which is with Allah is better and more durable
for those who believe and put their trust in their Lord.
[They] are those who avoid the most horrible sins and shameful deeds.
[They] forgive even when angered.
[They] hearken to their Lord and maintain the traditional prayers.
[They] conduct their affairs by mutual consultation.
[They] spend [for charity] from the sustenance We bestow upon them.
[They are] those who, when afflicted by an injustice,
[properly] defend themselves.
(Surah 42: 36-39)

When Dusty was little, he came to the stove and saw that I was making macaroni and cheese. "Mama, will you put some extra love in it?" he asked. I grinned, opened the refrigerator, got the bag of grated cheese, and added extra, medium cheddar love to the macaroni.

All the good and wonderful things we love will be in Heaven, but extra love will be in every detail so that Heaven will be much more amazing than we can imagine. Whatever we enjoy in this life is temporal, but the treasures of Heaven, as Jesus said, "will not be exhausted, where no thief comes near and no moth destroys" (Luke 12: 33).

In his essay "The Muslim Heaven," Abdulla Yusuf Ali wrote:

> How can we understand a psychological term like 'bliss' in general symbolical terms? If it is to convey the idea of satisfaction in any but abstract terms, we must have the symbolism of ordinary life, yet lifted up to ideas of refinement, delicacy, and satisfaction. The acts of eating and drinking are spiritualized and socialized. The choicest of meats, fruits, and drinks, which minister to the most sensitive taste, will be provided. Dress of most artistic taste will add dignity to social interaction, and there will be thrones and symbols of honor. There will be companionship –individual companionship, companionship of equal age, and general companionship. And those whom we loved in this life –mothers, wives, sisters, relatives, children, friends— will all add to our joy by their company in a transformed love superior to earthly love, as the Garden of Heaven is superior to an earthly garden. The condition of faith and good life is of course attached, for no disharmony can enter to mar the dignity of Heaven. Perfected love will not be content with self, but like a note of music, will find its melody in communion with others.[44]

In the once-secret Phoenix Project of the Philadelphia Experiment, sailors' bodies were reportedly fused with parts of the submarine used in a time-travel experiment. It was subsequently determined that it is important for people to remain within each person's given time-space lock. I think the Qur'an indicates that too whenever it speaks of companions of equal age (Surahs 38: 52; 56: 37). In Paradise, each person will feel comfortable and at-home in surroundings that are similar to the old homestead, whether it was a fifteenth-century, Cherokee longhouse; an eighteenth-century, pioneer log cabin; or a twentieth-century home of electric appliances. A person's earthly dwelling, environment, and culture may have been simple or elaborate, but the extra loving with which God recreates them will change even the sixth-century Bedouin tent into a mansion. All the best sights, sounds, tastes, textures, and smells that are familiar to an individual will be in his or her little corner of Paradise, but in a perfected and unimaginably beautiful state.

Bring us, O Lord, at our last awakening
Into the house and gate of Heaven,
To enter into that gate and dwell in that house
Where there shall be neither darkness nor dazzle, but one equal light;
Neither noise nor silence, but one equal music;
Neither fears nor hopes, but one equal possession;
Neither ends nor beginnings, but one equal eternity
In the habitations of Your glory and dominion;
World without end.
[John Donne (1572-1631) (England)]

62. WHEN MERCY COMES IN DROPS

He sends the winds like heralds of glad tidings, going before His mercy.
When they have carried the heavily laden clouds,
We shepherd them to a land that is desiccated.
[We] make rain to descend upon it,
and produce every kind of harvest from it.
Thus, shall We raise the dead. Perhaps you will remember.
(Surah 7: 57)

The day that Dottie, my baby chicken, was snatched away by a hawk, I sat on the porch crying and wondering why God had not saved something that He knew I loved so much. He could have saved her if He had wanted to, I thought. Suddenly a little chickadee smacked into the living room window and fell dead at my feet. I picked up the warm, soft, limp body and soaked it in my tears. God's little birds were always flying into the living room window and knocking themselves smack into eternity. Then I realized, I could have saved them if I had wanted to. I do want to, I thought. I decided to buy stained glass ornaments with suction cups and hang them in the window to advise the birds.

As I dug a little hole in the woods in which to bury the chickadee, I thought of how the wildlife had been so perversely affected by the drought.

"Something's wrong, God," I prayed. "This drought is wrong, and only You can fix it. You could fix it if You wanted to."

I covered the little bird's body with dirt, and as I placed a rock over the filled hole, something gently kissed my head. Then another kiss. And another. Rain. It was rain. And the raindrops seemed to carry a message: "I do want to." The following weeks were witness to the fact that the drought had ended for a while. Rain is a beautiful sight when it comes down in a soft veil of prismatic jewels. It cleanses the world around us and writes its poetry upon the earth.

Colors of spring returned to dry, brown plants; flowers exchanged their multi-colored smiles; and the water level danced to a forgotten height in the well.

People looked at me suspiciously when I told them that I had "one in the oven," but, in just twenty-one days, the single egg I had put in my incubator began to cheep. I watched the cheeping egg, and soon a crack formed. Then, a little hole appeared and a tiny beak popped out of the hole. It was dry inside the incubator, so, using an eyedropper, I gave the beak a few drops of water, which it eagerly drank. By the end of the day, the little miracle had struggled free from the egg. She was beautiful with colors of sienna and sand. I named her *Rain*.

> Thank You, Lord, for clouds to hug the dusty day.
> Thank You for raining kisses on the thirsty clay.
> Blessings are raining on every garden groomed.
> It isn't rain I see but fields of color bloomed.
> In each prismatic drop of rain, I see
> A fragrant café for every busy bee.
> I see wildflowers falling on the field
> As the sky drips its nourishing yield.
> Thank You, Lord, for showers of mercy gay,
> Reminders of Your grace for those who pray.

63. THE WONDERFUL WORLD OF CLOUDS

> Will (the sinners) wait until Allah comes to them
> in canopies of clouds, along with angels?
> The matter [of judgment] will then be settled!
> All matters are referred to Allah.
> The Companions of Paradise will be well that day, in their homes,
> with the nicest places for midday relaxation.
> That day the sky is rent asunder, with clouds, and angels descending,
> is the day that the dominion of truth is held by the Most Merciful.
> It will be a day of dire straits for the disbelievers.
> *(Surah 2: 210 and Surah 25: 24-26)*

"Mama, look! God cut the sunshine into strips and pasted them onto the clouds," two-year-old Dusty said about sunbeams.

Another time, he observed, "All the cloud monsters have gold fillings in their teeth."

Tana was also fascinated by clouds. "Angels, Mama, angels! They're lying on the clouds. Look; their hair is hanging down," she said of the sunbeams. "There's an angel sitting up there! I see his sandals!"

How wonderful to lie in the grass and watch the parade march by in canopies of clouds! Crocodiles and elephants. Puppy dogs and dragons. See the seal with the ball? Ooops! It's breaking up now, and it's turning into a school of fish.

One day, however, the parade of clouds will be angels, and they won't break up and turn into something else. First, Jesus the Messiah will return in a canopy of clouds to straighten out the mess down here (according to Acts 1: 9-11; and Daniel 7: 13-14). Muhammed (peace and blessings upon him) said, "The son of Mary will surely come down as a fair judge."[45] "He [Jesus in his second coming] will be a portent of the Time [of Judgment]; do not doubt it [but be prepared for that day]; follow Me [your Lord]; that is the Straight Way" (one interpretation[46] of Surah 43: 61).

The next time you look at clouds, think of Jesus (peace upon him and may he bring peace). If you are a sinner, don't wait until Jesus comes before you start thinking about submitting your whole self to God. When the sky opens up to reveal the spiritual dimension, and armies of angels descend in canopies of clouds, you'll know that you're too late! You're fuel for the fire, hotdog!

"You must change your lifestyle and your activities, and you must obey the Lord your God. If you do, He will not bring upon you the destruction He has promised" (Jeremiah 26: 13).

> God, grant me clear vision through the eyes of my childhood.
> God, grant me counsel from the mouth of my future, wiser self.
> Help me to hear with the ears of a schoolchild begging to learn.
> Spark the child within me to wonder at glorious day,
> And bless me with a child's peaceful sleep at night.
> Instill in me a child's marvel at the entertaining clouds,
> But prepare my soul for that brightest day
> When canopies of clouds bring Your great event.

64. WHEN HELL FREEZES OVER

> Truly, Hell is an ambush. For the transgressors [it is] a destiny.
> They will dwell therein for ages. They won't taste anything cool.
> There will be no drink except scalding water,
> and paralyzing cold [like freezer burn].
> [That is] a fitting recompense because they never expected accountability.
> They treated Our signs as false.
> *(Surah 78: 21-26)*

Brain freeze! That's the term used to describe the sharp pain that shoots up the side of your head if you have a sensitive tooth when you bite into ice cream. Rain, my baby chicken, got a total brain freeze when she made a dive for my iced tea. She lost her balance and tumbled head first into my glass. Only the ice cubes stopped her from sinking all the way to the bottom while her tiny legs kicked in mid-air. I immediately scooped her out, wrapped her in my shirttail, and got out the hair dryer. Relaxing in my hand, with her miniature wings spread and her head held back, Rain happily warbled as if the relief of the warm air from the hair dryer was worth the brain freeze.

Rain recovered from her dip in the drink. She enjoyed snuggling with her people, and we loved her. Her favorite thing was a pair of warm hands, and Tom's were the warmest. Sitting on the table, Rain would press against Tom's hand, and, when he moved it, she would walk sideways to follow it as if she were stuck with glue.

Rain was frail and probably would not even have hatched if I had not helped her break out of the egg. I tried to take good care of her; I needed the comfort of her affection to heal my broken heart after losing Dottie. Allah knows best, however. Still a peep-peep, she died in her sleep. I have the hope, however, that she is warm and happy in the eternal Garden. She had company on her journey to Heaven; our beloved cat Oris died the very same night. Life is an imperfect balance of joy and pain.

So, how about you? Do you hope for an eternity that is garden fresh, or are you headed for freezer burn? Even when the unbelievers think they are about to get relief from the eternal fire, they just find themselves in the deep freeze —without a hair dryer! In the Qur'an, Hell is described as having two extremes —boiling terror and nasty cold. Avoid the day when Hell freezes over.

> O God, You are immortal.
> Your existence will never cease. Your life is eternal.
> You will never succumb to that cold sleep
> From which a person never wakes.
> Your children will never gather round Your deathbed.
> O God, You are the immortal Father of all people.
> Your health never fails.
> Your benign shadow is cast over all our actions.
> You are powerful; we are powerless.
> You are strong; we are weak.
> Hear us when we call upon You.
> Accept the sacrifices of service we offer.
> We belong to You.
> We depend on Your protection.
> *(A prayer of the Wapokomo tribe of Africa)*

65. THE BETTER HALF

> Men are protectors of women
> because Allah has blessed some more than others,
> and men invest of their earnings [in caring for their families].
> Virtuous women, therefore, are devoutly obedient [to Allah]
> in discreetly guarding what Allah has entrusted to them.
> *[Surah 4: 34 (first part)]*

"A girl! I got beat up by a girl!"

My opponent sat on the floor and whined while I adjusted my boxing gloves and waited for another round. I don't know why he was so upset. If he had read the Qur'an, he would have known that women are more apt than men. Oh, did you think the Qur'an meant that God has blessed *men* more than women? Well, you can read it that way too. Some translators render the verse to imply that men are stronger or better than women. I prefer the translations that indicate that some men have qualities better than some women, and that some women have qualities better than some men. That makes a lot more sense to me.

The translations say, "discreetly guarding" or "secretly guarding" or "guarding in their husbands' absences" or a variety of other interpretations. I think the words mean for wives to quietly preserve the sanctity of their homes, without making a big fuss. When hubby is away, the virtuous wife doesn't run around celebrating while the tomcat is out of the house. At an investment seminar, the speaker was describing the wild lifestyle she was going to have when her husband knocked over dead and left her a generous sum from his life insurance policy. I don't think she qualifies as a virtuous wife. Wives should also not gossip and complain about their husbands (and vice versa).

The verse isn't just about wives, however. Daughters are also responsible for maintaining the dignity of the family name. Husbands and sons are just as responsible, but that's another story. It's coming up!

Women are capable of taking care of themselves, but there are times when women are more vulnerable. These times are due to the discomfort and inconvenience of the monthly cycle; pregnancy, childbirth, and being responsible for small children. Today, such difficulties are alleviated by modern pain medicines and feminine hygiene products; options for planned pregnancies; safer pregnancies due to better prenatal care and sophisticated birthing centers; easier childbirth with Lamaze classes and hypno-birthing;[47] and responsible childcare centers. In our modern society, a man's job is a lot easier than when the Qur'an was revealed. That means men can put more energy into buying chocolate and flowers!

A poet wrote that every man is a half in search of his better half. Muhammed (peace and blessings upon him) said, "When a man marries, he perfects half his faith; the fear of Allah perfects the other half."[48] We could also consider the hadeeth as vice versa. Marriage is a great commitment and responsibility; it has a way of keeping people straight.

Frank Sinatra sang, "I can't be right for somebody else if I'm not right for me." He should have added, "...but I can't be right for myself if I'm not right with God." Until a person is committed to God (blessed!), he or she is unable to properly commit to a spouse. The fear —which is the awareness of and reverence for God and His laws— keep the commitment viable and strong.

Devoted girls and women are valuable to the welfare and happiness of their fathers and husbands. Honorable men are, not only *required* to provide for them, but they also *choose* to do so. Men and women have various skills and talents. A husband may be better at some things; a wife may be better at others; together they complement one another. My husband is better at mechanics than I am, so I depend on him to help me keep my Corvair running smoothly, and he depends on me to make the persimmon pudding (as only an old hillbilly can). Tom is also better at electronics and electrical wiring, but I won't even let him help me do wallpapering or floor-tiling. Each marriage is unique, and a husband and wife should decide for themselves, without interference, what type of marriage they should have. The important thing is that the marriage be pleasing to God (blessed and exalted is He).

Tom was ashamed to take me anywhere after one of my boxing matches because I had so many bruises that people thought he was a wife-beater. When someone asked Tom how he felt about my kickboxing, however, he said, "I'm just glad she can take up for me."

> God of Love, thank You for the gift of love and romance.
> Thank You for creating someone special for me to love.
> May I never fail to feel awe and gratitude for the love of my life.

Help me and my spouse to always find in each other's eyes
Encouragement to face the difficult challenges of life.
Keep our love alive so we may always find in our embrace
A healing balm for the traumas that life sometimes brings.
Bless our marriage so that our love will always be
A witness of Your eternal love and amazing grace.

66. BEAT THE PROBLEM

Concerning females of whom you suspect improper conduct,
advise them, send them [each alone] to their rooms,
and then leave them [as a last resort].
If they return to obedience [to Allah's commands],
do not seek retaliation against them.

Allah is the Highest, the Greatest.
[Surah 4: 34 (second part)]

Tom's friend Goober Stungpoket had a wife who refused to control her outrageous spending habits. Time and time again, he counseled and admonished her. Sassy refused to go with him to a marriage counselor even after he slept on the couch for a week to give her some alone-time to think about her actions. He had no alternative but to *beat her* by cutting up her credit cards. When she had diminished the checking account, he closed it and opened a new one in his name only. When credit card applications came in the mail, and her credit was already ruined, Sassy forged Goober's name on the applications and got new cards. When Goober got the bills, he destroyed the cards, rerouted the mail to arrive at his parents' home, and sold Sassy's car to pay for her purchases. Next, Sassy took money from Goober's wallet while he slept, and she went on a wild shopping spree. Goober donated all her new, expensive clothing and jewelry to the Goodwill store. Nothing worked, and finally the marriage ended in divorce. Goober had to work two jobs to pay the debts Sassy had incurred.

Most translators, instead of "leave them" in the above verse, write "beat them" and explain that beating such a wife means "to beat her lightly" and should be done "only as a last resort." If I were to be beaten, even lightly, it would be a *very last* resort –if you get my drift. The Arabic *udribu-hunna* can also be defined as 'ignore them' or 'disregard them,' 'scourge them,' 'separate from them,' 'shun them,' and 'turn them away'. One interpreter says to "flick her with a tea towel," and I think that's silly! To me, 'leave them' makes the most sense.

Today we have marriage counselors and anger management classes and other self-help programs, unlike when the Qur'an was revealed. At that time, however, husband could not assault and batter his wife on impulse; he had to get permission from the Prophet (peace and blessings upon him). According to a report, "Whenever the Prophet permitted a man to administer corporal punishment to his wife, the Prophet did so with reluctance, and continued to express his distaste for it. And even in cases where it was necessary, the Prophet directed men neither to hit across the face, nor to beat severely, nor to use anything that might leave marks on the body."[49]

Physical punishment, was to humiliate, not to harm. The Qur'an shows this in the example of Prophet Job (peace upon him). When Job's wife advised him, "Curse God and die" (Job 2: 9), Job promised God that he would beat his wife as soon as he was back on his feet. God did not want Job to beat his wife, but He also did not want Job to break a promise to Him, so God advised Job, "Take a bundle of grass in your hand and beat with that so you won't break your promise…" (Surah 38: 44).

And what of husbands who behave poorly? As Islam is a religion of equality, I suggest that Surah 4: 34 works both ways! Watch out for that tea towel, fellers! In his article "Wife-Beating in Qur'an –the Modern Context," Dr. Javed Jamil explains:

> Though this verse is primarily addressed to men, its indirect application should also be there for situations where husbands are arrogant or disloyal to wives and are engaged in forbidden activities. There are various situations in the Qur'an where the instructions are either for men or women, but they need to be applied in reverse cases too.

The Qur'an also says:

If a wife fears cruelty or desertion from her husband, the couple will not be blamed [for their marital problems] if they come to an amicable settlement. Such an agreement is best [for resolving a bad marriage]. Even though people are deeply influenced by greed, you should do the right thing and use self-discipline. Allah takes notice of what you do (Surah 4: 128).

An "amicable settlement" may be, for examples, a decision to seek marriage counseling, to enroll in an anger management class or hypnotherapy sessions to control temper, or to separate until a resolution can be found for a specific situation. If a divorce settlement is inevitable, each spouse should take great care in coming to a fair and honorable agreement.

Finally, the Qur'an reminds that God (blessed and exalted is He) is the Highest and the Greatest, and one should not seek retaliation against a repentant spouse. When God forgives, you do not have the right to hold a grudge.

Only with God's guidance and prayerful submission to God's will can we discover the magnitude of God's wisdom for America and the world.

> Whenever my relationship hits a snag,
> Guide me and help me figure out what to do.
> Grant me strength for rocky days ahead.
> Help me mend the problems and keep my family together.
> Whenever life is difficult, and rocky cliffs I tread,
> May I feel Your grace holding safe my feet.
> However dark the sky and thorny the path,
> Enable me to keep my faith and to prevail.

67. WHEN BEING CALLED "DIRT" IS A GOOD THING

> Your wives are like your plantations.
> Approach your plantations as you wish.
> Always be mindful of [your responsibility to] the future.

> Fear and obey Allah. Be certain of your ultimate meeting with Him.
> Give good tidings to those who believe.
> *(Surah 2: 223)*

My wrestling a body-quaking, sputtering tiller to get my garden in shape would probably never have made it as a parable in the Qur'an. In my memory bank, however, is a more romantic image of Daddy walking be-hind Maude the mule as she pulled the plow. Although it was rugged work, there was a poetic gentleness to the firm hand of the farmer guiding the plow to impress deep, straight furrows into the generous soil. Daddy gathered the entire family to make life easier for Mother Earth as we picked up all newly exposed rocks, pulled any surviving weeds, and smoothed the soil with rakes. After the land was prepared, Daddy, with tattered, scuffed boots, walked carefully between the rows and offered gifts of lime and fertilizer to the rows' embracing arms. Next came the seeds. There is a world of artistry and poetry in a handful of seeds if only one can imagine and dream and hope. Daddy walked in careful, measured steps, dropping the seeds one by one in place; afterward, he used a hoe to tenderly cover each seed with a cloak of soil. Finally, remembering that all good things ultimately come from God, Daddy prayed for rain and for the emergence of tender, young plants promising food for us during the coming harsh winter.

A magazine article stated that "it is disingenuous to argue, as many contemporary Muslims do, that Islam is beneficial to women because it guarantees them social dignity and a protected legal status. On the contrary, the Koran repeatedly belittles women. …. And as for sex, the Koran tells men they can have it when they want it: "Women are your fields. Go, then, into your fields as you please (Sura 2, v. 223)."[50] Apparently, the author has never held a scoop of garden soil, smelled the aroma of its fertility, pondered the possibilities of its life-bearing future, or experienced the passion of a gardener, and he knows nothing of toiling behind an ass simply for the sake of improving the life and quality of a beloved field. The author has taken phrases out of context and perverted their meanings to conform to the limitations of his own knowledge, experience, and wisdom.

The whole of the verse instills in husbands responsibility, not only to lovingly tend to the needs of their wives, but also to consider the welfare of future generations; in so doing, the husband will not even risk producing children outside his own marriage, and he will be a responsible parent to his own children and to all children in a given community and within the global family. He will teach his son to respect girls and women and to relate to them with honor and dignity and to never attempt to exploit or abuse them. His son will safeguard the reputation of the family name when he reflects the lifestyle of his father, his role model. The devoted Muslim man will acknowledge his commitment to God (blessed and exalted is He) and to the Muslim community so as not to live a lie about God or to bring shame upon his family or the Ummah through immoral acts.

As Islam is a religion of equality, the verse should be understood also to mean that husbands are struggling cultivators, so wives should help them and support them in their endeavors. Wives should also acknowledge their responsibility to future generations and remember their ultimate meeting with God, thereby avoiding His wrath, and give good tidings to those who believe. Just as Mother Earth yields its beautiful and nourishing fruits and vegetables, wives and mothers respond to care and kindness from their husbands and children by loving and generous acts of tireless service to their families and communities.

The connecting energy that keeps the universe in order has been called "the Tao," "the Word," "the Spirit," "the Logos," and "the Circle of Life," among other things. Whatever name is found suitable, the energy can be found in a plot of cultivated dirt and a handful of seeds, and it can be found in the passion between a loving husband and wife.

> Bless Your servant, my spouse, O Lord,
> With health of body and of spirit.
> Let the hand of Your blessing be upon his/her head, night and day,
> And support him/her in all necessities.
> Strengthen him/her in all temptations, comfort him/her in all sorrows,
> And let him/her be Your servant in all changes,
> And make us both to dwell with You forever in Your favor,
> In the light of Your countenance, and in Your glory.
> *[Jeremy Taylor (1613-1667), a chaplain (Europe)]*

68. BRAINS AND ELBOWS

> .... Women have as many rights as responsibilities, in all fairness.
> Men have a measure [of responsibility] over women.
> Allah is Victorious, Perfectly Wise.
> *(Surah 2: 228, last part)*

Tom and I built our own house by ourselves, by the grace of God. I had gotten good at swinging a 16-ounce hammer when I worked in the furniture shop, and I had also learned to use many other tools and had developed some building skills.

Occasionally, someone from the neighborhood would stroll through the woods to see how our house was coming along. One day, a man came by, watched awhile, and then told Tom, "I would offer to help you build your house, but that wife of yours would put any man to shame."

Some people may say that I was an anomaly among women, but there are enough anomalies among people in general to show that if we stereotype and pigeonhole people according to gender, race, background, economic status, etc, society may lose out on some fantastic contributions.

Generally, men's and women's brains differ in such a way that they complement one another. From family to government, both feminine and masculine attributes are necessary for smooth operation. In our family, I depend on my husband for directions. I get lost so easily that, one time, I finally just parked at a gas station, had the attendant call my husband and tell him where I was, and then Tom had to come and find me and lead me back home. But I suppose the whole family would starve if I couldn't at least find my way to the garden and then plow and plant it, harvest the vegetables, cook the vegetables, and make the buttermilk biscuits.

Certainly there are skills that seem to elude men. Men's brains seem to be hay-wired in such a fashion that men don't notice things. Tom often launches a fruitless search for something he has misplaced. When he is finally so frustrated that he is almost bawling, I walk in and just pick up the object. It's usually in plain sight. I often tell him, "Tom, you couldn't find a naked woman in a burka fashion show."

Usually, he replies, "Maybe not, but I'd like to try."

There are a few things that women find difficult also. I personally cannot use an axe to chop down a tree; I could never get the swing of it. But Tom gave me a chainsaw for our wedding anniversary, so I'm good to go. Most women would find it difficult to fell trees, and that has a lot to do with the higher placement of her elbows, which means that her biceps are shorter. A man her size is usually able to build greater strength in his longer biceps, and thus he is better equipped to perform physical labor requiring upper body strength. Because of the awkward bulk of a woman's larger pelvic cradle designed for pregnancy, she cannot run as well as a man her size (generally speaking). However, because of a woman's higher hips and longer *tensor facia femoris* (the muscle alongside her hips and outside the pelvic crest), she is able to develop more flexibility and better thrusting power in her legs. When lifting is done correctly, a woman is generally able to more easily lift from the floor because of the higher hip placement, and she is able to develop more overall body flexibility, grace, and poise than most men are.

Men are assigned a measure of responsibility, including protection, over women because women are more vulnerable at specific times involving the discomfort and inconvenience of the monthly cycle, pregnancy, childbirth, and responsibility for small children, and even menopause. It is during such times that women should be able to depend most on the men in their lives for financial and moral support and for safety. Anytime those elbows get in the way, it's really nice to have a man around the house.

The Qur'an advises a mother to stay home with an infant for at least the first two years (Surah 2: 233), but a woman has the right to pursue higher education and employment before starting a family, and also after starting a family if the help of the extended family can insure the welfare of the children. Some women may choose not to venture into the workforce, but women should never become lazy and non-productive. Everyone has the responsibility to use the unique skills, talents, and opportunities that God provides, no matter where the elbows are located. Islam needs Muslim women who inspire, initiate, and command projects benefiting their homes, communities, community ummahs, the global Ummah, and society in general. To neglect one's talents is to waste divine gifts of God (blessed and exalted is He). Islam needs the brains and elbows of both men and women.

> I worship You in every religion
> That teaches Your laws and praises Your glory.

I worship You in every plant whose beauty reflects Your beauty.
I worship You in every event caused by Your goodness and kindness.
I worship You in every place where You dwell.
And I worship You in every man and woman
Who seek to follow Your way of righteousness.
[Zoroaster (6th century BCE), monotheistic reformer (Persia)]

69. DON'T MARRY A LOSER

This day humane/ethical things are made lawful for you.
The [kosher] food of those who were given the (Torah) is lawful for you,
and your [halal] food is lawful for them.
[Lawful for you men for marriage are] virtuous, believing [Muslim] women
and virtuous women from among those
given the (Scriptures) that was revealed before you.
You must give them their dowries and be honorable.
Do not commit fornication/adultery or take secret lovers.
If anyone rejects faith, his/her deeds are worthless.
In the hereafter, he/she will be one of the losers.
(Surah 5: 5)

After Goober divorced his first wife, he walked straight into another credit card marriage. His second wife was exactly like the first. He had to work three jobs to pay the credit card bills. After his second divorce, I told Goober, "Before you get married again, bring her to see me so I can look her over. I'll hook her up behind the tiller, and if she can't plow a straight row, throw her back!" Goober did not take my advice. Within just a few weeks, he was married to another loser. (Maybe he's the one who needs a beating – for being stupid!)

Jesus (peace!) taught that, because people are idiots, God made an allowance for divorce. Jesus said, however, that divorce was not part of God's original plan at the time of creation (Matthew 19: 8).[51] God (blessed!) says, "I hate divorce! It's a cruel thing to break the promises of marriage" (Malachi

2: 16). Muhammed (peace!) said, "Of all the things Allah allows, divorce is the most hateful."[52]

In my childhood church, the preacher used to say, "Let a believer marry a believer, and let two ol' devils get together and fight it out." Although the above verse is directed to men, it is equally true for the women. Gals, those cute dimples can be deceiving! In Islam, women are advised to marry within the Muslim Ummah in order to spare women from unnecessary grief –like having to put up with non-Muslim in-laws ridiculing her Prophet and her religion. If God (blessed and exalted is He) brings two believers of different faiths into a loving relationship, however, we should be happy for them and pray for God's blessings on them. Don't say stupid stuff that just hurts their feelings! The Qur'an does not expressly forbid a Muslim woman from marrying a believer from another faith.

Although Goober claimed to be religious, I don't think he tried to find a sincere, believing woman. He wanted someone gorgeous who looked hot in high fashion clothes. He looked for all the wrong things. The Qur'an says that it's better to marry an enslaved believer than to marry a free unbeliever (Surah 2: 221). We might apply this to our society as meaning that it's better to marry a believing woman without means of independence than to marry an unbelieving woman with a good-paying job and her own car; or, that it's better to marry a believing, old-fashioned, country gal than to marry an unbelieving, high-society chick. Goober always married beautiful women, but they were losers. Like a popular song says, "The beauty is there, but the beast is in her heart."

It's not easy in our society to find a moral, responsible person to marry. The Qur'an encourages marriage, but it never says to marry the first bimbo that struts your way, or the first creep willing to buy you a hamburger and fries. Take your time, and try to get it right the first time.

> Steer the ship of my life, Good Lord, to Your quiet harbor,
> Where I can be safe from the storms of sin and conflict.
> Show me the course I should take.
> Renew in me the gift of discernment,
> So that I can always see the right direction in which I should go.
> Grant me the strength and the courage to choose the right course,
> Even when the sea is rough and the waves are high.
> I know that, through enduring hardship and danger in Your name,

I shall find comfort and peace.
[Basil of Caesarea (329-379), a monastic hermit and bishop]

70. WHEN A DIAMOND IS NOT FOREVER

Marry those among you who are single
or the virtuous ones among your male or female slaves.
If they are in poverty,
Allah will give them means from His grace.
Allah is All-embracing, the All-knowing.
(Surah 24: 32)

Boy, did I lose my temper! Tana and I were at the mall with a boy whom she had met only a few weeks earlier. Like other teenage boys that she attracted, he was a slimy, sleazy, debasing, degrading, idiotic, ignorant, putrid, pimple-popping, testosterone-oozing, hormone-crazed, brain-dead jerk. Of all the nerve! He asked me to cosign with him to make payments on an engagement ring for Tana. I said, "Well, that would be ridiculous since she's not engaged. And I know she's not engaged because *I* say she's not engaged!"

Neither Tana nor the boy had yet finished school, neither had jobs, neither had money, and neither one of them had any sense.

"Marriage takes a lot more investment than buying a ring," I snapped. "If you want to be married, first finish school, get a job, and save money."

He showed Tana the ring he had selected. It was the cheapest one in the store! Tana looked at the ring and asked, "Where's the diamond?" The sales clerk provided a magnifying glass, and Tana studied the ring. "Hmmph," she said. "I thought diamonds were supposed to blind you by their dazzling sparkle, not because you have to look so hard to see them."

Tana told the boy, "I'd rather have a BIG cubic zirconium than a speck of diamond dust I can't even see. And I'm not even ready to get married. I just turned seventeen. I still want to be a kid for a while. But if you want to buy me a ring, buy one that you can afford; there are some bubblegum machines around the corner."

Marriage is an important part of Islam, so planning for marriage should be incorporated into the life of each single person. Boys and girls interested in marriage should plan for marriage years before finding their dreamboats. Whether or not you already have a sweetheart, you should have goals in your life to attain before marriage. Get achievements like a basic education, job placement, and a savings account. Once the commitment to marriage is made, have faith in God's promise to provide financial opportunities. God, however, is not Super Sugar Daddy. You have to take initiative yourself.

If a young man has a proposal, he should present himself to the young lady and her parents in a dignified and respectable manner. He should be able to explain how he intends to provide a home, however humble it may be. Even if he does not have a good income, if his intentions are honorable and he has goals for improving his life and making a living, and if he has good character and spiritual and moral values, then he's a keeper. If not, girlfriend, you can get a ring out of the bubblegum machine yourself.

> Have mercy, O Lord, on those enduring loneliness.
> Bless each lonely heart with someone with whom to share love.
> May each benevolent seeker of love be rewarded
> with a family that returns love and shares life in beautiful ways.
> May each one who is blessed with a good spouse and family
> be filled with enduring gratitude for the Heaven-sent gift
> of a family that never runs dry of unconditional love.
> Bless the home where Your name is the banner of hope.
> Have mercy on each one shattered by a stormy relationship.
> Hear the anguish of the fervent prayer spoken in desperation.
> Grant to each petitioner the humility to apologize,
> The grace to forgive, and the wisdom to know when to walk away.

71. THE SHOUT HEARD AROUND THE WORLD

> Among His signs is that He created you from dust,
> And then, behold, you were human beings dispersed.

> Among His signs is that He created for you mates
> from yourselves so that you may dwell in tranquility with them,
> and He has put love and mercy among you.
> Truly, in this are signs for people who ponder.
> *(Surah 30: 20-21)*

There's an old 50's song that tells men, "If you wanna be happy for the rest of your life, never make a pretty woman your wife; from my personal point of view, pick an ugly girl to marry you." One of the singers says to another, "I seen your wife; boy, she's ugly!" The husband answers, "Yeah, she's ugly, but she sure can cook."

When he was thirty years old, I told Dusty, "You have to get married before I can die. Surely you can find some ol' gal who can stand you. I don't care if she's bow-legged and snaggle-toothed; marry an ugly girl and be happy about it."

He got it backwards though. He found a beautiful girl, but she couldn't cook. I asked him, "Do you have to go back after seven years of burnt toast and marry the ugly one?" He whined, "They didn't have an ugly one, Mama." What a shame!

Dusty met Aishah in the Philippines on May 3 and married her on May 10. Yes, in the same year. He had to marry her before she came to her senses. It wasn't the shotgun heard round the world, but I sure was shooting my mouth off about it. What a relief! I was so glad that somebody was crazy enough to marry that whopper of a boy I hatched!

I wrote about the wedding in an e-mail that I sent all over the world. One foreign correspondent replied, "Sister Linda, what wrong with you? You son fine hulk of man –not whopper of man hatched. Congradlations on new daughter. She spit image of beauty."

Tom and I knew each other eight weeks before we married. Now we have been married so long that people can't tell us apart, and our kids are older than we are. I figure I've attained a high enough level of insanity to be able to give advice on having a long and happy marriage.

The first secret to a successful marriage is to be right with God (blessed and exalted is He). You can't be right for somebody else until your life is right in terms of God's will and purpose for you.

Once you find that special someone, make sure that you share the same values and morals. Discuss various issues, and, though you don't have to agree on everything, your views should be based on the same spiritual rationalization.

Childhood memories hold secrets to the individuals that people have become. Sweethearts can learn about one another by sharing fond memories and haunting regrets. If his favorite memories are of his mama's cooking, then maybe he needs to stay home with Mama a while longer. The bride-to-be may have some hidden phobias if one of her memories is that of her three, older brothers tying her hands and feet together behind her back; taping her mouth shut; wrapping her, head and all, in a thick quilt in hot weather; shoving her under the bed all the way to the wall; and then leaving her in the house alone while they go out for ice cream. (What mean brothers I had! I was glad when they got wives to civilize them.)

One of the few pieces of advice Mama gave me was to spend enough time with a fellow to get to know his bad habits, and then ask yourself if you can live with those habits all your life. Do his false teeth clatter when he eats? (Mama always hated that.) Does he pick his ears with his car keys? (She didn't mind that so much.)

Does she sniff and blow her nose all the time? I asked Tom if he would still love me if I had a nose like a pear. I thought of getting a nose transplant and opt for a nose big enough that I could actually breathe through it. Tom said he would love me no matter how big the nose I pick.

Is smoking a habit of either spouse-to-be? I think that a non-smoker should not marry a smoker. The non-smoker may regret it later in life when he or she is sick from breathing secondary smoke, and the smoker is too breathless to carry the sick spouse to the doctor.

Discuss with your spouse-to-be exactly what both of you expect from the marriage. What kind of marriage do you each want? What do you expect from one another? Consider all the what-ifs.

Before Dusty and Aishah became married, Dusty called home for advice on what questions to discuss before the handsome couple finalized the marriage contract. Housework was one of the things I told them to discuss. Who will do what? If the husband won't do his share of chores, the wife will eventually become resentful at being married to a house instead of a man. I also wondered about money management. Dusty had a genius IQ, but, when it came to money, he didn't have a lick of sense. Aishah was better with money, so it was decided that she manage expenses. She allowed Dusty a weekly allowance, and he was fine with that.

In an ocean of time and space,
You discover one endearing face,
With a smile so pure, so innocent,
You know it must be Heaven-sent.

Aishah's money management skills and Dusty's big mouth, working together, became more and more important as they both volunteered much of their time to da'wah and zakat work.

Aishah did learn to cook, and she cooks quite well. Still, Dusty does his share of the cooking, and they share other responsibilities too.

Also, realize that you are not just marrying one person; you are marrying his or her entire family. Make sure that you can stand the family members or at least can move far away from them. Tom quipped that he could never tell any horrible mother-in-law jokes because none of them were true. My parents were Tom's parents too.

Enter marriage with the pure intention of pleasing God (blessed!). Marriage itself should be an act of worship, and each marriage partner should remember that his or her spouse is also a brother or sister in God's spiritual family. Remember that the kindness and respect that you owe to believers in the global family are also owed to believers within the marital family.

We invoke Your gentlest blessings, our Father, on all true lovers.
We praise You for the great longing that draws
The soul of man and woman together
And bids them leave all the dear bonds of the past
To cleave to one another.
We thank you for the revealing power of love,
Which divines, in one beloved,
The mystic beauty and glory of Humanity.
We thank You for the transforming power of love,
Which ripens and ennobles our nature,
Calling forth the hidden stores of tenderness and strength
And overcoming the selfishness of youth by the passion of self-surrender.
Grant them with sober eyes to look beyond
These sweet days of friendship to the generations yet to come
And realize that the home for which they long
Will be part of the sacred tissue of the body of Humanity
In which You are to dwell, that so they may reverence themselves
And drink the cup of joy with awe.
[Walter Rauschenbusch (1861-1918), Baptist minister (USA)]

72. MEET THE DEVIL AND REJOICE

> Do people think that, simply because they say, "We believe,"
> they will not be tested? We tested others before them,
> and Allah recognizes those who are true,
> and He recognizes those who are false.
> *(Surah 29: 2-3)*

The difference between an old sot and an alcoholic is that an alcoholic goes to Alcoholics Anonymous meetings, and an old sot just don't care how drunk he gets. Daddy's friend Sudds Spitzwoter was a worthless, old sot. One night he figured on going frog gigging. He sharpened a stick and got himself a canning jar full of moonshine (corn liquor from a backyard still). Sudds carried his stick, a bucket, and his jar of moonshine through the woods and to a creek slithering with nightlife. He stayed in the woods for hours, drinking and stinking, and stabbing bullfrogs. He took out his pocketknife, cut off the frogs' hind legs, and threw the maimed, little bodies back into the creek. Once he had a bucketful of frog legs, Sudds headed back to his house.

Sudds set the bucket of frog legs in the refrigerator, threw his soggy boots into the box of firewood, and then flopped into bed with his stinking clothes on.

Deep into the night, Sudds woke up to distant sounds of bullfrogs. The sounds got closer and closer, and as they did, the croaking sounds began to gradually form words. "Crrrr-ribit." "Crrrr-I regit." "Crrr-I wa'legit." "Crr-I wan my legits."

Sudds sat up. He saw shadows moving in the moonlight that flooded the room. More and more writhing shadows formed. Sudds was too scared to move as the room filled up with legless frogs croaking, "Crr-I want my legs! I want my legs!" They were squirming all over the room and onto his bed and oozing out of the dresser drawers.

Suddenly a hideous, screeching laughter pervaded the room. As Sudds watched, shadows materialized into a demonic specter, which sat on the foot of the bed. The devil's teeth gleamed yellow in the flooding moonlight. His forked tail swept back and forth through the air. Sudds yelped, and then he realized that the devil had hold of Sudds's legs. Sudds screamed and tried to yank his legs from the devil's grasp. The devil thrust his head back and rolled laughter like a repeating revolver. As the devil held tightly to Sudds's legs, the croak-speaking frogs covered Sudds with their twisting, dragging bodies.

"I ain't gonna drink no more! I ain't gonna drink no more!" Sudds squealed. "I ain't gonna drink no more!"

The devil's insidious laughter bounced off the walls as Sudds struggled to free himself from the nightmare that gripped him by the soul. Finally, Sudds realized that he was kicking his legs freely into the air, and that his own shrieks were the only sound. He sat up, slapped imaginary frogs from his face, and looked around the room slowly brightening from the rising sun. Sudds grabbed his car keys, ran out the door, and drove straight for my parents' house.

"Bill, I ain't gonna drink no more!" Sudds began, and then he told Daddy the whole story.

How long do you think Sudds's commitment lasted? I'm not sure, but the last time I saw Sudds, he was as loaded as a skunk full of stink. The reason the devil was laughing with such ludicrous delight was because his job was done. He had Sudds right where he wanted him. The devil didn't have to bother coming up with temptations and whispered suggestions.

Dusty has a favorite saying: "If you haven't met the devil lately, you're going the wrong way." In other words, the devil does not need to confront those who are already going in his direction. He is free to mock and ridicule them. When people are trying to live righteously, however, the devil has to be more creative.

God (blessed and exalted is He) does not instigate evil, but He allows evil to confront us. Such tests give us opportunities to glorify God and to grow in strength and also to prove our faith as a witness to others. Confrontation and struggle has been an important factor in every major event. Jesus (peace upon him) faced opposition from the time he was born, but God used this opposition as part of His plan, and God's plans are always best. Muhammed (peace upon him) faced obstacles throughout his mission, but it was through adversity that the Islamic Movement progressed and eventually evolved into its Golden Age. Instead of making slow, lackadaisical progress, the Prophet's followers trail-blazed a dynamic legacy after being trained on the obstacle course of persecution and oppression. The superficial followers who didn't make the team were replaced by those who could carry the burden and push the cause of Islam forward.

Instead of complaining about the evils of the "wicked West," the bias of the secular media, the constant slander by certain religious groups, and the prejudices, stereotyping, and discrimination Muslims daily encounter, we should rejoice that we are being subjected to the same testing and adversity as Jesus, Muhammed, and the other prophets of old (peace and blessings upon them all). In the mysterious parallels of the time-space continuum, we are actually experiencing our religious struggle along with the prophets, and that should be considered a great honor. The important thing is how we respond to the struggle. We should make every effort to turn adversities into opportunities for growth and for da'wah. Just as the original Islamic movement succeeded in overcoming all obstacles to become the dominant force in Arabia, each of us can contribute to the American Islamic movement until success is realized and we can continue toward establishing the Global Renaissance, a new Golden Age affecting the entire planet.

"Do your little bit of good where you are; it's these little bits of good put together that overwhelm the world" (Desmond Tutu).

> O Allah, bless us with the wisdom
> To find opportunities in our adversities
> So that through our patience and endurance
> Others may see the Light of Your magnificent ways.

73. LET GO AND LET GOD

> Here [in the Qur'an] is a simple statement to humanity,
> and a guidance and instruction to those who fear Allah.
> So do not despair or become depressed.
> You will come out on top if your faith is genuine.
> *(Surah 3: 138-139)*

This life is no picnic, and sometimes it serves up one problem after another. Some people freak out when they get just a taste of trouble while others patiently choke down whole meals. The tasty tidbits I get make alien abductions to outer space banquets seem normal. An entry from my diary, if I had time to write a diary, might go something like this:

> The chickens woke me up at three o'clock in the morning, screaming, "Bloody murder! Squaaaaawk! Bloody murder!" I grabbed the shotgun from under the bed and released the safety as I darted for the back door. I forgot all about that stupid, half-deflated, blow-up pool, and stumbled right into it, dousing my nightgown with algae and water bugs. The shotgun flew out of my hands and across the yard. It went off and shot the flowers right off the azalea that Tom had planted for my birthday. I pulled myself out of the water and groped in the dark for the shotgun. I found it and finished the lap to the chicken coop. The alien varmint had already been frightened back into the woods, but all of Freddy's beautiful, tail feathers were everywhere except on him, and all the chickens were pitching a hissy-fit. I hugged each one, sang them a chicken song, and set them back on their perches.
>
> I rinsed the tadpoles out of my hair, changed my gown, and slithered back into bed for a bit more sleep before getting up to make buttermilk biscuits. As I was taking the bread out of the oven, the rest of the family clomped into the kitchen and complained about a restless night.
>
> Tom looked out the window and said, "Well, Linda, something tore all the flowers off your bush."
>
> Tana popped over to the window and said, "Whatever it was stomped down my pool."
>
> Dusty just staggered around saying, "Huh? Huh?"
>
> "It must have been an alien from outer space," I said as I tried to finish breakfast, with everybody ganged-up in my way.
>
> Dusty said, "Huh?"
>
> Dusty left for his job, Tom packed for his next road trip, and Tana ran off to a friend's house —without permission. I said my late-as-usual morning prayer, and then tended the chickens, rabbits, goats, cats, ducks, rats, and the pig-dog (the ugly dog that makes a rather pretty pig). Then I had to replant my peppers that the crazy raccoons dug up. Why do they do that?

I went back into the house and started loading the dishwasher as Tom carried his bags to his vehicle. Within minutes, a blur zipped past the window. I looked outside and saw Tom running across the yard with a chicken stuck in his back. Nugget hates Tom's sandals. Nugget gets his kicks out of untying shoestrings; he chases and flogs anybody wearing shoes without strings. I hollered out the back door, "All you have to do is pick him up and give him a hug. He can't spur you if you're hugging him."

Tom didn't hug the rooster, so I had to go dig Nugget out of Tom's flesh. "I told you all you have to do is hug him."

Tom said, "How can I hug something stuck in my back?"

I protected Tom until he could leave for work.

I checked my e-mail, and my nutty editor, aka "Last-Minute Man," sent me some work. "There's no hurry," he wrote. "I just need it within the hour." Good grief! I received another e-mail from a fan: "Stop writing! You don't know what you're talking about. You're an idiot!" The other eighty-seven e-letters were junk mail. I got the last-minute writing done, and then settled down at my drawing table.

The phone rang. "Mama," whined a voice, "I'm at the hospital."

"Dusty? Did you have a wreck?"

"Remember my customer who got mad yesterday because I couldn't fix her phone? She came back today with a baseball bat and tried to bash my brains out."

Getting my hopes up, I asked, "She found brains?"

I hung up the phone and went back to my art. "PeeWee!" My cat PeeWee had stepped in my watercolors and walked across my illustration. I managed to dab out her tracks before having to rush to my doctor's appointment.

"Doc, you gotta find something for these killer headaches that hurt for days."

"You should have a brain scan," the doctor told me. "You may have a sinus tumor."

"Whoa, Doc! Isn't that what Scully had on the 'X-Files' TV show? The only way she got cured was to get abducted by aliens, and that hasn't happened to me in a long time. Besides, in fixing her disease, the aliens got her pregnant. Holy catfish, Doc! I got one in the oven now, and it's due; I gotta get home."

I got back to the house, and the cats had surrounded the incubator, which had a little window in the top. With eyes like flying saucers, the cats peered through the little window as an egg wiggled. Soon a beak was sticking out of the shell. The beak looked thirsty, so I used a dropper and gave it some of my iced tea. After several hours of struggling, the little chicken pecked its way to daylight. I dried it, sang to it, and tried to keep the cats from using it for a squeak-toy.

I tried to catch up on prayers, but I only got two rak'ats (verses of prayer) done when I noticed a ruckus outside. Fortunately, I had two rak'ats in the shotgun. I grabbed the gun and dashed out. The rabbits Pepper and Hugs Hunny were darting frantically as a fiendish, alien hawk was trying to nab one of them. I aimed the shotgun and fired at the hawk. The Amens bounced off the hawk like slimy, pool water off a greasy duck, but at least the hawk got the message and left.

The phone was ringing when I got back into the house; it was Tom. "We'll have to cancel our camping trip. I'm already behind schedule." He explained that, in delivering new trucks, he had made the first delivery that evening, and then had to take a shuttle bus to an airport, traveling to get another truck. On the way to the airport, the bus driver had hit a deer and refused to stop to see if it was okay. Tom got to the airport, rented a car, and returned to the dazed deer, still lying in the road. Tom bandaged the deer's leg before it finally came to its senses. Suddenly, the deer jumped up, head-butted Tom, and chased him back into the car. The deer darted into the safety of the woods, and Tom got back to the airport just in time to see his plane taking off without him.

I figure the only way I'm going to get a vacation is for aliens to kidnap me and take me to another planet.

After collecting vegetables from the garden, feeding all the animals and putting them up for the night, and chasing the raccoons out of the house, I slithered into the tub. Just as I began to commune with Mr. Bubble, the doorbell rang. Maybe it was my imagination, I hoped. The bell sounded again. Finally, I crawled out of the bubble bath, put my stinky clothes back on, and wobbled to the door. A UPS package glared at me from under the porch light. "Oh, no!" I shouted. "I missed the UPS man –the only person in the universe that visits me regularly. Now I'll have to order something else."

I collapsed into bed. Around midnight, someone yelled at me from beneath my bedroom window. "Linda! You gotta hide me out! Somebody's trying to kill me!"

I jumped up and peered out the window into the darkness.

"It's Slim Witt," said the voice; "You gotta hide me out!"

"What's going on, Slim?"

"Some boys are chasing me; they're gonna kill me. You gotta hide me out."

"Oh, good grief," I whined to myself. I threw some clothes over my nightgown, went downstairs, and opened the door. Slim was shaking and crying and muttering nonsense. I took him upstairs where he curled into a fetal position and started bawling. All the racket brought Dusty out of his hole in the basement. He got into his car and went up to the road to investigate about what Slim was ranting.

Dusty came back for Slim because the police were looking for him. Details of the incident gradually came together. Tana had decided to spend the night with a girlfriend –without permission. Slim had decided that he should have a wife, so he went after Tana, alien caveman style. He knocked her down, grabbed her by the hair, and started dragging her to his car, with her kicking and screaming. When two other boys ran to help Tana, Slim threw her down, and got back in his car. He backed down the road, poised, and then accelerated forward, and finally ran off the road to run over the boys. The impact threw one boy up into the air; he came back down on the hood of Slim's car, rolled off, and then lay injured in the grass. The other boy got into his pickup truck, chased Slim down the road, and then crammed into the back of Slim's car until the car was smashed like an accordion. That's when Slim got out of his car and ran through the woods to my house.

Tana was in an ambulance, and the injured boy –with broken legs and serious, internal injuries— had to be airlifted to a major hospital. There were eight police cars, seven fire vehicles, four ambulances, a helicopter, and half the neighborhood at the scene.

Dusty had just left our house with Slim when two firefighters, helping the police look for Slim, came to the house. Our neighbor Adem Baumb, who is crazier than a rabid raccoon, came running out of the woods, waving his hands and yelling, frantic with excitement. One of the firefighters said, "Well, that boy's crazy; that must be Slim." The other fighter said, "Yeah, let's nab him," and they rushed after Adem.

"No, that ain't Slim," I yelled. "That's Adem Baumb; he's always crazy!"

I finally got Adem calmed down enough to send him home, and I managed to get a couple hours sleep before Tana called for me to bring her home from the hospital. She had a broken foot and painful, back injuries. And I'm out of chocolate.

Well, that's a sample of my normal day-to-day routine. Some people ask me how I keep from going insane; others ask me if I am getting help for my insanity. My professional help comes from the Qur'an, which tells me to give my "whole self" to God (blessed and exalted is He) and that everything truly belongs to God. If God wants to wake *His* body up in the middle of the night and throw it into a nasty, half deflated, kiddy pool, and then shoot the flowers off *His* azalea, that's His right. If He wants to let *His* wild, mutant, alien creatures harass *His* rabbits and chickens, that's His business. If He wants to let *His* kitty make 'puddy-tat' tracks across *His* illustration, then He will help *His* artist figure out how to fix it.

The point is, everything we are and everything we have truly belong to God (blessed!), so when everything is SNAFU (Situation Normal: All Fouled Up), we need to remember that everything is in God's care. Let Him do the worrying. Let go of your worries, and Let God take control of your burdens.

Aliens, go home!

> Our Lord, do not condemn us if we forget or fall into error.
> Our Lord, do not put upon us a burden
> like that which You put upon those before us.
> Our Lord, do not put upon us a burden greater
> than we have strength to bear.

Erase our sins and grant us forgiveness. Have mercy on us.
You are our Protector. Help us against those who challenge our faith.
(from Surah 2: 286).

74. SIGN OF TSUNAMI

Then Satan made them fall from (Paradise).
Satan caused them to be cast from that [perfect realm] in which they were.
We said, "All [humanity], get out and live
with bad feelings among yourselves.
On Earth will be your dwelling place
and your means of survival for a reckoned period of time."
Adam received words [of guidance] from his Lord,
and (his Lord) forgave him.
He is the Responder and the Most Merciful.
We said, "All of you [all humanity],
descend from here [the original Paradise].
You will receive guidance from Me. If you follow My guidance,
You will have no fear or grief [in the hereafter].
Do you think that you should enter Paradise without difficulties
like what came to those who passed this way before you?
They faced suffering and adversity
They were so shaken that even the messenger
and those who joined him in faith cried,
"When will Allah's help come?"
Truly, the help of Allah is near!
(Surah 2: 36-38, 214)

Candy wrapper and bottle top games are terrific; I always win a chance to "Please try again." If I ever do get a winning number, I hope I can double my reward the way Mama did when she won a sewing machine. Her name was pulled from a drawing she had entered at a store. When she returned to the store to claim her prize, she found that the sewing machine was just the mechanism without a stand or cabinet. The store salesman then tried to sell her an expensive sewing cabinet. Mama took only what she had won, left the store, went home, and built a cabinet herself.

Whether or not, at the end of a day, a believer has won the game of spiritual jihad, each new day brings another chance to "Please try again." When a person finally gets it right, the success itself is a gift. You can double your reward by acknowledging that all successes are by the grace of God (blessed and exalted is He) and that He is able and willing to increase your successes. You don't have to buy into any other plan; the divine plan is all you need.

Humanity's second chance began when Adam and Eve got kicked out of the Garden. Known as 'Eden' in Judeo-Christian tradition, the Garden, I think, was (and is) an alternate reality existing in a different dimension. It is the "new creation" (Surah 21: 104), which is a perfected Earth established without struggle and with an entirely different kind of governing sciences. The "new creation" is the Earth which the humble shall inherit. At least, that's the way I figure it.

Because of the order to get out or descend some think that the Garden, or Paradise, is up in the sky, but the phrase could mean 'descend from rank or prestige.' Regardless of where the Garden is, it is in our present existence that we receive our chances to try again. We play the game in this world of struggle, where we must battle daily pests and occasional monsters.

The physics, chemistry, and biomathematics of our universe have been set in motion by their Creator (blessed!), and He does not interrupt the natural forces in order to save people or other living creatures from disaster. For example, He does not suspend gravity in order to keep an avalanche from falling on a village. If He did, our world would be more chaotic than it already is. Anything is possible for God, but He has created for us a world in which everything is not possible. It is not possible to have a positive without a negative, a high without a low, an upward without a downward, an action without a reaction. Our God of Impossibilities does intervene on occasion. Sometimes we do not even realize God's intervention, and we use the word *miracle* in reference to an unexplainable rescue from inevitable disaster.

Natural tragedies –like the tsunami of 2004, earthquakes, volcanic eruptions, and even accidents and diseases— result from the natural order of our world and are part of the struggle. Sometimes specific disasters are allowed as punishment, but nature itself shows us that disaster in general is not a divine scheme of punishment. The struggle affects the lives of, not only people, but also plants and animals, and certainly God has no reason to punish or test wildlife. Plants and animals are without the ability to choose to do good or evil, so if a dogwood tree, for example, suffers from a plant pathogen, God is not punishing the tree for annoying the bees.

Nature has answers, and even natural disasters have something to teach us. Despite death and destruction left in the wakes of disasters, Earth benefits in ways that may seem minor. In the total scope of the perfect order of nature, however, these benefits are tremendous. Hurricanes, for example, bring fresh water and nutrients to estuaries that would not survive without them; and, without estuaries, the food chain of the entire planet would be disrupted with devastating results for all life.

In the spring of 2005, Death Valley burst into gorgeous bloom, including flowers of plants unseen for over a hundred years and never before photographed. This resurrection was due to the unusual desert floods prior to spring. Only God (blessed!) can be sure how the earth will benefit from these new, old plants, but someday, insh'Allah (God willing), we will figure it out.

The people of the Moken Islands depend on the sea for their livelihood. When the tsunami of 2004 hit, the Mokens had already fled to safety. Their village was destroyed, but their lives were saved because they read the billowing pages of the sea. The elders saw and heard the signs the sea gave them, and they finally convinced the stubborn youth of the impending danger. The Mokens believe that it is the responsibility of the sea to cleanse the earth and that it was only doing its job by hosting a tsunami. Because of the Mokens' view of life, there is no word for *worry* in the Moken language and no word for *when*. The Mokens experience each moment as it comes. A word for *want* is not in their language because the Mokens appreciate each blessing as it comes. When the tsunami took all they owned, the Mokens simply began to imagine the new possibilities that lay ahead in their rebuilding.

For believers, natural disasters and other calamities within the struggle are tests, which are opportunities to exercise, exhibit, and strengthen faith. The possibilities of variety and changes that disasters deliver along with their destruction is a sign that God, the Ultimate Renovator, reveals His own power in the spiritual variety and changes in the lives of believers. Sometimes inner selves have to be renovated so people may attain the dynamic personalities God has envisioned for them. Whenever the struggle brews a storm within your spirit, just think of the possibilities.

"Your prayer cannot change the order of the universe, but it is possible that praying will alter your being. If there is a revolution in your inner self, it will not be strange, then, if the whole world changes too" (Muhammad Iqbal).

> O Almighty God, have mercy on me from Your unfailing love.
> With Your amazing grace, erase my transgressions.
> With Your bountiful compassion, blot out my sins.
> Create in me, O God, a pure heart and a steadfast spirit.
> Restore to me the joy of Your salvation and grant me a devoted attitude.
> *(Psalms 51: 1, 2, 10, 12)*

75. VEIL OF HONOR

> O Believers, do not enter the Prophet's houses
> until permission is given to you for a meal.
> Don't wait [in the house] until (the meal} is prepared,
> but enter when you are invited.
> After you have eaten the meal, leave without engaging in frivolous talk.
> Such [behavior] annoyed the Prophet,
> but he was too shy to tell you to leave.
> Allah, however, is not embarrassed by the truth.
> When you [men] ask (his wives) for anything,
> ask them from behind a veil [of piety].
> That increases the purity of your hearts and theirs.
> It is not right for you to annoy Allah's messenger.
> [You should] not marry his widows after him at any time.[53]
> Truly, such a thing in Allah's sight is a serious error.
> *(Surah 33: 53)*

When I took my daughter to school one day, I noticed on the 19th century, school building "Boys Entrance" and "Girls Entrance" carved above the doors on opposite ends of the school. Of course, now all classes are mixed-gender, but I thought how much simpler Tana's life would have been if boys and girls still attended separate classes. Some of the boys in her class have made rude comments that would be classified as 'sexual harassment' if anyone cared enough to pay attention to her complaints. Such comments have been upsetting and distracting for her. She also told me of a very embarrassing day when the boy-and-girl class was taught feminine and masculine hygiene, facts of sexual activity, and sexual responsibility (which was reduced to the use of condoms). Certainly, the concept of an invisible but effective veil should be taught at home, and then be continued in school with gender-separate classes, except for some appropriate activities for the sake of learning graceful, social skills between the genders.

According to whose commentary is consulted, the above instruction to "ask from beyond a veil" pertains only to the Prophet's wives or to all Muslim women. The reference to the Prophet's wives, according to scholars, is to emphasize their greater responsibility as role models for all other believing women. The verse, however, seems to be directed to the men, so I wonder why men don't have to wear blinders? Men are usually the ones who can't keep their eyeballs where they belong.

The literal veil is an object of controversy, but who could argue against the need for a metaphorical veil –a veil of honor for appropriate gender behavior? Islamic leaders discourage close, working relationships between men and women, but the fact remains that men and women do work closely together and always will. The more logical approach is to inculcate within society the values and morals that are necessary for developing and maintaining decency, respect, and self-discipline. In the "veil" ayat, the greater burden seems to be placed on the men to take responsibility for their actions. That's quite different from the *old* American way of thinking that "boys will be boys" and that women are responsible for curbing the men's lack of restraint. The *new* American way of thinking is that women have the right to be just as disgusting as men. In God's way of thinking, nobody –male or female— gets a free pass on being disgusting.

It is said that dating is un-Islamic, but I think rather it is 'the modern concept' of dating that is wrong. In earlier centuries in America, proper courtship began when a young gentleman asked the parents of a young lady for permission to "call on her." This meant visits to the girl's home while her parents guarded her chastity. If romance stirred, the relationship continued at church picnics and community dances. If the couple was well suited, the gentleman asked the parents for "her hand in marriage." Today, however, most American teenagers do not observe any type of dating etiquette. They simply "hang out" and "run around" and "hook up" with no supervision and little, if any, moral instruction. The result has been, according to one report, 40% of births in the USA to unwed couples. Parents need to once again become the "veil" and take responsibility for chaperoned dates governed by rules of proper etiquette and moral responsibility.

Scientists have concluded that a twenty-first-century person's brain is not developed enough to consistently exercise rational judgment until a person becomes age 25 —not the age of 15 or 18 or 21 of previous generations. A supervised atmosphere should be maintained for people under age 25, whether those people are in school, the military, or the work force. Parents should be able to retain some amount of legal control over their children after the age of 18 and until age 25, and schools and employers should exempt students and young employees from situations (ie, an unsupervised, after-hours project) where temptation and a lapse in judgment can have devastating results. Job training programs need to include a code of conduct that is an expected part of an employee's job performance, and the same concept should be part of a supervisor's training. Part of this code of conduct should serve as a "veil" between men and women in order to establish and maintain proper relationships on the job.

From home to school and to courtship and from higher education and job skills programs to employment, the concept of a metaphorical veil can be implemented as self-discipline, self-restraint, and self-respect are inculcated into the character of the upcoming generation. If it doesn't begin today in a century already plagued with adultery, promiscuity, rape, incest, pedophilia, and sexual harassment, how shocking and decadent the world of the 22nd century!

Help us, Almighty God, to find solutions
To keep children conceived in situations of rape, adultery, and promiscuity
From falling into the same pit of immorality
From which their innocent lives began.

76. BELOVED POISONS

> They ask you about intoxicants [eg, drugs, alcohol] and gambling.
> Say, "There are some sin in them and some benefit."
> They ask you how much to give [in charity].
> Say, "As much as you can spare."
> These are [examples of] how Allah clarifies His signs
> so you may ponder this life and the life after.
> O Believers, intoxicants, gambling, [idolizing] stones,
> And [telling the future by] arrows are all evil acts.
> They are Satan's tools. Avoid them so you may be successful.
> Satan's plan is to incite enmity and hatred among you
> with intoxicants and gambling.
> [He wants to] hinder you from the remembrance of Allah
> from ritual prayer.
> Will you abstain?
> *(Surah 2: 219 and Surah 5: 90-91)*

When I was growing up, our neighbor Smoky Hempfield had ducks that used to come into our cornfield and eat the seed corn that we had planted. One day Daddy bought a box of cherry bombs, and then he sat in a chair by the garden and waited for the ducks. As soon as the ducks came waddling after the seed corn, Daddy started lighting the cherry bombs and throwing them at the ducks. The tiny explosions scattered the ducks in all directions. The seed corn was saved, but then we had a bigger problem. The cherry bombs had set some of the ducks' tail feathers on fire. The ducks then ran through the woods and set the woods on fire. We quickly made field-straw brooms and carried buckets of water into the woods. We dipped the brooms into the water and beat the flames. It took us hours to put out all the little fires. The moral is, in bombing ducks, the calamity is greater than the benefit. Intoxicants and gambling are like that too.

A little wine with meals aids digestion and helps blood circulation, and whiskey has been used as a sedative and as a disinfectant. Consumption of alcoholic beverages, however, leads to dependency (alcoholism) and drunkenness, which leads to violence, poor judgment, social misconduct, family problems, poverty, and moral ruin. Drunkenness is an evil dragon with fetid breath, retched exploits, and hideous legacies. The poison of alcoholic beverages is loved and glorified, however. It is dressed in stunning bottles with glitzy designs. Seductive ads present an array of alcoholic poisons as glamorous, macho, or sporty, depending on the audience. Getting drunk is considered a rite of passage by partying teenagers, and adults hoist their deified vessels in celebrations and indulgent parties.

According to one set of statistics, one out of ten people who drink becomes an alcoholic, and about 14.5 million people from age twelve in the USA now suffer from alcoholism (now called "alcohol use disorder"). Alcohol is the third leading cause of preventable death in the USA. Alcohol use disorder affects one's family life, job security, and social life, and may result in physical incapacity, insanity, or death. About 6.6 million children in the USA has at least one alcoholic parent, and family members may suffer from violent abuse as well as financial ruin. Violent behavior associated with alcohol use is blamed for 49% of murders, 52% of rapes, 21% of suicides, and 60% of child abuse. In the workplace, 47% of industrial injuries and 40% of industrial fatalities are linked to alcohol consumption.

Prophet Muhammed (peace and blessings upon him) cursed ten people in connection with wine: the wine presser, the one who has the wine pressed, the one who drinks the wine, the one who transports it, the one accepting the transport, the one who serves it, the one who sells it, the one who benefits from the price paid for it, the one who buys it, and the one accepting the purchase."[54]

In our society, the limited benefit of liquor has been replaced with modern food preservatives, disinfectants, painkillers, and sedatives. Now we are only left with the sin. Similarly, drugs are of great value for medical purposes, but drug abuse and use of dangerous substances have disastrous results. The illegal drug business, accompanied by greed and power-lust, has resulted in corruption within corporate, political, and social systems.

At the time of the Prophet (peace and blessings upon him), gamblers shared their winnings with the poor, so some good came of gambling. In today's society, the public lottery is a great source of income for the state, and the revenue is used for such things as schools and roads. Gambling, however, ruins the individual who becomes addicted and foolishly wastes his or her time and money, and the welfare of the gambler's family is seriously jeopardized.

Gambling doesn't always involve money, however. What is intended as innocent flirtation, for example, is a gamble with morality. The same is true of indulging in pornography or watching a movie with filthy language.

Tobacco products control the mind and lifestyle of an addict, and their use is certainly a gamble with one's own life and the lives of those with whom he or she resides. Snuff and chewing tobacco cause mouth diseases and tooth decay. Cancer from smokeless tobacco can change a handsome face into a monstrous atrocity and send the user's promising future to rot in a closed casket.

Anything addictive weakens the mind and makes a person vulnerable to Satan's suggestions. Stay away from "recreational drugs," tobacco, pornography, and other traps. A person indulging in such things is apt to become hooked, and then he or she becomes a slave to one of the false gods poisoning our society.

The people who usually suffer the most from intoxicants and gambling and other addictive products and activities are the children. Many parents don't have enough sense to raise their kids. A high school teacher snatched a smutty, romance novel from the desk of one of his students. The teacher advised the student that he would not tolerate such literature in his classroom. To validate his conviction, he read a passage aloud to the class. It was explicit in describing a sexual encounter, and the language was obscene.

The teacher asked the student, "Does your mother know you read this trash?"

The student answered, "It's my mother's book. She read it and then gave it to me."

The saddest gamble of all is made by pregnant women who smoke, drink, and/or use drugs. An infant's nervous system and circulatory system are formed during the first six weeks of fetal development. Tobacco, alcohol, and drugs can seriously affect the permanent health of the brain and heart. Cigarette smoke (whether first-hand or secondary) can cause birth defects. Alcohol during pregnancy causes the frontal lobes of the brain not to form properly. This condition, known as FAS (fetal alcohol syndrome), sets a child on a course of lifelong difficulties, including lack of impulse control, lack of decision-making skills, abnormal vulnerability to harmful ideas, inability to accept responsibility for his or her actions, bizarre obsessions, and lack of social skills. Drug use during pregnancy can also cause serious health and mental problems, but a baby with FAS faces more severe problems than even a crack baby does. About one in one hundred babies in the USA is born with FAS. Children born with such prenatal defects often become wards of the state and have bleak futures. They are often unsuccessful as adults and become dependent on welfare programs. They often turn to crime and other unacceptable lifestyles. As the curse of substance abuse continues, victims of prenatal defects often become parents of children like themselves.

How can a moral, responsible, humane society continue making available the poisons that are destroying that society and its children? Such a decadent society makes an enemy of God and is heading toward a disastrous end. "[Prophet Jethro said,] 'O my people, just because I alienate myself from you [because of your lifestyle], do not let that cause you to sin. [You could] then suffer a fate similar to that of the people of Noah or of Heber or of Salih. You are not far removed from the people of Lot [of the infamous cities of Sodom and Gomorrah]. Ask forgiveness of your Lord, turning to Him in repentance. My Lord is indeed flowing with mercy and loving kindness'" (Surah 11: 89-90).

A nation that continues to ignore or reject God and His laws is a nation in constant and never-ending turmoil. Abraham Lincoln warned, "The only assurance of our nation's safety is to lay our foundation in morality and religion." Freedom without the discipline of integrity and morality enslaves the free with their own decadence.

If you have truly surrendered to God (blessed and exalted is He), you do not have the right to jeopardize the life that rightfully belongs to God. And you certainly do not have the right to jeopardize the health and welfare of others around you. God created humanity to be His representatives on this planet at all times. You cannot fairly represent God if you have a stupid cigarette sticking out of your face or if you are hoisting a martini? If you use any addictive substance or are engaged in an addictive, dangerous activity, rededicate yourself to God and seek His guidance in perfecting your life. Get professional help if necessary to rid your life of substance abuse or dangerous activities.

"Say, 'I seek refuge with the Lord of the Dawn. [I seek refuge] from the corruption of created things. [I seek refuge] from the corruption of darkness as it spreads. [I seek refuge] from the corruption of those who blow on knots [in practicing black magic]. [I seek refuge] from the corruption of the envious one as he practices envy'" (Surah 113: 1-5).

Together we can make a difference and change the society in which we live.

> There can be no count of the number of fools,
> No count of the thieves and fraudsters,
> No count of those who shed innocent blood,
> No count of the liars who take pleasure in deceit,
> No count of those who spread malice and hatred.
> By the grace of Your name,
> May Humanity be lifted higher and higher.
> Grant Your consideration, O Lord,
> So that virtue may reign in every human heart.
> *[Nanak (1469-1538), founder the Sikh religion (India)]*

77. KEEP YOUR SOUL GREEN

> Say, "Truly, my prayer, my service of sacrifice, my life, and my death are for Allah, the Cherisher of the Worlds."
> *(Surah 6: 162)*

One spring/summer season, I went every day to the same spot in the orchard to pray, and I prostrated directly on the ground. When the weather started getting colder, the grass began to yellow –all except for a wide circle around where I prayed. That circle stayed green while all the rest of the grass eventually turned brown. It stayed green until it got too cold for me to pray outside. Only after I stopped praying there did it finally turn yellow and then brown. If my prayers did that for the grass, imagine what your prayers do for your body and your soul. The positive energies that prayers bring into your personal bubble has an effect on your whole life.

The life of this world is always bombarding us with temptations, evil suggestions, and opportunities to darken our souls with the evil that lurks. Keep your soul lively and green by dedicating your whole self to Allah, making Him the beneficiary of all your prayers, your sacrifices, your total being, and even your death. Only in this way are you prepared to battle the evil forces around you.

When the sins in my soul are increasing, I lose the taste for virtuous things.
Yet even at such moments, Lord,
I know I am failing You and failing myself.
You alone can restore my taste for virtue.
Many false friends are willing to encourage sin.
I depend on Your friendship to provide strength of mind
To resist and defeat sin.
[Teresa of Avila (1515-1582), Carmelite nun]

78. UMMAH TO THE THIRD POWER

All of you, hold firmly to the rope of Allah.
Do not be divided [into sects].
Remember the grace of Allah on you when you were enemies,
and He made friendship among your hearts.
[Remember when,] by His grace, you became as family.
You were right on the edge of the pit of the fire [of Hell],
and He saved you from it.
Thus, Allah clarifies His signs for you, so you may be guided.
(Surah 3: 103)

One Sunday, in a restaurant, I was wearing my shirt that says, "Muslims love Jesus too," plus, of course, my hijab. A man came up to our table and asked, "So, you're Muslim?" After I replied yes, he started talking about the importance of religious freedom and how upset he was about the New Zealand mosques shooting in 2019 in which more than fifty people were killed.

I said, "There are 4,200 religions in the world but One God for everybody; nobody has a monopoly on God." He was so impressed with that statement that he repeated it as if he was trying to memorize it.

In Arabic, the word *ummah* means 'the faith family'. That same word is in the Hebrew Bible and is often translated to 'nation' or 'community'. Jesus spoke Aramaic, and he most likely used the word *ummah*, which was translated to the Greek *ekklesia*, and then to the English *church*.

In my way of thinking, there are three kinds of ummahs. First, Muslims may belong to a local mosque or Muslim community that is their personal ummah. Second, there is the universal ummah to which all Muslims belong. One reason the salat (formal prayer) remains in Arabic is so that no matter where a Muslim goes anywhere in the world, he or she can participate in the prayer. There is no such thing as mosque membership. If you are a Muslim, you are automatically a member of any mosque in the world.

The third type of ummah, to me, is the greater universal ummah of all believers regardless of what various religious paths they follow. I don't claim any sect because sectarianism puts God's truth in boxes of our own making. All truth is God's truth, and we should accept truth wherever it is. I am able to accept any truth I find in any sect or any religion or in science and certainly the truths we find in nature. If I see any truth in any religion, I am suddenly a Christian, a Jew, a Bahai, a Hindu, a Buddhist, a Sikh, or any other religious person that has a layer of light to share. Ultimately, my religion is Islam, but I believe in showing respect and appreciation for all religions of light.

I invite you to embrace all believers, regardless of religion, in a greater universal ummah. Don't waste your time trying to decide which religious groups will be blessed with Heaven and which groups are doomed for Hell. It's way above your pay grade. Leave that job to Allah. Your job is to love people, be kind, and strive for peace throughout the world.

> God, help us to know those who seek You to be their guide.
> Show us other faith communities that are precious in your sight.
> Certainly, there are those among us where Your existence is denied.
> So, we pray that such denial will disappear with new light.
> Doctrinal questions may sometimes cause us to divide.
> So, remind us that it is our priority for our love to unite.
> Though we differ, may we compete in doing good works which will abide.
> May our common submission to You be ours and Your delight.
> Please help us to overcome our foolish pride.
> May fruitful fellowship take precedence over our desire to be right.
> Dear God, we ask that wisdom You would provide
> So that loving our neighbor will always keep us aright.
> *("A Prayer for Faith Communities" by Michael Wright)*[55]

79. I WANT MY FINGERTIPS BACK!

> I call to witness the Day of Resurrection.
> I call to witness the self-reproaching spirit.
> Does humanity think that We cannot assemble his/her bones?
> Certainly, We are able to put together in perfect order
> even the very tips of his/her fingers.
> *(Surah 75: 1-4)*

If there was one person in the world I never wanted to look like, it was Ted Kopple, the news reporter with a head like a prune. But I look more like him every day.

When my hubby Tom gets out of bed in the morning, he waddles down the hallway as stiff-legged as the Frankenstein monster. I say, "Good morning, Frank."

He looks at me, with my face all screwed up and wrinkled from sleep, and says, "Good morning, Ted."

Life just has a way of sapping the kick out of a body.

When Tom and I were renewing our foster parenting license, part of the process was getting fingerprinted for FBI investigation. I was surprised to find that I no longer had fingerprints. I used to have fingerprints. I was fingerprinted when I joined the air force, again when I joined the air national guard, and my captors fingerprinted me when I was captured as a spy on a training mission. This time, however, my fingers only made blobs. According to the officer scanning my fingers on the new, electronic, fingerprinting device, I had worked so hard all my life that my fingerprints had completely eroded.

I almost cried. Because of hard labor, I had lost something uniquely mine. I thought also of Mama who had certainly lived a much more difficult life of struggle and strife than I had, and I felt sad for her.

Then I thought about all the things I had achieved with my hands. I had built furniture and a house; refinished antique furniture; completed masonry projects, including a rock chimney; refinished rooms, with new floor tile, wallpaper, and hand-painted murals; grown vegetables and flowers; developed unique photographs in my darkroom; made the best soap in the world;

created fine art and illustrations; written manuscripts; and established a long list of other accomplishments. Still, I missed my fingerprints.

American geneticist E. B. Lewis discovered, in 1978, that eight genes, with only minor variations in the genetic code, are present in all species of the animal kingdom. Mammals, fish, fowl, and even insects all share the same master control genes that sculpt each basic body plan. These genes are called 'homeobox' genes –'hox' for short. They comprise the command center for the creation of each body. Hox genes produce proteins in a developing embryo. The proteins begin a developmental cascade by binding to specific DNA sequences; that in turn causes other targeted genes to produce their own proteins. The new proteins act as messengers that inform each cell what it is to become. For example, a Hox gene initiates the sending of messengers to one segment of cells to tell the cells to form either an arm, a wing, or a fin. The Hox genes are active along a creature's body in a specific order, from head to rear, tracking the spine.

Perhaps the Qur'an refers to the Hox genes when it says, "He/she was created from a gushing fluid. [This fluidity began] from between the backbone and the ribs" (Surah 86: 6-7). In the embryo, the Hox genes are located between what is to become the spine and the ribs, and they gush forth fluid-like in sending messages according to the body plan. The Hox genes are the master switches for turning on sets of other genes that, in turn, regulate the creation of distinct regions of an animal's or a human's body.

Prophet Muhammed (peace upon him) stated, "There is nothing of the human body that does not decay except one bone. From the bone at the end of the spine, each human body will be recreated on the Day of Resurrection."[56] Perhaps, without ever knowing anything of DNA science, the Prophet (peace!) was alluding to the Hox genes.

In another hadeeth, the Prophet (peace!) said, "Allah will say to the person who will have the minimum punishment in the fire on the Day of Resurrection, 'If you had things equal to whatever is on the earth, would you ransom yourself with it?' The person will reply, 'Yes!' Allah will say, 'I asked you a much easier thing than this while you were in the backbone of Adam, and that was not to worship others besides Me, but you refused and insisted on worshiping others besides Me'."[57]

Consider the words "in the backbone of Adam." Congruent with the backbone of Adam was the DNA pattern, the Hox genes, for all Humanity. Genetic scientists have already determined that all Humanity has descended from the same two parents, and that the Hox genes have been inherited from one common ancestor. Intentional references to the area along the spine and to the tailbone (the area of the Hox genes) are used in the Qur'an and Hadeeth, but the full meaning could not have been understood until the age of DNA science.

God (blessed and exalted is He) promises that someday our bodies will be completely restored —even the tips of our fingers —fingerprints and all. The significance of that promise, however, is beyond what is physical. The implication is that each person will be recreated as a unique individual; we won't be cookie-cutter people. We won't lose our personal identities, physically or psychologically. When your Hox genes get a fresh breath from the Creator, and you are fully resurrected, you'll be back to your old self. God does promise, however, that He will remove any negativity that remains in our minds. So we will be better than brand new; we will have spiritual fingerprints that can never be eroded from an environment of negative forces.

"Good night, Frank."

"Good night, Ted."

> Even though my limbs are stiff, I am thankful to awaken to a new day.
> My aches and pains fade in proportion to my gratitude to God
> And as I recall how I must serve Him today.
> *[inspired by "The Day's Duties" (Iraq)]*[58]

80. BECOMING YOUNG

> It is Allah who sends the winds to beckon the clouds,
> and We herd them to a land [that seems] dead
> and revive the earth after its decay.
> Thus will be the resurrection.
> Listen for the day when a caller will call from a near place.
> On that day, they will hear a blast in justice.
> That will be the Day of Resurrection.
> Truly, We give life and death.

To Us is the final goal.
(Surah 35: 9 and Surah 50: 41-43)

When I was little, Mama would draw paper dolls for me. They were beautiful, little girls wearing lace dresses and petticoats, shoes with buckles, and dainty bonnets over fountains of curls. Mama's life was difficult, and she never had the opportunity to develop her artistic talent. She often said that she would become another Gran'maw Moses, an American folk artist. Gran'maw Moses had sacrificed the prime of her life to raising her family before beginning a late career.

Long after all of us children were grown and out on our own, I asked Mama to draw paper dolls for me. I wanted to honor her by using the drawings on greeting cards. I gave her nicely woven, drawing paper and a soft, artist's pencil, and she awkwardly began to recall some long-forgotten strokes. Then her gnarled, arthritic hand trembled as the pencil wandered into shapeless, jittery patterns.

"I can't," Mama said as tears painted her face with streaks of yellow and orange reflected from the glow of the crackling fireplace. "My hands are too old," she mourned as she realized her talent had faded away with all the other dreams of her youth.

The American artist Picasso once said, "It takes a very long time to become young." Actually, it takes a lifetime and also the death-time, and then the resurrection returns youth and vitality. My theory is that in cosmic time, the Day of Resurrection is already happening for those who have crossed over to the spiritual life unaffected by our Newtonian time.

The scientific term for the Day of Resurrection is 'the Omega Point'. Some scientists believe that the continually expanding universe will reach a final time-space singularity and the universe will begin collapsing upon itself. The universal computations within creation will shrink until all power is compressed into energy powerful enough to reach the Omega Point when the entire historical universe –past, present, and possible— will be resurrected along with all the minds and bodies that have ever lived.

Mama did not have to wait until the Omega Point, however, to be resurrected. The spirit is not confined to our experience of time and space which is mere illusion. I believe that, in God's real time, Mama is already in our future –a time beyond the Omega Point— and she is already enjoying eternal life with our future, resurrected selves.

I try to imagine Mama, now gone from this life, sitting in Paradise, drawing paper dolls and doing all the other creative things she could never enjoy in this life of constant struggle. She has been revived by the breath of the Eternal Word and the nourishment of the Living Water.

Teach me, O Lord of Resurrection,
The lessons of Your season of Spring.
Instill in me the hope
That death does not equal an end to life.
As my body succumbs,
Remind me that I am not entering an endless winter,
But simply another season in the unfolding mystery of life.
Greet me with forgiving grace
As my soul spills from the womb of winter.
At the feast of the numinous spring,
May I taste with delight
The freshness and vitality of new birth
In the land of Your new creation.
Resurrect me to be fully alive
In the presence of You my Lord.

81. HOW LONG IS FOREVER?

Consider time! Truly, humanity is at loss.
The exceptions are those who have faith and perform
righteous deeds and unite in teaching truth and patience.
Has there not been a time over humanity
when he/she was nothing —not even a mention?
One day, He will assemble them.
"O assembly of spirit-beings,
you certainly misguided many of the people."
Their buddies among people will say,
"Our Lord, we profited from each other, but we reached
our span [of living], which you set for us."
He will say, "The fire will be your dwelling place
where you will stay continuously, except as Allah wills.
Truly, Your Lord is Perfectly Wise, the All-knowing."
(Surah 103, Surah 76: 1, and Surah 6: 128)

A great blue heron skirted across opaque ripples. A gator's eyes bulged barely above the water's pollen-and-duckweed scarf. Gossamer wings of dragonflies flickered in the dappled sunlight. My canoe scattered a flurry of waterbugs from their synchronized swimming.

My arms were strengthened, and my hands calloused from the previous weeks of farming, so I was good to go on the oars. Working in the sun had already given me a redneck tan —everything tanned except what had been covered by overalls and a T-shirt with one sleeve rolled to pack a stick of teaberry gum.

I stopped rowing just to listen to the stillness. A thousand sounds of nature harmonized to make a song of silence. Suddenly, the lively water-world launched a fish. The streaking shimmer rocketed upward to snatch a mosquito from the food chain. Plop! The shimmer sank back into its murky milieu.

Considering time in a Carolina swamp, time seems nothing but a box from which our spirits long to escape. Time is simply one factor of our created world. Time is a virtual-reality book from which we experience one passage and then another and then another, moment after moment. All time —past, present, and future— was created in the beginning. In our linear view of time, however, we experience each frame as it emerges from the reel of time. In a canoe, a traveler may see an alligator's eyes emerge from the murky swamp. The boater knows that the whole gator is there, but, hopefully, she experiences only the one visible aspect. Time seems to stand still as she cautiously paddles by, but if the mighty jaws emerge in another instant of time, emergent time may be gone in a flash for the nature gal. And then there is eternity.

When I was a little kid nagging my daddy to do something for me, he would promise that he would do it "right now in a little bit." I could not figure out exactly what time that would be, but I was sure "right now in a little bit" would eventually come.

For each person, the grand finale will come "right now in a little bit," and God (blessed and exalted is He) warns that the unforgiven sinners will reside in the fire "forever, except as Allah wills." God's reality is not confined to time as we know it, so we have no way of knowing what "forever" means. The words "except as Allah wills" give us something significant to ponder because they may indicate that "forever" may be a definite experience for each individual.

Abdulla Yusuf Ali explains, "Eternity and infinity are abstract terms. They have no precise meaning in our human experience. The qualification, 'except as Allah willeth,' makes it more intelligible, as we can form some idea —however inadequate— of a Will and Plan, and we know God by His attribute of Mercy as well as justice."[59]

Be certain that you are ready for your personal grand finale because it is sure to come "right now in a little bit." In fact, in God's reality, it is already here. Although physically and intellectually, you are confined to this illusive reality, your soul is in touch with the numinous reality. Depression and hopelessness may sometimes be symptoms of souls in distress as they face the reality of an eternal future of misery. God (blessed and exalted is He) has already written our lives, and we are simply living the chapters. That does not mean, however, that we are unfairly held responsible for a destiny over which we have no control. Some scientists believe that there are alternative, pre-written chapters that we authenticate or eradicate according to the various choices we make. In quantum physics, an unselected possibility becomes a vacated wavelength. There is no predestination from which a person cannot escape; instead, one chooses from many life-plans.

When a person listens to his or her soul, he or she may be warned and advised to choose another path —an alternate possibility in the choose-your-own-ending biography. Each individual must take a good look at the chapters he or she has already authenticated. If those chapters seem to be leading to a sad ending, salvation can still be obtained from our Heavenly Biographer when the star of the biography turns to the Lord of Happy Endings. God (blessed!) has sent us His revelations and His prophets to guide us on our choose-your-own-adventure lives, and in His amazing plan, we can find the best chapters for our lives.

In our realm of existence, quite often the best chapters of life become vacated wavelengths of unrealized blessings. Sometimes we inadvertently make bad decisions and screw up our lives. Sometimes other people make bad decisions, selfish choices, and even commit crimes that seriously affect others. Governments declare unjust wars and commit acts of oppression and injustice. Natural phenomena, such as hurricanes, floods, and tornadoes, may suddenly wreck the lives of families and entire communities. Our natural resources are exploited, wilderness areas are raped, and the wild kingdoms are abused and destroyed —all leading to a domino-effect of afflictions for the entire planet, including human welfare.

God (blessed and exalted is He) promises a resurrection and a new creation. In theoretical quantum mechanics, at the Omega Point, everything throughout history will be resurrected. If vacated wavelengths are resurrected, then, when the faithful inherit the earth, they will also inherit new opportunities to make the best choices for peace on earth and good will for all God's people and for His creation. Maybe we will get a chance to set things right. Maybe aborted babies will be born. Maybe murdered children will live. Maybe victims of diseases, starvation, and disasters will be victorious. Maybe wars will be averted. Maybe the vast buffalo herds of the American West will not be vanquished. Maybe the dodo, quagga, and spectacled cormorant[60] will not become extinct. Maybe the world will exist in harmony. Considering time, all things are possible.

> O Lord, in You we put our trust.
> To You we turn in times of need.
> To You we shall go at the moment of death.
> Do not allow us to be deceived and misled
> By the designs of those whose hearts are evil.
> Forgive us for the evil in our own hearts.
> You alone are mighty; You alone are wise.
> *[Prophet Muhammed (peace and blessings upon him)]*

82. FOLLOWING THE CROWD

> We guided the Children of Israel across the sea.
> They happened upon a people devoted to their own idols.
> (The Israelites) said, "O Moses, create a god like their gods for us."
> He said, "You certainly are a people without any sense.
> These (idolaters) indulge in fragmented ruins.
> What they practice is all in vain."
> He said, "Should I seek for you a god other than Allah?
> It is Allah who has favored you above all other nations."
> In his absence, the people of Moses used their ornaments
> to make the image of a calf.
> It seemed to moo [because of a wind instrument designed into its nose].

> Could they not see that it neither spoke to them nor showed them the way?
> They accepted it [as a god], and they sinned.
> When they became remorseful and realized their error, they said,
> "If our Lord does not have mercy on us and forgive us,
> we shall indeed be among the lost."
> *(Surah 7: 138-140, 148-149)*

Daddy's friend Perky Addlehead was driving past the fairground when fair-goers were looking for parking spots. At that time, the fairground didn't have a parking lot, and surrounding landowners sold spots in their fields, front yards, or anyplace else a car would fit. Nearly every house had a sign out front to tell the cost of parking in the yard. Perky rolled down his car window and started yelling, "Follow me; park free. Follow me; park free." A line of cars began following Perky as he drove farther and farther away from the fairground.

Finally a fair-goer yelled out his car window, "Where the heck are you going, man?"

Perky yelled back, "I'm going to the river to fish. Parking is free down there." Perky laughed out loud and then sped off before he could get beat up. What an example of blind following!

I helped build furniture before the shops used electric nail guns, and I swung a sixteen-ounce hammer all day. I also unloaded the delivery trucks bringing nails, and I lifted two fifty-pound kegs of nails at a time. I could have lifted them one at a time, but I was in the precarious position of having to constantly impress the men as I was the first and only woman in the machine room.

One day I opened a new keg of nails and started to work. It started out to be a bad day as I kept bending the nails and having to pull them back out.

The boss came over, saw a big pile of bent nails, and said, "Linda, why are you bending so many nails today?"

I said, "I don't know; this wood must be really hard."

He got one of the nails out of the keg and held it up and studied it. He said, "Well, this nail is already bent!"

I looked at it and saw that it had a curve to it. No wonder I was having a hard time driving those nails straight!

People are like that too. Once they have gotten crooked, it's difficult to get them to go straight. Once I saw the curve in the nail, I was able to adjust my hammer swing so that I was more likely to drive the nail straight. In the same way, if you understand a person's crookedness, you can aim your words in a fashion that may help drive them to the Straight Way.

Just like today's children (young and adult), the Children of Israel wanted to follow the crowd. The Israelites saw a cult which was a fragment of a ruin, which may have been an Egyptian mining camp remaining after Egypt had been ruined by the plagues. Even though the One True God had shown His favor to them, the Israelites thought it was really cool to have golden images –gods they could see and touch. Modern people are the same way; they use material things and concepts as false gods just because these gods are cool and fashionable. Do they not see that the gods of the pop culture cannot speak to them of truth and justice and cannot show them the Way? As Muslims, we must remind them of God's reality and help them understand that the pop culture is a fragment of a ruin of a sinful nation.

> Our Lord Allah who is in Heaven, holy is Your name.
> Your Kingdom reigns in Heaven and on Earth.
> As Your mercy is in Heaven, make Your mercy on Earth.
> Forgive us our sins and errors.
> You are the Lord of good people.
> Send mercy from Your mercy,
> And send healing from Your healing so there may be a cure.
> [Prophet Muhammed (peace and blessings upon him)]

83. CONTRIBUTIONS GREAT AND SMALL

> (Believers) could not contribute any amount –great or small—
> or cut across a valley [ie, go out of the way to do some good deed]
> without such deeds being ascribed to their credit
> so that Allah may reward each deed with what is best.
> (Surah 9: 121)

There's a saying that "a writer isn't always writing when he or she is writing." It means that, no matter what a writer is doing, he or she is always thinking about something to write. The same is true for an artist, and, as an artist and a writer, I sometimes drive myself crazy thinking about something to draw or write. My head is always swarming like it's full of killer bees.

I mentally wrote this parable while I was repairing some stairs at home. The first thing I had to do with the stairs was rip up the old carpeting that covered it. Actually, I ripped up half of it; I got a sinus infection from all the dust and bacteria released into the air, so Tom ripped up the other half so that he could get a sinus infection too. Being miserable together helps make the marriage work. Next, I had to pull out the one-inch, finishing nails that had held the carpet in place. Some of the nails came out really straight, so I saved those to use for something else. If there was any curve or crook at all in them, I threw them away, because it's difficult to drive a cooked nail straight.

As I was removing the nails from the stairs and separating the straight nails from the crooked nails, I recalled a news report I had seen sometime in the past. I don't remember from what country it was broadcast or why; I just remember that it showed people who had just lost their homes to a catastrophe. The people were wailing because they had lost everything they owned. But then the women went into the rubble and started dragging out boards with nails in them. They pulled out the nails and began bending them back straight so that the people could rebuild their homes with the used nails. When you see victims with that much perseverance and determination, how can you not want to help them? When you see devastated people with that much hope, how can you not have hope yourself?

We should always pray for devastated people, and prayer does a lot of good. Sometimes people speak of prayer as if it's a small thing: "I can't do much, but at least I can pray." If you had a meeting with the President of the United States so that you could ask him to do something, you would think that was a really big deal. Prayer gives you the opportunity to meet with God (blessed and exalted is He) and ask Him to do something, and He has a lot more pull than the President. Prayer is a powerful tool, but our putting action behind our prayers is important also. One of the things that impressed me about the news report was that the reporter squatted down with the women and helped them straighten the nails as he reported the news. He was doing something besides just talking about the incident; he was putting action behind his report. Our prayers, our charity, the donations of our talents and skills, and our time and energy are all contributions, and we will each be rewarded for our contributions, great or small.

> Teach me, Creator, how to tread softly as the grasses grow.
> When storms shake and shiver me, keep me steady as I go.
> May I meet the wild world with spirit firm with Your power,
>   And with a heart as generous and lovely as a flower.
> Teach me, Creator, how to speak cheerful notes like the lark.
> Give my legs a mission joyful like the sound the crickets spark.
> Like the oak with outspread arms, let my life provide a place
> Where passing souls can rest and learn of Your amazing grace.

84. PRAYER WITH LEGS

> Among His signs is that He sends the winds as heralds of glad tidings.
> They give you a taste of His mercy so that ships may sail by His command
>   and you may seek His bounty so you may be grateful.
> *(Surah 30: 46)*

When I was growing up, we didn't have a lot, but we had plenty. People were more industrious in those days and knew how to get by with just a little. For one thing, people worked hard and grew their own fruits and vegetables and canned much of their harvests. In the summer we had fresh produce, and in the winter we had canned foods.

An old couple lived on the other side of the woods from us. They didn't have much money, but they did have a quaint, little house with a nice garden in the back yard. Their supper table was always covered with different kinds of fruits and vegetables, and the old man said the same prayer every evening at the supper table: "O Lord, bless those poor starvin'-to-death people all over the world. We got mighty fine vittles here, and we sure do thank You, Lord. Amen."

Toward the end of summer, most people start getting tired of squash and okra everyday –like the children of Israel got tired of manna in the wilderness. One summer day the old man came in from working outside, he sat down at the supper table, and saw the all-too-familiar platters of fried squash and okra. He prayed, "O Lord, bless those poor starvin'-to-death people all over the world. We got mighty fine vittles here, and we sure do thank You, Lord. But, Lord, if it ain't too much trouble, I sure would like to have a big pot of possum stew. Amen."

Every evening for nearly three weeks, he prayed the same prayer. Finally one evening when he started to pray, the old woman said, "Hold up there, old man. I'm gonna say that thar prayer today." So they both bowed their heads, and the old woman said, "O Lord, bless those poor, starvin'-to-death people all over the world. We got mighty fine vittles here, and we sure do thank You, Lord. But, Lord, if it ain't too much trouble, send this old man a pot of possum stew so he'll shut up about it. Amen."

The very next evening, the old woman set platters of fried okra and squash and biscuits on the table, and then she went to the stove and picked up a big pot. The old man smelled something good as soon as he walked into the house. His eyes were big; his mouth was watering. The old woman set the pot right smack dab in the middle of the table. The old man couldn't wait. He lifted the lid, and, lo and behold, it was possum stew! The old man was so tickled that drool was running down his beard. But then he started scratching his head and pondering. Finally he said, "I just don't get it. I prayed for possum stew every day for nigh three weeks, and the good Lord didn't pay me no never mind, and then here you come up a praying one time, and, lo and behold, you get your prayer answered straight away. What I want to know is, how's come?"

"Well, I'll tell you how's come, old man," the old woman started. "The good Lord answered my prayer because I put legs onto my prayer! But you know what? Them possums is a whole lot harder to catch than you might think."

God (blessed and exalted is He) does not operate a made-to-order industry; sometimes His answer to a prayer comes with a label that says, "Some assembly required" or "Batteries not included." The old woman had put legs onto her prayers by going out and trusting God to help her catch a possum and then make that stew herself. Sometimes trusting God to answer our prayers means putting legs onto our prayers and doing things for ourselves. God (blessed!) is the wind within our sails, but it is up to us to hoist the sails and seek His bounty.

Lord, make us instruments of Your peace.
Where there is hatred, let us sow love;
Where there is injury, pardon;
Where there is discord, union;
Where there is doubt, faith;
Where there is despair, hope;
Where there is darkness, light;
Where there is sadness, joy.
Grant that we may not so much seek to be consoled as to console,
To be understood as to understand,
To be loved as to love.
For it is in giving that we receive,
It is in pardoning that we are pardoned,
And it is in dying that we are born to eternal life.
[Attributed to St. Francis of Assisi (1182-1226)]

85. ELECTORAL REFORM TO PRESERVE DEMOCRACY

They are told,
"Come to what Allah has revealed. Come to the messenger."
They say, "We are satisfied with what our fathers did."
Nonsense! Their fathers did not know anything,
and they did not follow the right way.
(Surah 5: 104)

After multiple visits to the doctor, Daddy went to another appointment for the same ailment. Daddy said to the doctor, "If you had a headache and took an aspirin tablet every day, and the aspirin never did help your headache, wouldn't you want to try something else?" The doctor agreed that he would try something different. Daddy said, "Well, that's how I feel about you, Doc. You don't seem to be doing me much good, so I figure I ought to try something different."

My daddy was a simple, mountain man without much education, but he had enough sense to know that if something isn't working, there needs to be a change.

Our ancestors decided that the President should be chosen by the electoral vote based on a number determined by each state's total number of Congressional and Senate members. To insure that the most populous states would not determine the Presidential election, our nation's founders allotted two senators for each state, but this has enabled small states to have too great an influence in respect to their populations. If a candidate receives even one more vote in the popular vote, he or she is given *all* the state's electoral votes. In this system, a Presidential candidate can lose the national popular vote but win the election by the electoral vote.

In the House of Representatives, legislators go behind closed doors to carve up districts in such a way as to keep incumbents in office. Sometimes gerrymandering is done solely by one party; other times both parties work it out together. The goal is to preserve the power of those already in power.

The two-party monopoly is failing to preserve fair democracy. Many politicians are out of touch with the values and concerns of the average American. The Democratic and Republican parties are tainted with greed and corruption and influenced by corporate and special interest groups.

Should we stick with the electoral process designed for us by ancestors who had no knowledge of 21st century problems and no guidance toward foreseeing a generation so different from their own? We should be cautious in changing anything our nation's founders have set in place because of the ageless value of their wisdom and knowledge. When it is obvious, however, that a process is not working and that, because of it, our own democracy is slipping away, then we should not be satisfied with the process just because our ancestors followed it.

There is an urgent need for organizations, including Muslim organizations, to begin taking serious steps toward bringing the electoral process into reform and to end the two-party monopoly. The gerrymandering to protect incumbents must end, and the President should be elected by direct popular vote. Campaign money needs to be controlled and divided fairly so that citizens can be equally exposed to each candidate's message. Although there needs to be a criterion for placing a candidate on the ballot, candidates outside the Republican and Democratic parties should be given an equal opportunity to win without votes being wasted. This can be accomplished by giving the voter the opportunity to cast a first and second choice with an automatic fix so that if the voter's first choice is not elected, the voter's second choice would automatically benefit.

Such changes in the electoral process would require a Constitutional amendment, and, in order to insure a more democratic future for the next generation, citizens need to begin campaigning now. The first step is for citizens to become more educated in the government process and to insure that our children are being educated in schools that adequately teach civics and government.

> I defend the honorable attributes of democracy.
> I defend voices whether they agree or oppose my own voice.
> I defend the right of those who speak against the light by which I live
> As much as I defend my own rights and freedoms.
> *[inspired by "Sound and Light" (Wales)]*[61]

86. WAR STORIES

> You must fight, in the way of Allah, those who attack you.
> Do not break the rules [of fair fighting].
> Allah does not love those who go too far.
> Why would you not fight, in the cause of Allah, for those who, being weak, are oppressed men, women, and children, who are crying,
> "Our Lord, rescue us from this society of oppressive people.
> Send, from You to us, someone who will protect.
> Send, from You to us, someone who will defend"?
> Fight them until there is no more oppression
> and until the religion is free for Allah.
> If they stop fighting, let there be no more trouble,
> except against those who continue being oppressive.
> *(Surah 2: 190, Surah 4: 75, and Surah 2: 193)*

Some blockheads claim there was no Jewish Holocaust or that it was not as bad as reported. I've always known about the Jewish Holocaust of WW2.[62]

Daddy was a marine in WW2, and he brought home horrifying photographs. Gaping mouths screamed silently, and haunting eyes stared sightlessly from mountainous heaps of desiccated corpses. Naked, starving survivors, standing in a row of living death, looked like splintered corn stalks ravaged by a curse of locusts.

Daddy brought home another photograph that was permanently exposed and developed in the darkroom of my memory. It was a lovely picture of a young Japanese woman and her child. I often got that picture from a box Daddy kept tucked in a drawer. I was mesmerized by the haunting faces, and I often asked Daddy to again tell me the story of how he came to have the picture.

Daddy was a flame-thrower in the Marine Corps. In Japan, his division discovered a cave where the enemy Japanese soldiers kept munitions. The marines invaded the cave, shot the guards, and set up explosives to destroy the munitions site. All the marines left the cave, except for Daddy, who was to light the fuse and be the last man out. The fuse ablaze, Daddy raced through the cave. He stopped sharply when he heard a moan. A Japanese soldier was still alive. Within seconds the cave would explode. Daddy hefted the enemy soldier over his shoulders, and then he ran for his life. He barely cleared the opening of the cave when the explosion happened, hurling Daddy and the soldier into the air and then slamming them into the dirt. Daddy used his own body to shelter the soldier as rocks and shrapnel plummeted.

The turbulence finally ended, but the soldier was mortally injured. Daddy gently rolled him over and held him in his arms while they both lingered there in the warm sand spotted with smoldering embers. The soldier fumbled for something in his pocket. Daddy got it out for him. It was the photograph –apparently of his beautiful wife and child, softly radiating sweetness and innocence. The young Japanese soldier died, in Daddy's arms, looking at the picture of the people he loved most –the people who would never even know that he had spent the last seconds of his life breathing his love for them. I hope that, when I get to Heaven, Daddy will introduce me to that beautiful family.

By the end of six ghastly weeks of that glorified invasion, Daddy's own life slaked the bloodthirsty sands of Iwo Jima. Riddled with shrapnel, he lay among severed heads and limbs of both American and Japanese warriors who were finally companions in a voyage of souls. Wanting to control their own fateful demise, many Japanese soldiers clutched hand grenades and exploded their own bodies against a background of hellish fury.

Shot with cameras instead of guns, born were the heroic and valiant images that would mask the reality too horrific to publish in newspapers and history books. For the civilian populations, the war faded like old newspaper clippings, but, for the veterans of the battlefield, the real-life drama replayed itself in the movie house of the mind. Miraculously, Daddy survived, although it was five years before he would walk again. Many years later, he would occasionally use his pocketknife to cut out pieces of shrapnel that had worked their way near the skin's surface. He relived the horrors of WW2 until the day he died. Will humanity ever become civilized enough to figure out solutions to conflicting agendas without blowing each other to smithereens?

The Qur'an specifies that war is permissible only in self-defense and in the defense of innocent others and within the confines of regulation. Followers of the Islamic religion, however, are among those guilty of transgressing the limits of war. The *irhabists* (terrorists defaming the name of Islam) have been misled and are misleading others in their unjust declarations of a false "jihad" against non-Muslims. Also, Muslims killing other Muslims because of sectarian and political differences is far from the Prophet's vision for Islam. All such violence is a lie about Islam.

Our own United States government has also fallen way off track in keeping humanitarian ethics in mind. The US government increasingly displays itself as the world's big bully. We citizens must fight such transgression with the might of voice and pen as well as the voting ballot. Letting the truth be known may be our best weapon against a corrupt government. We can support our troops best by supporting truth and by holding our government leaders accountable. Otherwise, the gallant hoisting of the flag on Iwo Jima must share history's pages with such revolting images as those from Abu Gharib.

On an online news media, author Yousef Drummond reported Christopher Sheppard's experiences and reflections concerning the War in Iraq. Sheppard told this story:

> Three years ago, I was a Marine Corps captain on the Iraqi/Kuwaiti border, participating in the invasion of Iraq. Awe-struck, I heard our howitzers thunder and watched artillery rockets rise into

the night sky and streak toward Iraq —their light bathing the desert moonscape like giant arc welders.

As I watched the Iraq war begin, I completely trusted the Bush administration. I thought we were going to prove all of the left-wing antiwar protesters and dissenters wrong. I thought we were going to make America safer. Regrettably, I acknowledge that it was I who was wrong.

I believed the Bush administration when it said Iraq had weapons of mass destruction. I believed its assertion that Iraq was trying to buy yellowcake uranium from Africa and refine it into weapons-grade uranium for a nuclear bomb. I believed its claim that Iraq had vast quantities of biological and chemical agents. After years of thorough inspections, all of these claims have been disproved.

I believed the administration when it claimed there was overwhelming evidence Iraq was in cahoots with al-Qaida. In January 2004, then-Secretary-of-State Colin Powell admitted that there was no concrete evidence linking Saddam Hussein and al-Qaida.

I believed the administration when it grandly proclaimed we were going to bring a stable, Western-style liberal democracy to Iraq, complete with religious tolerance and the rule of law. We never had enough troops in Iraq to restore civil order and the rule of law. The Iraqi elections have produced a ruling majority of Shiite fundamentalists and marginalized the seething Sunni minority. Iraq dangerously teeters on the brink of civil war. We have emboldened Iran and destabilized the entire Middle East.

I believed the administration when it claimed the war could be done quickly and cheaply. It said the war would cost only between $50 billion and $60 billion. It said that Iraqi oil revenue would fund the country's reconstruction. I believed President Bush when he landed on the USS Lincoln and said, "Major combat operations have ended."

[In 2006:] The war has cost the American taxpayers $250 billion and counting. The vast majority –94 percent— of the more than 2,300 United States service members killed in Iraq have occurred since Bush's "Top Gun" proclamation. The cost in men and materiel has been far beyond what we were led to believe.

I volunteered to go back to Iraq for the fall and winter of 2004-2005. I went back out of frustration and guilt —frustration from watching Iraq unravel on the news, and guilt that I wasn't there trying to stop it. Many fine marines from my reserve battalion felt the same and volunteered to go back. I buried my mounting suspicions and mustered enough trust and faith in my civilian leadership to go back.

I returned disillusioned by what I saw. I participated in the second battle of Fallujah in November 2004. We crushed the insurgents in the city, but we only ended up scattering them throughout the province. The dumb ones stayed and died. The smart ones left town before the battle, to garner more recruits and fight another day. We were simply the little Dutch boy with our finger in the dike. In retrospect, we never had enough troops to firmly control the region; we had just enough to maintain a tenuous equilibrium.

I now know I wrongfully placed my faith and trust in a presidential administration hopelessly mired in incompetence, hubris, and a lack of accountability. It planned a war based on false intelligence and unrealistic assumptions. It has strategically surrendered the condition of victory in Iraq to people who do not share our vision, values, or interests. The Bush administration has proven successful at only one thing in Iraq: painting us into a corner with no feasible exit.

I will never trust any of them again.[63]

I pray that we in the United States will be able to regain some measure of warranted confidence in our leaders. Most US Americans want what is right and are willing to do what is right. Unfortunately, many, it seems, are too easily misled about what is right. They allow their minds to be controlled by political propaganda and media hype. Americans need to **think** and be more informed —not simply trust the soundbites of the six o'clock news, but dig into the facts and consider various perspectives. As a nation, let's not be fooled again!

We can use the guidance of the Qur'an to determine whether a war is just and necessary and whether a war is being fought with reasonably humane morals and ethics. Glorious and inspiring photographs, such as that of the flag-raising on Iwo Jima, should not blindfold us to the ghastly realities of war. An unwarranted war's insatiable appetite for disaster can never be appeased despite the overwhelming devastation and agonizing death vomited by blood-gorged clashes.[64]

> Our Sovereign Lord,
> We ask Your blessings on the believing men and women
> who serve You while also serving their country.
> Instill in them a sense of dignity and responsibility.
> Help them use good judgment and quick thinking in difficult situations.
> Send Your healing to the minds of those exposed to the horrors of war.
> Send Your strength to the bodies of those mutilated
> by the destruction of war.
> Send Your peace to the hearts of those robbed by the carnage of war.

87. ABORTION MEETS 21st CENTURY IJTIHAD

> We originated Humanity from a product of mud.
> Afterward, We placed him/her as a seed in safe lodging.
> Next, We fashioned the seed into a mass of blood,
> and then We fashioned the mass into a lump,
> [that looked like] something chewed [like chewing gum].[65]
> Next, We added bones and clothed the bones with flesh.
> We then developed all this as a new creation.
> Blessed is Allah, the Best of Creators!
> *(Surah 23: 12-14)*

When I was pregnant, I was asked, "What are you hoping for?"
I said, "A baby human."

Of course, she meant whether I hoped for a boy or a girl, but I was more concerned about having a healthy, normal child.

In my high school was a boy cruelly called 'Frog'. His odd features attracted unpleasant stares and insensitive comments. He had webbed fingers and toes, and his face had a peculiar, amphibious look to it. He died in a car wreck when he was only nineteen, but I thought about him in the seventies when the TV show "Man from Atlantis" was popular. The fictional character had descended from survivors of the legendary, ancient city's collapse into the sea. In the show, Atlantis was a thriving underwater world whose citizens had adapted through evolutionary changes providing gills and webbed fingers and toes. Frog's life may have been more pleasant if, instead of being considered a freak, he had been associated with the hero in "Man from Atlantis."

When we are resurrected to begin our lives in the perfected creation, God will correct the mistakes of nature, which are incidental to the struggle burdening this crumbling world. My schoolmate Frog may enjoy a perfected body, or perhaps we 'normal humans' will enjoy perfected minds in a way that we can see beauty in such odd differences. Frog's water-world appearance may have been interpreted as a sign reminding us that water was the material bond shared by all life. "…We created every living thing from water…" (Surah 21: 30).

When I gathered the hens' eggs, I often put them in my pocket, and sometimes I got busy doing other things and forgot about them. More than once, I reached into my pocket for my pocketknife and stuck my hand into an ooey-gooey mess of broken eggs. I laughed, dumped the pocket's scrambled contents, and washed my overalls. If I had planned to put the eggs in the incubator, however, I would have been much more conscientious and careful. I would have handled the eggs as if they were already alive.

Human embryos are regarded much the same way. If a baby is wanted, a good mother learns and practices as much as she can in regards to caring for herself and her baby throughout the pregnancy and afterward. She plays music on her belly, sings to the child in her womb, and even exposes her belly to bright light so that the baby can begin learning to see. If a baby is unwanted, however, it's lawful in our society to have an abortion. Of course, there are medical and circumstantial reasons for abortions too, and often a decision to abort is a traumatic but necessary decision.

Some Islamic scholars claim that abortion is permissible until after the sixteenth week when, they say, a fetus receives his or her soul. They make this conclusion based on a statement attributed to the Prophet (peace upon him). The hadeeth explains that a baby begins as a fertilized ovum in the uterus of the mother for forty days, it grows as an embryonic clot for forty days, it grows as a morsel of flesh for forty days, and then an angel is sent to blow the *ruh* (life energy, spirit, breath, soul) into the body and to record the child's future to include years of life, deeds to be performed, provisions to be enjoyed, and happiness and sadness to be known.⁶⁶ Some scholars believe that the *ruh* as 'soul' is breathed into the fetus at 120 days of age, until which time the embryonic life is not a living entity, and therefore aborting him or her does not equal killing. Other scholars claim that aborting an embryonic life, even prior to his or her soul being endowed, is destroying life and the potential for life and therefore is a crime.

The term "forty days" is a Scriptural term used for an indefinite amount of time, so I think the Prophet (peace!) was not trying to speak with scientific accuracy, but simply with general and common lingo. He made a vague reference to a three-step process in the development of a baby in the womb.

Accepting the term "forty days" as an indefinite amount of time, we cannot conclude that three times forty will give us a timeline as to when the soul enters the body. It does not matter anyway, because souls are already created in God's reality, and we cannot use our linear perspective of time to overwhelm God's reality of time-space continuum in which all that is to exist already exists.

At 120 days, the sixteenth week of pregnancy, the fetus exhibits *quickening*, which is fetal movement. It may be that *ruh*, in this case, is not the soul, but an awareness of 'life energy'. This awareness most certainly comes in tiny measures beginning the sixth week of pregnancy, which begins the embryonic stage. At this time, early brain chambers form, heart tubes fuse, and heart contractions begin. These can be seen on ultrasound.

Life begins with the fertilization of the ovum, which becomes a developing ball of cells called a *zygote*. Within a week of fertilization, the zygote evolves into a *blastocyst* attaching to the uterine walls. With bracketed expansion, the ayats may be interpreted to mean, "…We placed him [or her] as a seed [a blastocyst, week 1] in safe lodging [implanted on the uterine cavity]."

The meaning could continue, "Next, We fashioned the seed [the blastocyst] into a mass of blood [the placenta and vascular network, week 4]…." At week four of pregnancy, three different layers of cells are developing; these are called 'germ layers.' The ectoderm layer evolves into the nervous system (including the brain), skin, and hair. The endoderm layer evolves into the lining of the gastrointestinal tract, the liver, pancreas, and thyroid. The mesoderm layer evolves into the skeleton, connective tissues, blood system, urogenital system, and muscles. This evolving process is completed about the end of the tenth week, and then the fetal stage begins, during which the formed structures continue to grow and develop.

The next line could be understood to mean, "...and then We fashioned the mass [of germ layers] into a lump [which is the embryo, week 6, with the embryonic period lasting weeks 6 through 10], [that looked like] something chewed [like chewing gum in which teeth marks resemble *somites* along the back of the developing embryo]."

"Next, We added bones and clothed the bones with flesh [with the fetal period beginning at the end of week 10.] We then developed all this as a new creation [a newborn infant]."

All scholars agree that abortion at any time for frivolous reasons (such as, economy, fetal gender, career conflict) is haram (forbidden). In an extremely difficult situation, however, some Muslims may consider abortion. Until a family experiences such a situation itself, it cannot know the desperation wrought in a case of rape, mental instability of the pregnant female, grave possibility of birth defects, life-threatening situation of the pregnant female, or other such difficult circumstances. Each local ummah should provide respectful counsel in such matters, and then be supportive of the woman or couple after a decision is made, even if the decision is to have an abortion.

Traditionally, *ijtihad* (interpreting Qur'an and Sunnah for their value to contemporary needs and diverse societies) has been left to specially trained scholars called *mujtahids*. Today, however, the average Muslim has information at fingertip level with the worldwide web and is finding it necessary to do his or her own research and then to practice ijtihad daily in his or her personal life. In our fast-paced world and diverse Muslim cultures and lifestyles, Muslims cannot wait for the mujtahids to make decisions that may not even relate to one's specific lifestyle. In the case of abortion, the USA government's decision to uphold "the right to choose" has placed the right to ijtihad in the hands of the individual American citizen. The responsibility of such a choice cannot be taken lightly, because liberty without integrity can enslave a people in the corruption of their own self-centered interests.

Some people may be able to justify a hasty abortion before the sixth week, saying that the pregnancy is little more than a mass of dividing cells. A more informed and responsible decision is required after the sixth week in order to justify aborting an entity that has brain chambers and a heartbeat. The decision to abort is extremely more difficult to justify after the tenth week when the germ layers have evolved into definite human shapes. The mujtahids are behind the times, so average people must arm themselves with the academic knowledge and spiritual integrity required to make responsible, informed decisions.

> My soul is an embryo developing
> In the womb of Paradise lost.
> With hope, I labor toward my birth
> Into Your reality, O Lord.
> Until I awaken whole and free,
> Unencumbered by feet of clay,
> Speak to me from wise, old trees,
> Sing to me from cheerful birds,
> Wash me with white rain,
> And hold me with soft grass.
> I am not yet born.
> I fear walls that cage me,
> Deceit that lures me,
> And hate that crushes me.
> I am not yet born.
> Save me.

88. CONSIDER ADOPTION

> …He has not made your adopted children
> [the same] as your [biological] children.
> Such are the words from your mouths,
> but Allah speaks truth, and He shows the way.
> Attribute them to their [biological] parents;
> that is better in the sight of Allah.
> If you don't know who their parents are,
> they are your brothers [and sisters] in faith and your dependents.[67]
> No blame is on you if you make a mistake;
> what matters is the intention in your hearts
> Allah is the Most Forgiving, the Most Merciful.
> *(Surah 33: 4-5)*

Tana

an angelic face, but her halo was always crooked, and her wings were bent.

Tana was approaching her fifth birthday when Tom and I met her for the first time. We spent about an hour with her, and then our adoption worker Lucy told us Tana's situation and problems, including fetal alcohol syndrome. At the end of our meeting, Lucy instructed us, "Talk it over and let me know what you decide."

I turned to Tom and said, "It's okay with me. Is it okay with you?"

"Sure," Tom agreed.

I turned back to Lucy and said, "Okay."

"Okay what?" she asked, puzzled.

"Okay, we'll adopt her," I answered.

Surprised, Lucy said, "But I thought you wanted to talk it over first."

"We just did," I informed her.

That's how our adoption of Tana began. She was in a foster home with fourteen children who also needed permanent homes. The most difficult part of the adoption was walking out of that foster home with only one child. Feeling hopeless and rejected, some of the children cried and asked us why we did not want to adopt them too.

Tom and I had always planned on having one or two brats by birth and adopting one or two more. From an early age, I had been mindful of the need for good, adoptive homes. Much of my awareness and concern was linked to an accident I witnessed as a youngster.

Daddy took the family for a Sunday afternoon drive through the mountains. In those days, narrow, mountain roads brought their roller-coaster-like ups and downs and twists and turns right to the edge of straight drops that led miles down, down, down. Sometimes the ride was so treacherous that Mama would curl up in a ball on the floorboard so she couldn't see out the window. She would sit there and squeal.

We were coming down a mountain when a pickup truck passed us. In the truck bed were twelve children of stepladder ages. Their parents were in the cab, and the mother held a newborn on her lap. With the sudden jolt of a ruptured tire, the truck pitched over the side of the mountain. The children in the back were thrown helter-skelter through the brush as the vehicle plummeted downward. Apparently, the family had been visiting family or friends, because the truck also tossed out an array of home-canned goods. Jars of shelly beans, watermelon-rind jelly, and colorful chow-chow fell among the wildflowers.

Another motorist headed down the mountain road to find the nearest phone and call for help. One by one, the scattered children crawled out of the entanglement of wild growth and made their way up to the road. Daddy cautiously ventured down the treacherous mountain cliff to see if he could help those in the cab. It was a long wait while Daddy inched his way down and then back up. He told us that the parents and baby were dead. "The truck is on top of the woman," he said. "Her head is sticking out, and her legs are lying beside her head."

After the police and ambulances arrived, we headed back home in silence. As soon as I got to my bed, I lay down and cried, trembling from the horror of the episode.

Throughout the coming weeks, TV news reporters covered the story. One of the things repeatedly reported was that those twelve surviving children needed an adoptive family –hopefully one family who would take them all. I never learned if those children were ever adopted, or if they got to stay together. Theirs is just one sad story in a continuum of tragedies.

In the United States, there are over 123,000 children waiting to be adopted, and there are thousands more orphans and foster children all over the world who need good homes. The Prophet (peace and blessings upon him) and the Qur'an implore us to provide for these homeless children, but Muslims in general are not taking the challenge seriously. In fact, many Muslims believe that adoption is anti-Islamic, and they point to the above Scripture as the reason. Well, hang on; we're going for a ride up the mountain of rational thinking.

At the time of the Revelation, the primary purpose of these ayats (verses) about adoption was to curb the demeaning practice of referring to one's freed slave as his or her son or daughter. In the USA, African Americans whose heritage is that of slavery, now carry the names of slave owners, and most have no idea of the parental heritage lost in the aftermath of the slave trade. According to Islam, slaves have the right to know and keep their parents' names. (Islam also abolished slavery on a time-release plan.)

Abdulla Yusuf Ali wrote, "Freed men were often called after their master's name as the 'son of so and so.' When they were slaves, perhaps their fathers' names were lost altogether. .... 'Brother' is not objectionable, because brotherhood is used in a wider sense than fatherhood and is not likely to be misunderstood."[68] Ali explains that the overall purpose of the passage "is to destroy the superstition of erecting false relationships to the detriment or loss of true blood relations. It is not intended to penalize an unintentional slip in the matter, and indeed, even if a man deliberately calls another his son or father, who is not his son or father, out of politeness or affection, God is Oft-Returning, Most Merciful. It is the action of mischievous parties which is chiefly reprehended, if they intend false insinuations. A mere mistake on their part does not matter."[69]

The ayats also give an adopted child the right of choice when he or she becomes of an accountable age. Prophet Muhammed (peace!) had an adopted son Zaid. When Zaid's family located him, the Prophet gave Zaid the option of returning to his birth family or staying with the Prophet (peace!). Zaid chose to remain with the Prophet, but his birthright was not denied to him. Of course, many adopted children today must be protected from criminally unfit, birth parents, but the children still should have the right to information about their birth parents.

Another purpose of the ayats is to allow marriages between members of the adoptive family and members of the adopted child's birth family; in a small community, this may be an important concern. Another purpose is to prevent accidentally incestuous marriages; if an adopted child does not know who his or her birth parents are, the child could grow up to marry his or her own sibling. One more purpose is to protect the legacy of a man killed in combat or of any honorable man who deserves to have his name remembered, but this benefit does not extend to men who have fathered children out of wedlock or who have deserted their families.

Although many situations that existed during the Revelation do not exist today, the instructions still serve as examples of how to handle similar situations. Adoption in this country came to be regulated so that official records were sealed by the courts, and a child would not be permitted to know the names of his or her birth parents or their whereabouts. This has created psychological problems for the child who grew up wondering why his or her parents did not want him or her, or why they could not care for their child, or what happened to them, or a multitude of other unanswered questions. There are also health concerns; ie, the lack of medical history and the possibility of accidentally incestuous marriages. Today there is even more concern in this area due to such things as sperm banks, surrogate motherhood, and fertilized egg implants. With these plus a great number of children born out of wedlock, the probability of accidental incest is increasing.

The method of adoption which would best satisfy the concerns of the Qur'anic passage is 'open adoption', now legal in most states. This is the healthiest and most rewarding for all concerned. The birth mother (and birth father if he is involved) can choose the couple she wants (or they want) to raise the child, and she (or they) have visitation rights and the opportunity to be involved in the child's life. There are many reasons why a mother might choose to place her child in an adoptive home, but adoption is usually a loving choice made by a mother in a difficult situation who wants what is best for her child. Regardless of any mistakes she may have made which contributed to her situation, she should not be criticized for making the difficult, unselfish, and heroic choice of adoption. Although, for issues of privacy and legality, the child would take the last name of the adopting parents, the child would also keep possession of his or her original birth certificate with the names of the birth parents. An open adoption creates a unique and wonderful type of extended family, and a healthy relationship can be successfully established among all those involved in an open adoption.

Most children needing homes are not waiting for open adoptions, but instead are abandoned by or taken from unsuitable parents, and some are orphaned. Certainly, there is no blame on adoptive parents who rescue such children even though the birth parents' names may be kept from the adoptive parents. Today, the number of children growing up in foster care and never knowing the security of a permanent home is a national and global tragedy and disgrace. Any couple capable of providing a loving, nurturing home to a child lost in the system should do so. How can Muslims expect God to be merciful to us if we neglect such helpless victims?

> Have mercy, Allah,
> On the most innocent victims of this world of struggle.
> Inspire more families to have the courage and compassion to adopt.
> May we be merciful to the children,
> As was Prophet Muhammed (peace and blessings upon him),
> Who was adopted by his kin,
> And as was Messiah Jesus (peace upon him and may he bring peace),
> Who had an adoptive father.
> Bless foster and adoptive families,
> And make their efforts successful for the sake of the children.

89. JIVE TALKING FROM A ROCK 'N' ROLL DERVISH

> O Humanity, We created you from one male and one female,
> and made you into nations and tribes so you may get to know one another.
> Truly the most honorable among you in the sight of Allah
> is the most righteous of you.
> Allah has full knowledge and is well aware.
> *(Surah 49: 13)*

If it weren't for oldies rock 'n' roll playing on the radio, I don't think I'd ever muster enough energy to clean the stinking house. There's just something about "shoo-bop-shee-bop" and "ram-a-lam-a-ding-dong" that gets me into the swing of things! Rock 'n' roll is an important aspect of my time-space link!

Some deadbeat commentators would have us believe that all forms of musical expression are haram (forbidden). If God (blessed and exalted is He) disapproves of music and dance, why did He not mention it in the Qur'an? Why does He not silence the birds, crickets, and other musicians of nature? Why does He not cripple the peacocks, roosters, butterflies, and other natural-born dancers?

God (blessed!) created sound and hearing, and, as representatives of God on earth, we are destined to continue the creation by making new sounds that reflect the glory of God. He also created sight and motion, so we are destined to create poetic motion as an art form. These are not just freedoms; they are responsibilities as God's servants. God (blessed!) would count as an evil deed any involvement in music with filthy lyrics or any form of lewd dancing. It stands to reason, then, that God would bless someone for listening to symphonic music, enjoying ballet, which is poetry in motion, or enjoying a traditional heritage such as square dancing or ol' timey, cowboy music (which I love), or even classic rock with clean lyrics.

Wonderful diversity abounds in God's tapestry of humanity! Every tribe and nation can be identified by its unique food, costume, language, dance, music, and art. How sad it is, then, that deluded jurists would have societies forsake all that makes them unique and become one blended and bland tribe. Throughout history, Europeans invading other lands tried to "civilize" inhabitants by inculcating the European culture. Can you imagine a world where everyone is British? Yikes! Compare the modern, Cherokee, gambling casinos with the pictures of the fascinating, proud, and unique Cherokees sketched by artists traveling to the "New World" in the fifteenth and sixteenth centuries. Much of the Cherokee heritage of music, dance, and costume is now reserved for the entertainment of tourists rather than to glorify the Great Spirit and to honor the ancestors. What a sad loss for all humanity!

The people of Meccah and surrounding territories enjoyed music, dancing, and singing —particularly that of the Abyssinians who were invited to perform for special occasions. Prophet Muhammed (peace and blessings upon him) enjoyed music and dance.

Aisha explained, "Once on an Eid day, the Abyssinian slaves came and began dancing in the mosque. The Holy Prophet called me. I placed my head on the Holy Prophet's shoulder and watched the performance. The Holy Prophet allowed me to watch them until I became tired of watching and turned away."[70]

A woman came to the Holy Prophet, and he asked Aisha, "Do you know her?"

Aisha replied, "No, O Prophet of Allah."

The Prophet said, "This is the female, professional singer of (a certain tribe). Would you like for her to sing?"

So the singer entertained them.[71]

Anas explained, "Black slaves were dancing in front of the Messenger of Allah and singing the following words: 'Muhammed is a pious person.' The Holy Prophet didn't catch the phrase and asked what they were saying. He was told, 'They say that Muhammed is a pious person.'"[72]

People should have the right to enjoy and reflect their unique musical heritage, but some jabberwocky jurists have misunderstood and misrepresented such hadeeths as the following:

The Prophet was reported as saying, "From among my followers, some people will consider these to be lawful: immoral sex, wearing silk, drinking alcoholic beverages, and using musical instruments."[73]

I think the Prophet referred to music associated with immoral sex, drinking, slinky clothing, and, in today's world, recreational drugs. We must avoid the lifestyle associated with, for example, beer-drinking, rebel-rousing, honky-tonk music. Scholars such as Shawkawni, Ibn Hazm, Ghazalli, Abu Bakr al Arabic, and Qaradawi have all said that music, in proper context, is permissible.

The Qur'an honors David (peace!) and the Psalms, which were poetic lyrics accompanied by music. Muhammed (peace!) was reminded of the Psalms when he heard Abu Musa's prayers:

After the Prophet had heard Abu Musa Ashari beautifully and

melodically reciting his prayers and worship at night, the Prophet commented, "Abu Musa has indeed been given one of the musical wind instruments of the family of David."[74]

Music was a favorite, cultural tradition of Arabs contemporary to the Prophet (peace!). Music, songs, and dance were frequently used in worship rituals, festivals, and funerals. Singing kept cadence in times of war and in driving camels and in work-related activities. Hadeeth is plentiful in showing episodes of the Prophet's enjoyment, approval, and encouragement of music. For examples:

A slave girl belonging to Hassan ibn Thabit came to us on Eid al Fitr. Her hair was unkempt, she carried a tambourine, and she was singing. Ummi Salamah rebuked her, but the Holy Prophet said to her, "Ummi Salamah, leave her be. Certainly, every nation has a holiday, and this is our holiday."[75]

Aisha arranged the marriage of an Ansari girl. When the Holy Prophet attended the ceremony, he asked, "Have you sent forth the bride?" When they replied that they had, he asked, "Did you send a singer to accompany her?" When Aisha said that she had not, the Holy Prophet said, "The Ansar cherish singing. It would have been better if you had sent along a singer for her."[76]

When the Prophet passed by a clan of Bani Najjar, he saw some slave girls playing the daff[77] and singing, "We are the singers of Bani Najjar. We are fortunate enough to have the Prophet as our neighbor today."
The Prophet told them, "Allah knows that my heart feels affection for you people."[78]

Salama ibn al Akwa told the following story:

At night, we headed for Khaybar in the company of the Holy Prophet. A man from the group said to Amir, a Hida poet, "O Amir, will you let us hear your poetry?"
Amir began singing, "O Allah, were it not for Your guidance, we

could not have been able to offer salat and pay zakat. Please forgive our past sins and any sins we may commit in the future. We are ready to offer our lives for Your cause. Grant us perseverance when facing an enemy and pour Your mercy upon us. May we refuse to surrender when the enemy challenges us to fight; may they cry for help against us."

The Holy Prophet asked, "Who is that singer?" They told him that it was Amir bin al Akwa, and the Prophet prayed, "Allah, bless him."[79]

Imam Ghazzali, in *Alchemy of Happiness*, stated:

The hearts of men have been so constituted by the Almighty that, like a flint, it contains a hidden fire, which is invoked by music and harmony and renders a person beside himself with ecstasy. These harmonies are echoes of that higher world of beauty, which we call the world of spirits. They remind humanity of his relationship to that world and produce in him an emotion so deep and strange that he himself is powerless to explain it. The effect of music and dancing is deeper in proportion as the natures on which they act are simple and prone to emotion. They fan into flame whatever love is already dormant in the heart, whether it be earthly and sensual, or divine and spiritual.

Abul Kalaam Azad, an Islamic scholar and theologian of India, stated in *Ghubarr-e-Khaatir*:

I can always remain happy doing without the necessities of life, but I cannot live without music. A sweet voice is the support and prop of my life, a healing for my mental labors. Sweet music is the cure for all the ills and ailments of my body and heart.

There are some forms of musical expression –ie, filthy lyrics and "dirty dancing" –that are certainly degenerate and should be avoided and protested. Traditionally, however, song and dance are important aspects of every culture, and there is no genuine evidence to suggest that music and dancing are haram when performed with respect to modesty, dignity, moderation, and what is considered normal and decent in a given society.[80]

The Qur'an encourages us to study nature for God's signs; nature has the answers. When we listen to the sounds of nature, we usually find rhythmic sounds that are soothing, calming, and that speak to us of God's majesty. Our music, then, should have the same qualities. Some sounds of nature, however, are alarming and unsettling. One of the most horrendous sounds I've ever heard is the pitiful scream of a rabbit being ripped apart by a mountain lion. The high-pitched wail seems as if it could tear the sunset right out of the sky. Perhaps there are situations for which it is appropriate for music to speak to us in ways that alarm us to global tragedies, rock our souls, and roll us to action. Personally, I hate that rap crap, even when it is called *Nasheed* (Islamic music). Rap music sounds like somebody wants to shrink my head and put it on a stick. If a musician is earnestly trying to glorify God, however, whether we personally like the style, we should not judge but pray that God will use the music for good and that, if a certain style is not pleasing to God, God will help the musician to evolve his or her style into what is acceptable to God (blessed and exalted is He).

To a young Muslim confused about pop culture, I would say that the most important thing is to totally submit your whole self to God (blessed!) and to daily recommit yourself to Him. When you give every part of your life to God (blessed!), He will guide you and help you make the right choices. Obey your parents and consider the advice of your spiritually attuned elders. Every person in the family of God is on his or her own unique, spiritual journey. If you are truly living for God, you are where He wants you to be at any given time on your unique journey. Sometimes the road is not clearly marked, and you may fall into a ditch. When you have latched onto the hand of God, He will pull you up in His own time. He may allow you to stay in the ditch just long enough to see the snakes and scorpions for yourself, thereby making you wiser. He has given you wisdom and Scriptures to help you discern for yourself right and wrong. Do not be distracted by senseless ranting; keep focused on God (blessed!), and He will not forsake you.

One more point to the youth: The music you make popular today will be *your* classics of tomorrow. Choose wisely.

<blockquote>
You put words in our hearts and minds.
With words we can describe the glory of Your creation,
Our words can reflect Your glory.
</blockquote>

You put music in our hearts and minds.
With music we can echo the beauty of Heaven,
Our music can express our deepest wish.
How can someone as insignificant as me
Express the vastness and wonder of Your creation?
How can someone as imperfect as me
Dare to hope for a place in Heaven?
My only answer lies in the words and the music,
Which You Yourself have given me.
[Nanak (1469-1538), founder of the Sikh religion (India)]

90. A VEIL OF ART

To no person does Allah speak
unless by inspiration, or from behind a veil,
or by the sending of a messenger to reveal,
with Allah's permission, whatever Allah wills.
He is the Highest and Wisest!
(Surah 42: 51)

As a child, I was fascinated by a picture that hung over a mantle board in our old, family homestead. Before I was even born, Mama had gone to a church revival where the picture was displayed. The congregation was told that the picture would be given to whoever had donated the most pennies by the end of the week. Mama took in ironing and other odd jobs, and she donated all her hard-earned pennies. At the end of the weeklong revival, the picture was hers.

The serene picture illustrated Jesus (peace upon him) meditating on a hilltop overlooking Jerusalem. Soft, muted colors seemed inspired by sullen clouds crowding competitively around the moon. The picture was always out of my reach except when Mama took it down to dust and clean, and then it seemed to me like some mysterious part of Heaven had been brought down for me to experience for a moment. Now the picture hangs in my own house, and it still draws me into it with its mysteriously numinous appeal.

I never had any mental blocks to prevent me from seeing and appreciating the beauty of the artist's message or to prevent me from having the correct perspective of the illustration. When I was little, I asked my older sister if Mama's picture was really a picture of Jesus (peace!). She said, "No, it's just an artist's interpretation." I always understood that the purpose of the picture was to give a message *about* Jesus –not to *depict* Jesus himself. I grew up in a Southern Baptist church where no images were displayed –no pictures, no statues, not even a cross— in order to abide by the commandment, "Thou shalt not make unto thee any graven image, or any likeness of any thing that is in heaven above, or that is in the earth beneath, or that is in the water under the earth" (Exodus 20: 4, KJV).

The meaning of the Torah commandment was obvious one day when I had a difficult time focusing on my prayers at someone's house. On the walls, pictures of Jesus (peace!) hung right beside pictures of glorified racecar drivers and honky-tonk singers. It was a stark reminder of the idolatrous world in which we live.

Whether inside a church, synagogue, temple, or mosque, permanent portraits or figure art should not be displayed in the prayer area. A worshiper should not be distracted from contemplating his or her relationship with the awesome God (blessed and exalted is He) whose essence can never be captured or properly represented by any image. Sometimes, however, *temporary* graphics may be appropriate for educational purposes in a place of worship. Outside the places of worship, respectfully done illustrations are a visual way of communicating messages about God and His prophets and other servants.

A prominent, Islamic authority, Dr. Hasan Qazi Muizidin, reminded me that the king and prophet Solomon (peace upon him) supervised the creation of images and that "Solomon's sunnah cannot be anti-Islamic." Surah 34: 12-13 tells of the building of Solomon's temple, which contained "images" or "statues," as indicated by the Arabic word *tamasil*. Dr. Muizudin says, "Our jurists of today have already begun to point out the lapse of the earlier jurists and do sanction the permissibility of pictures, photographs, and sculptures if the images are not to be worshiped."

In the age contemporary to Prophet Muhammed (peace upon him), the pagan majority had caused a social mentality that prevented people from being able to see such images without associating them with idols and idol worship. According to Ibn Abbas, "All the idols that had been worshiped by the people of Noah were worshiped by the later Arabs. …. The names [of the idols] had been taken from pious men from among the people of Noah. When the pious men died, Satan inspired the people to make and place images at the places where the pious men used to sit. The images were called by the names of the men they represented. The images were not worshiped, however, until after all those people [contemporary to Noah] had died. The origin of the images gradually became obscure, and people began worshiping them."

Prophet Muhammed (peace!) forbade images of people and animals because the tradition of idolatry prevented the proper perspective of such art. According to some ahadeeth, he would not even allow decorative arts on cloth or furniture if the art included images of living creatures. Such restrictions on art led to the inspiration for the classic, geometric and symmetrical Islamic art.

What defines Islamic art today, however, is evolving due to inadvertent opportunities of the electro-gizmo age. Although the world still has idols, they are usually in the forms of writhing rappers, sports meatheads, and strutting celebrities. The idols of the ancient pagans are relics of a time before electricity shed light on our artificial world. Islamic artists are now liberated to incorporate all images of natural creation into their art as long as the art is done with proper respect. "If someone wants to make a picture of an animate being, with no intention of competing with God as Creator or for its [the image's] glorification or respect [beyond what is Islamicly proper], there is no prohibition of doing so; there are numerous sound traditions *(ahadeeth)* in this regard" (Yusuf al-Qaradawi).[81]

Certainly, the new art forms do not get to fly without challenge and controversy by conservatives who believe that tradition should dictate what defines Islamic art. Such critics recite conventional Islamic laws forbidding representations of humans and animals. In his article "Challenge of Conservatism," Maqbool Ahmed Siraj advises the ultra-conservative reactionary:

> To err on the conservative side is considered a great merit in matters of interpreting Islam, among clergy in India. They vie with each other to produce a more-conservative-than-thou interpretation, no matter how out of sync it is with the time and society [in which] the Muslims are living. The clergy generally treats the new technologies with utter disdain. When cameras arrived a century ago, photography was declared *haram* (illegitimate) by the conservative ulema.

Over the century, this interpretation was extended to television, cinematography, videography, animation, and cartoons. Cue is mostly taken from the Prophet's prohibition of making images of living objects. Perhaps the holy Prophet [peace upon him] wanted to warn his followers of dangers inherent in sculpting idols. The clergy needed to ask the simple question [of whether] the Prophet made the mirror a taboo. To the contrary, he often carried a mirror, among his personal belongings, to dress himself. Isn't it that the new technology is nothing but a production of image which can be preserved, printed, digitized, embossed, engraved, or transferred into so many other forms and useful purposes? There was need to be guided by the saying in which the Prophet [peace!] encouraged girls to have dolls as they learnt cultural mores. He would not have certainly meant cutting the Muslims away from cultural, scientific, and educational benefits of emerging technologies.

The Prophet (peace!), I think, would not want to deprive Muslims of the sensitivity and beauty of Islamic artists glorifying God by reminding art appreciators of the variety of His creation. Adrienne Haywood-James pointed out, "Intent, for many, is what defines the contemporary Muslim artist's platform. Islam defines intent [according to a hadeeth]: 'Deeds are considered by intention, and everyone will be requited according to what he intends. He, whose intention is to please Allah and His messenger, will be rewarded for pleasing Allah and His messenger' [Bukhari]."[82]

Modern technologies of printing and publishing, photography, video imaging, television, and the internet have made images an important and unavoidable part of our lives. Pictures of various leaders appear on banknotes and coins and on office walls. Portraits of major figures from Shi'ite history are important elements of Shi'ite observances, and such portraits adorn both public and private areas. Reportedly, a fatwa issued by Grand Ayatollah Sistani (Iraq) even allows depictions of Muhammed and other prophets (peace upon them) as long as the pictures are made with the utmost respect. The Muslim community must be reminded never to fall prey to the temptation to idolize any such depictions. The purpose of such art should be for illustration rather than adoration.

Mama's picture of Jesus (peace!) was not an idolatrous image; rather the painting illustrated the passionate rumination of Jesus over his beloved

Jerusalem. The illustration instills in the viewer a sense of calm and peace despite the encroaching shadows of gloom, and it encourages hope to pensive souls. Such art provides a veil through which God (blessed!) may speak to the viewer who sincerely seeks the message the artist tries to convey.

Although anyone can become skilled in artistic techniques and use of tools and materials, the sensitive, creative aspect of art is a natural talent that cannot be learned; therefore, being an artist is a gift of nature, and the signs of God are imbedded in nature. Certainly natural talent can be misused, but it is the duty of a believing artist to use his or her talents to glorify God (blessed!). That does not mean that an artist cannot make a living in, for example, advertising, but it does mean that the artist must be conscientious about what product or service is being advertised. For example, advertising *safe* tires is in keeping with God's glory; advertising *inferior* tires is not, if the artist knows or should reasonably suspect that the tires may be dangerous. A Muslim artist, then, can serve God (blessed!) while working in non-religious commercial or graphic arts as long as aspects of the specific projects are not incongruous with the divine treasure.

Religiously inspired, Islamic artists of the visual arts include decorative designers and crafters, calligraphers, and illustrators. Of these, illustrators (like me) are the ones most often attacked. "Artists will be the first to go to Hell!" an irate Muslim announced to an artist in Washington, DC. The Muslim artist soon learned to keep his art a secret from other Muslims. A publisher of Islamic books lost money on a series of illustrated, children's books that told stories about the lives of some of the prophets. Some of the books were returned with nasty notes about the evils of drawing pictures of the prophets, even though the pictures were simply vague, suggestive images used in illustrating events in the prophets' lives. Many readers lacked the reasoning skills to be able to differentiate between images to be idolized and illustrations that served as veils through which God (blessed!) may remind us of the love He sent the world through the ministries of His prophets (peace!)

God is the Master Artist (blessed and exalted is He), and, in His wisdom, He has chosen human artists to illuminate His messages. Visual images have the ability to permeate souls encrusted with the glitz and debris of a chaotic world. Art inspired by God (blessed!) is a veil of energy, color, and composition. The divine voice travels with the speed of light, from every artistic stroke to the eye of each beholder, and echoes in the chambers of minds emptied of vain thoughts and ready to be filled with the Master's pictographic sonnets.

> O Lord who is the all-pervading glory of the world,
> We bless You for the power of beauty to gladden our hearts.
> We praise You that even the least of us may feel a thrill
> Of Your creative joy
> When we give form and substance to our thoughts and,
> Beholding our handiwork, find it good and fair.
> We praise You for artists, the masters of form and color and sound,
> Who have the power to unlock for us the vaster spaces of emotion
> And to lead us by their own hands into the reaches of nobler passions.
> We rejoice in their gifts and pray that You spare them
> From the temptations that may beset their talents and skills.
> Kindle in their hearts a passionate pity for the joyless lives of others,
> And make them rejoice when they are worthy
> To hold the cup of beauty to thirsty lips.
> Allow the artists to be reverent interpreters of God to Humanity.
> Bless them for seeing Your face and hearing Your voice in all things.
> Help them unveil for others the natural beauties
> That are often passed unseen
> And the sadness and sweetness of Humanity
> To which our selfishness has made us blind.
> [Adapted from a prayer by Walter Rauschenbusch (1861-1918),
> Baptist minister (USA)]

91. HE SPOKE IN SUNLIGHT

> If all the trees on earth were pens
> supplied by the ocean plus seven more oceans,
> the Words of Allah would not become exhausted.
> Allah is Victorious, the Perfectly Wise.
> *(Surah 31: 27)*

In southeastern USA, swamp waters are blackened from the inky, tannic acid, and cypress trees are perched like fountain pens in wells of murky water. Draped with feathery, Spanish moss flagging in a summer breeze, the trees remind of quill pens. I think of the scene as God's own illustration of the above passage from the Qur'an.

The "ocean" refers collectively to the five oceans. With modern knowledge of the globe, we now know the significance of the number in "seven more oceans." If the *seven* continents were replaced with liquid so that our entire planet was covered in ink, there would not be enough ink to document all the knowledge and wisdom of God.

The Qur'anic verse inspired me, and I began a landscape of the cypress trees in the Carolina swamps. I covered the canvas with color as I painted the sky and water. While that was drying, I sketched the trees onto layout paper so that I could transfer the carefully planned drawing onto the painted background. I was using photographs from a magazine, and I noticed an unusual, bare branch on one of the trees. The shape of the branch was very similar to the Arabic script for the name of Muhammed (peace and blessings upon him). I decided to add that odd branch into my painting as a sign that Muhammed (peace!) had indeed washed his soul in the baptism of the Living Water and that he was the instrument through which God inked the Qur'an.

Later in the day, I noticed that the evening sunlight streaming through my studio window had splashed itself in a graceful array on the canvas. Shimmering through the leaves on the trees outside my studio, the sun danced on the oil rendering of water and bore an amazing resemblance to the Arabic word for *God*. Just days earlier, I had read an article that presented the question of what defines Islamic art. As I sketched the Arabic *Allah* onto my painting, I thought, Allah (blessed and exalted is He) defines His art. I painted *Allah* as a reflection on the water beneath the setting sun in my painting. The finished painting was a remarkable testament to God's creative majesty.

"If you tried to write a list of His wonders, there would not be enough space. If you tried to tell of them in a story, there would not be enough words" [Psalms 40: 6 (40: 5, Christian Bible)].

God's infinite Word cannot be confined to paper and ink and bound within a single Book. The Universal Qur'an, with all its majesty and holiness, is a love letter from an endless volume of sonnets. The power of God's Word is not derived from the printed pages, but from the breath of the

Divine Presence speaking to each individual soul and giving life to the revealed Words. All the preaching in the world cannot activate the Words for one who refuses to listen to the still, quiet Voice of the Creator. We must preach beautiful sermons, in deeds as well as words, and then trust God (blessed!) to inscribe His Words on the hearts of the wise. But first, we must listen ourselves, and we must also look and find God's illustrations all around us.

"If you tried to count Allah's blessings, you would not be able to number them all. Allah is the Most Forgiving, the Most Merciful" (Surah 16: 18).

> Blessed Creator, You are the Merciful One
> Whose bounty cannot be measured.
> Help me, not to simply read, but to experience
> The Living Word You have revealed
> And also to hear Your quiet voice
> Speaking endless Words to my soul.
> All that I am is by Your grace alone.
> I present my hands into Your hands.
> I present the work of my hands into Your will.
> Guide my thoughts and hold my hands.

May whatever I write, draw, or mold be truly Yours.
Thank You for talent, inspiration, and discipline.
Take me into Your loving embrace
And make me fully Yours.

92. ROTTEN APPLES OF APOSTASY

Certainly, those who believe, and then disbelieve,
and then believe again, and then disbelieve,
and then continually increase their doubts will not be forgiven by Allah.
He will not guide them on their journey.
To such hypocrites, give the good news that a dreadful penalty awaits them.
(Surah 4: 137-138)

One early fall morning I had a hankering for an apple, but the orchard was already bare. I had a half-Schnauzer, half-mutt dog named 'Trash'; Tom had found her as a pup inside a sealed box discarded in the county dump. (Some people are so sub-barbarian!) I stood on the front porch with Trash and stared down at the barren orchard. I said, "Trash, I sure would like to have an apple right about now." The dog perked up, looked beyond the orchard, and then took off. I didn't think much of it, but I probably should have. In the past, Trash had brought home somebody's shoes, several craft projects from a Bible school class, and a huge, juicy steak with grill marks on the bottom.

About an hour later, I looked out the window and saw Trash struggling to drag something up the driveway. "What in the heck is she dragging home now?" I walked outside, across the yard, and met Trash halfway down the driveway. She had a full bag of apples in a grocer's mesh sack! The apples were battered from being dragged down the road, through the woods, across the creek, and up the driveway, but what more could anybody expect from a mutt named Trash?

I not only had an apple for a snack, but there were also enough apples for a pie. It was days later before I had a chance to make the pie, and I began by peeling the apples. There were bruises evident on the outsides, so I cut away those places. I cut the apples in half and found worms in some seed cavities. I carved out the seed cavities and any places the worms had made messy. Bruises on the insides had started to rot, so I cut away those places. Some apples already had rotten spots that were infesting other apples. I finally gave up on the pie. I had only enough to make a small dish of stewed apples.

Backsliding does the same thing to people. Some people are so weak that if they get a few bruises on the outside, they push Islam aside. They may come back eventually, but sometimes those old bruises begin to rot, and the flippant, half-believers forsake Islam again. They may return for a while, but by then the worms of a perverse lifestyle have begun eating away at everything central to true faith. Their doubts only increase, and they are of no value to the Ummah. In fact, they create only confusion and chaos and even endanger the faith of others —just like the rot of one apple can infect an entire sack of apples.

The issue of how Muslims should respond to apostasy is controversial. Some believe that apostates should be punished by death. They cite specific examples in which apostates were put to death during the time of Prophet Muhammed (peace and blessings upon him). One example is Sahih Bokhari, a Jew who accepted Islam, and later reverted to Judaism. Another example is that of a female apostate, Umm Marwan, who fought in the battle of Uhad. In these examples and others, however, the apostates were not put to death because of their apostasy, but because they had joined forces with the enemies at war against the Muslims. They had committed dangerous acts of treason and aggression in a time of war.

The Qur'an does not command death for an apostate; instead, it proposes religious freedom. There are also a great many Sunnah stories that indicate that apostates should not be punished. One such story is that of Abdullah bin Saad. He accepted Islam and became a Qur'anic scribe, but later he apostatized and fled to Meccah where he ridiculed Islam and defamed the Prophet (peace and blessings upon him). When Meccah was conquered on the 9th of Hijri, Abdullah bin Saad was captured, and some of the Prophet's companions insisted on his execution. Instead, however, the Prophet pardoned him.

After the conquest of Meccah, about twelve apostates were captured. Only four of them were beheaded, not because of apostasy, but because of acts of treason and violence against the Muslims. The Prophet (peace!) pardoned the others, who had acted peacefully toward the Muslims even after the apostates had returned to their former faiths.

The treaty of Hudaibiah included a provision whereby, if a person from Medina should abandon Islam and seek refuge with the pagan Quraysh in Meccah, he would be allowed the freedom to do so.

When the direction of prayer changed from Jerusalem to the Ka'bah, many Muslims were so shocked that they left Islam, but none of them were punished.

A man named Mujah, part of the delegation of the king of Yamamah; a Christian lady named Waled; and a man named Jalas are just a few of the many apostates who were not punished but were allowed religious freedom. Only dangerous hate-mongrels and riot-inciters were ever punished.

The enemies of Islam tell a great many rotten lies about Islam and about Muhammed (peace and blessings upon him). We must diligently cut out the lies and replace them with truth. If we don't, the image of Islam will continue to rot in the eyes of non-Muslims, and there won't be enough good reputation left even to bake a peace pie.

> O Allah,
> I am your servant,
> Son of Your male servant,
> And son of Your female servant.
> My forehead is in Your hand.
> Your judgment is exact;
> Your decision about me is just.
> I ask You, by every name of Yours,
> By which You have called Yourself,
> Or revealed in a Book of Yours,
> Or taught to any of Your servants,
> Or reserved within Your unrevealed knowledge,
> To make the Qur'an a spring to my heart,
> A light in my chest,
> That it may remove my sadness
> And erase my anguish.
> *[Prophet Muhammed (peace and blessings upon him)]*

93. THE E PLURIBUS UNUM CONNECTION

> Truly, as for those who have divided their religion into sects,
> do not participate with them.
> Their matter is with Allah. He will tell them what they did.
> *(Surah 6: 159)*

One morning, I was awakened early by a frantic commotion of birds. I got up and looked out the window. A long, blacksnake was wrapped around a tree branch and was inching his way toward a robins' nest. Birds of all colors had united in one big effort to give that snake a fit. They were swooping and diving and pecking and clawing at the slinking menace. Even the blue jays –known for disrupting other birds' nests— had joined the jihad of protecting the robins' eggs. I decided to join the jihad too! I went outside and got the water hose, adjusted the nozzle to "blast," and blasted the snake. The birds' clamor became more excited as they cheered for me. The snake finally gave up, slithered back down from the tree, and crawled under the tool shed in disgrace.

We humans should take the birds' ummah as an example of how we should protect one another from the evils around us. Instead of squabbling over differences, we must unite in a jihad against every slinking menace.

A grownup Tana went to the local video store and chose a movie with "adult language and themes" (whatever that means). Frieda Watcher, the storeowner, said, "Tana, you put that movie back right now!"

Tana protested, "I'm over eighteen!"

Frieda said, "I don't care if you're thirty-eighteen. Your mama doesn't want you watching a trashy movie like that, and I'm not renting it to you."

Frieda was not a Muslim, but right then she was part of my ummah. She was looking out for my kid and my family values. Of course, it would have been even better if Frieda had looked out for everyone by not having such a movie available in the first place. Frieda was like a destructive blue jay helping protect a robins' nest. All people need to hold themselves responsible for safeguarding the moral and ethical values of one another regardless of individual religious differences.

While not making a judgment about those who follow the teachings of a certain sect of Islam, I never give a straight answer when someone asks me, "What kind of Muslim are you?"

Usually I answer, "I don't know, but if you can tell me what kind of Muslims Abraham, Jesus and his disciples, and Muhammed were (peace upon them all), I think I can figure it out."

If I'm having a weird, brain-scrambling kind of time, I say, "Well, I've been spinning in circles all day, so I think I might be one of those Whirling Dervishes."

After praying, I came out of the woods with dirt on my forehead and knees. Imam Etsamah Dudi was visiting and asked me, "Are you a mystic?"

I said, "No, I'm just a crazy woman who prays in the woods."

God (blessed and exalted is He) didn't call me into a sect; He simply invited me into the Light of Islam. It's okay to belong to a group of like-minded believers, but when the differences split the religion into warring factions, Muslims are simply aiding and abetting our enemies.

There are four ways one can divide the religion: (1) accept some aspects of the religion and flush other aspects down the black hole; (2) act piously on special days and live like a hell-cat on other days; (3) separate one's life or society so that some areas are regulated by religious values and other parts by blast-it-all-to-hell values; (4) focus on sectarian differences so as to blow the unity of the universal Ummah into smithereens.

Islam cannot bandage and heal the world while the Ummah suffers from continuously infected, self-inflicted wounds. Islam in America cannot grow into a healthy, blossoming plant while thorny weeds sap nutrients from the soil of fertile minds. We cannot yank up the weeds without damaging the roots of established Islam, but we can clip the weeds at the soil line and continue clipping them until the roots simply starve. What I mean is: we can't knock off all the Muslims who focus on differences, but we can cut them off —stop paying attention to their divisive rhetoric— until they change their focus to reconciliation, unity, and understanding.

Muslims in America must unite in a dynamic way, and here is my suggestion: As Islam is in its pioneering stage in America, I think that we Muslims should follow the example of those successful, early pioneers who settled in America where they could live, worship, and work together, by the grace of God, in a self-sustaining society. Religious groups of Mormons, Mennonites, Quakers, Waldensians, Moravians, Amish, and others established independent communities governed by each group's religious values and ethics. They had their own churches, farms, stores, and businesses.

Hundreds of lovely, wooded acres are for sale in North Carolina and other beautiful states. Muslims could buy such land and collectively invest in and begin establishing an Islamic village. Inhabitants would share community gardens for fruits and vegetables; barns and pastures for raising goats and cows for milk; hens for eggs, and emus for meat; support their own entrepreneurial shops and businesses, including Islamic arts and crafts studios; and in other ways they would establish a halal lifestyle. The village could be started by Muslims whose children are grown. They could begin by setting up a 'camper village' and purchasing bulldozers, cement mixers, and other equipment and building supplies. Participants could live in campers while they planned and physically built a permanent settlement. When the village is well established, younger Muslims could begin moving in as a school, recreational center, and other family-oriented facilities are prepared.

The idea of putting the community back into communion is a solution that would benefit all of America. American neighborhoods with community gardens, farms, shops, etc in which everyone has a contributory share would give each individual a purpose that would help direct him or her away from crime and moral corruption. By establishing such Islamic villages, Muslims could create the model community for all peace-loving Americans regardless of religion.

Islamic land in America? Are we just going to dream about it and talk about it and write books about it? Pioneers, stop dreaming and start swinging. It's time to begin trailblazing a path to the future of Islam. Put your differences aside and cooperate in a united effort. "E Pluribus Unum" ("Out of many, we are one") is not just the motto of the United States; it is an ideal of Islam. "Truly, this, your community, is one community, and I am your Lord, so worship Me!" (Surah 21: 92).

> Send Your peace, O Lord,
> Which is perfect and everlasting,
> So that our souls may radiate peace.
> Send Your peace, O Lord,
> So that we may think, act, and speak harmoniously.
> Send Your peace, O Lord,
> So that we may be contented and thankful
> For Your bountiful gifts.
> Send Your peace, O Lord,
> So that amid our worldly strife,
> We may enjoy Your bliss.
> Send Your peace, O Lord,
> So that we may endure all, tolerate all,
> In the thought of Your grace and mercy.

Send Your peace, O Lord,
So that our lives may become a divine vision,
And in Your light, may all darkness vanish.
Send Your peace, O Lord, our Father and Mother,
So that we, Your children on Earth,
May all unite in one family.
*["Prayer for Peace" by Pir-o-murshid Inayat Khan (1882-1927),
Sufi musician (India)]*

94. DON'T SETTLE FOR INTERCESSORY MOON-SIGHTING

We have measured for the moon phases until it returns [appearing curved] like an old, dried-out date stalk.
(Surah 36: 39)

A hillbilly in Chicago, I was introduced to some new things (well, they were new to me): push-button coffee with pre-measured sugar and cream, suited to an average of tastes; doughnuts filled with a generic jelly that had an apple-cherry-grape blend of flavors, suited to an average of tastes. These are just a couple examples of the artificial and commercial world in which we live —a world that lacks the personal touch that each of us craves.

The Qur'an urges us to get in touch with nature in order to see and understand God's signs, but many of us rely on intercessors instead of experiencing nature for ourselves. Instead of participating with the earth to raise our own vegetables, we have made the grocer our intercessor, and most of our groceries are suited to an average of tastes. Commercial apples, for example, have been genetically altered to combine flavors into a standard apple that looks good and has a long shelf life.[83] Instead of wading through feral, nature-hugging streams or climbing rugged, cloud-kissed mountains or traversing the mysterious depths of ethereal seas, we depend on PBS as our intercessor. Instead of sharing a breath of frosty, morning air face-to-face with wild creatures, we allow the wildlife photographer to be our intercessor. Instead of exercising our natural, creative skills by, for example, making our own clothes, we use Walmart as an intercessor.

By being out of touch with nature, intercessor-dependent people are out of touch with God as the Creator (*Al Khaliq*). One of the results of this is a lack of imagination. For example, if there is need for only one generic apple, there is no need for the imagination to produce varieties; therefore, the divine gift of imagination remains dormant and eventually dries and desiccates. One of the greatest links we have to God (blessed and exalted is He), as beings made in His numinous image, is imagination. As God's representatives on Earth, it is our duty to exercise our imaginations in order to protect, sustain, and evolve the creation in such areas as engineering conservation programs, managing and respectfully using natural resources, improving life through discoveries in science and medicine, and creating new sounds (music), new forms (art), and new motions (dance and drama).

I believe our intercessor-dependency is one reason for crime. At a Muslim convention, I witnessed something rather shocking. I was helping attend the exhibit for the Zakat Foundation and was busy speaking with visitors. I noticed a woman entering the exhibit area, but it was common for visitors to enter the exhibit to see things displayed on tables. Suddenly, the woman reached between the curtains separating the exhibits, and, in a split second, she was running down the aisle, carrying a dress on a hanger. She disappeared into the crowd before I realized what had happened. The vendor of the adjoining booth was selling dresses from a rack along the curtained divider. I reported the incident to the merchant, and he determined that the woman had ripped away a 400-dollar dress. How does that relate to intercessor-dependency? I think it unlikely for a person to have stolen the dress if she had ever plowed and planted a field of cotton or tended a silkworm farm, pulled the shuttle of a loom, or used her own hands to sew a dress and tediously stitch the beads and sequins into an intricate design. When we are too far removed from nature and creativity, we are distanced from our natural instinct to follow God's will.

The moon offers a fascinating adventure to envelope us in God's creativity. As the Qur'an poetically describes, the moon makes its choreographed journey, lodging in the twenty-eight stellar "mansions"[84] of the Zodiac. Finally it appears to us as a thin, curved remnant, which is also the shape of an old, dry, withered date stalk or palm leaf. The moon's journey is a sign that we too should seek God's mansions of wisdom and enlightenment as we each travel on a personal spiritual journey until we return to Him as withered souls seeking His grace in the gift of salvation.

The arguments about the moonsighting for events and seasons distract us from the more significant message of God's omnipotence. Because it has no beginning and no end, the perfect circle etched into the sky by the full moon symbolizes God's eternal quality. When we see only the sliver of moon in the sky, we are reminded that what we know of God (blessed!) is only a fraction of what truly exists, the unseen mystery. As we watch the lunar phases, we are reminded that, as we sojourn on the spiritual path, God reveals more of Himself to us. When we see the full moon, we realize that in eternity we will see God as He truly is and experience His glory in all its wonderful fullness. Acknowledging the dark side of the moon, we consider that certainly there are mysteries of God that may never be known to us.

The science of astronomy is a gift from God (blessed!), and we should make wise use of it, but the astronomer should not serve as an intercessor that prevents a person from experiencing a personal, numinous, lunar landing. Seek the sliver of moon for yourself and remember how you were once an infant just beginning an adventure in life. As the moon swims through its phases, let the mystic moonlight paint you with meditations of all the times God has met your extended hand with His full embrace. Remember when you came walking to Him, and He came running to you. And finally, let the thin, curved return of the moon remind you of the Day of Resurrection, which is a day of hope and a new beginning for all those who stay in touch with the Creator (blessed and exalted is He).

"Ramadan is the month in which was revealed the Qur'an. The Qur'an is guidance for humanity. It is evidence of that guidance and a criterion [for knowing right from wrong]. Every available person should spend the month fasting. A person who is sick or traveling may substitute other days. Allah wants to help you and not make things difficult for you to complete the given number of days for His glory and to increase your gratitude. You should be grateful for that" (Surah 2: 185).

In the phrase "every available person," *available* is translated from the word *shahida*, which means 'presence, knowledge, and declaration'. Abdulla Yusuf Ali translates it, "…every one of you who is present (at his home) during that month…." Zafar Ishaque Ansari translates it, "…those of you who live to see that month…."

I prefer to think of "every available person" as referring to anyone with presence of mind to seek the spiritual as well as physical bounties within God's creation. Such a person seeks knowledge to make rational conclusions concerning God's signs. He or she strives to be a living declaration (a testimony) to others of God's Living Word that continues to be recited by all the majestic wonders of His endless universe.

Prophet Muhammed (peace and blessings upon him) said, "Fast with sighting [the moon] and break the fast with sighting it. If it is cloudy, complete thirty days of [the month of] Sha'aban."[85] Even the cloud-covered moon reminds us that there are times when knowledge and understanding are hidden from us, but when we stay focused on His will even in uncertain times, we will see the clouds depart and His radiance come forth.

For your personal moon-sighting adventure, find a cornfield and sit in it; take some doughnuts filled with real jelly. Plan a picnic and take the family into the country. Strap on a backpack and climb a mountain. Or pray on a silent hillside with your friends. Step away from your artificial world, absorb creation, and imagine.

> I am thankful for the moon and the night sky.
> The moon is a symbol for the complete circle of life.
> As I gaze upon the moon's craters and shadows,
> I lift my heart in a prayer of thanksgiving for all cosmic miracles.
> *[inspired by "For the Moon" by Alice Springs (Australia)]*[86]

95. THE GREAT ISLAMIC SMOKE-OUT

> O Believers, do not squander your collective resources in vain.
> Promote commerce with mutual good will.
> Do not destroy yourselves. Truly, Allah has been Most Merciful to you.
> *(Surah 4: 29)*

As a kid, my brother Ron got caught smoking Daddy's cigarettes. Daddy then made him sit in a chair and smoke one cigarette after another. Ron turned green, was so sick he was moaning, and was woozy from all the halogen-laden smoke surrounding his fat head. That taught me a lesson: don't get caught. I always hid behind a blackberry bush in the field and rolled my own rabbit tobacco. I turned green enough from that. (If you don't know what rabbit tobacco is, I can't explain the yuckiness of it. Just don't smoke anything you find growing wild in a field.)

After developing heart disease and emphysema, Daddy himself stopped smoking. After having smoked most of his life, however, Daddy still died from tobacco-related illnesses. Just three years later, Mama died too. Although she never smoked, her cancer was likely caused by years of recycling Daddy's exhaled cigarette smoke into her own lungs.

Tobacco claims the lives of over five million people per year, globally. In the USA, 1,200 Americans die per day because of smoking. In 2005, the tobacco industry spent fifteen billion dollars on advertising to keep people smoking and to attract more people to fill their bodies with slow-death poisons.

Is smoking a sin? I think so, and here are seven reasons why.

1. You have no right to pollute what rightfully belongs to God (blessed and exalted is He). Cigarettes contain 600 ingredients that are poisonous or emit poisonous fumes when burning. One of these is ammonia, which is deviously added by the manufacturers in order to make your brain absorb more nicotine, thereby strengthening addiction's possession of you. If you submit your whole self to God, your body —as well as your heart, mind, and soul— belongs to God (blessed!). Do not ruin God's property.

2. Addiction to tobacco products is a form of idolatry. You cannot be a servant of God and also a slave to cigarettes or other tobacco products. We are assigned the responsibility of being ambassadors for God. How can you adequately represent God (blessed!) if you have smoke boiling out of your nose as if you're a demon from Hell?

3. Wasting property is a sin. The average addict spends $1200 annually on tobacco products. Your personal resources are part of the collective resources of your local ummah and the global Ummah, and you do not have the right to waste the Ummah's property on vanities.

4. You are ordered, "Do not destroy yourselves." Some translators depict the ayat, "Do not destroy (or kill) one another." It is predicted that within this century, over 500 million people will die from diseases directly related to tobacco products. Smokers are not only killing themselves, but are also killing those around them. If a non-smoker has to continually be subjected to another's cigarette smoke, the effect is as if the non-smoker smoked three cigarettes per week. That includes the innocent child of smoking parents! Babies of smoking parents are more likely to die of sudden infant-

death syndrome and suffer from respiratory problems. Even in-door pets have been known to develop cancers and other diseases due to their owners' smoking. Tobacco products, including snuff and chewing tobacco, kill more people than AIDS, murder, suicide, fire, alcoholic beverages, and illegal drugs *combined*. Tobacco products are the #1 cause of preventable deaths. More Americans have been killed by tobacco products than by the terrorists targeted by the current war on terror; yet, the federal government refuses to initiate a war against the tobacco companies.

5. Use of tobacco products means that you are funding a demonic organization. By purchasing tobacco products, you are contributing to the corrupt, greedy, spiteful, despicable, and devious tobacco industry, which uses deceptive manipulation to gain new suckers as their products are destroying their current consumers. The tobacco industry was the #1 contributor in the 1996 and 2000 US Presidential elections. Many politicians are slaves to the tobacco industry, and that is a huge reason that tobacco products are still legal to manufacture, promote, and distribute, even though they are killing American citizens every day. As more Americans wise-up, however, American tobacco companies target people in countries even less active in educating their citizens about the dangers of tobacco use.

6. It is a sin to waste time. Purchasing a tobacco product, opening the package, removing the product, and sticking the tobacco or snuff inside your cheek; or sticking the cigarette or cigar in your mouth, and then striking a match or using a lighter to initiate the death-sparks; and then spitting or puffing are all a frivolous waste of time, and Muslims are commanded not to waste anything the Creator (blessed!) has given us.

7. Smoking demonstrates a lack of love and mercy. Smoking is anti-social and is a form of hate as it shows disregard for the safety and comfort of others. Thanks to anti-smoking campaigns and laws, four out of five people in the USA do not smoke, and most of these cannot tolerate cigarette or cigar smoke. Even in countries less active in promoting the anti-smoking cause, two out of three do not smoke. It is now common for restaurants and other public places to ban smoking, and if you are a smoker, your employer may assign you an outdoor site to confine your smoking. That's because nobody wants you around with your stinking cigarettes! Wise up!

The mouth is a gatekeeper for the body. Nobody smokes his or her first cigarette, chews his or her first wad of tobacco, or tastes his or her first shot of whiskey and is pleased with the taste. The taste buds say, "Spit it out!"

First-timers should listen to their mouths. Likewise, the nose detects the unpleasant fumes and odors and is repulsed. The nose knows!

I cringe when I hear TV news reporters describe Ramadan as "a time when Muslims refrain from eating, drinking, and smoking." Smoking? Muslims shouldn't be smoking in the first place! Giving up cigarettes for Ramadan, and then going back to them after Ramadan makes as much sense as wallowing in depravity during the Mardi Gras with the intention of asking for forgiveness when the party is over. Believers (of all faiths) should be better than that. If you are a smoker, consider one aspect of Ramadan as the Great Islamic Smoke-Out, and quit for good.

> O Lord, forgive me for my sins, my ignorance, my excesses,
> And that of which You know more than I do.
> O Lord, forgive me for my wealth, my error, my intention,
> And all that is within me.
> O Lord, forgive me for what I have done
> And for what I have not done,
> For what I have kept secret
> And for what I have done openly.
> You are my God! No god is there but You!
> *[Prophet Muhammed (peace and blessings upon him)]*

96. THE CONFUSED HAJJI

> Safa and Marwah are among the symbols of Allah.
> Those who visit the (Holy Mosque) during the pilgrimage
> or at other times may walk around (the hills).
> They have not sinned [as pagans did in the past].
> Whoever obeys his/her own good conscience can be assured that
> Allah is Appreciative and Aware.
> *(Surah 2: 158)*

My son Duston went on hajj, but instead of getting my son back, I got a bald, bearded man in a dress. Dusty had gone early for hajj, so he was able to associate with the people and absorb some of the culture. After visiting a street market, he returned to his hotel room and showed his purchases to his roommate.

"Look at this thobe!" Dusty said. "This is what the Arab men wear. Isn't it great!"

The roommate was impressed. "I'd like to have one of those."

"Well, let's go get you one," Dusty invited. He removed his American clothes and put on the thobe.

As the two strange Americans made their way to the street market, everyone was friendly, but people were especially friendly to Dusty.

"Look how everyone smiles extra big when they see me," Dusty bragged. "It's because I'm dressed like an Arab. We need to get you one of these thobes so you'll fit in too."

The roommate was excited as they approached a vendor selling clothes. "Do you have any thobes?" the roommate asked.

"No," the street vendor answered, and then pointed to Dusty; "but I have pajamas like he's wearing."

Dusty finally got a real thobe and proudly wore it several days before he was advised that he was supposed to wear pants under it.

It may be a no-no to think of God having a good, belly laugh, but God (blessed and exalted is He) created laughter (Surah 53: 43). I imagine that He is occasionally humored when He studies the living cartoon characters He has created. It's comforting to know that, as long as we are doing the best we can and obeying our own good consciences, God (blessed!) is not going to squash us for goofing up. "Whoever obeys his/her own good conscience can be assured that Allah is Appreciative and Aware." Those words are especially comforting for people like me who try to live righteously but can't seem to fit into the boxes that others have made for them. God's gift of laughter is good medicine for those who manage to find the funny side of life's glitches.

> Dear Lord, it seems as if You are so madly in love with Your people
> That You would not want to live without us.
> You created us with our peculiarities and quirks.
> You made us able to laugh and be goofy.
> And you loved us every one.
> When we turned away from You, You warned us,

And when we repented, You forgave us.
Yet You are God and really have no need of us.
Your greatness is made no greater by our creation.
Your power is made no stronger by our repentance.
You have no duty to forgive us, no debt to repay us.
It is love, and love alone, that moves You.
Help us become more deserving of Your amazing love.
[Patterned after a prayer by Catherine of Siena (c. 1347-1380)]

97. THUMBS UP FOR ABRAHAM

When (Abraham's son) had attained an accountable age,
(Abraham) told him, "O my son,
I have seen a vision in which I offer you in sacrifice.
What is your opinion?"
"O my father, do as you are commanded.
You will discover, Allah willing, that I will be loyal."
(Surah 37: 102)

Tom and I needed an acre cleared for planting our orchard. We called Stumpy Whackfield to bring his bulldozer. We showed Stumpy what we wanted cleared, and I specifically said, "Go just to that longleaf pine tree and no farther." I went into the house and settled at my drawing board.

An hour or so later, Stumpy banged on my door to get paid for his work. I went out to take a look. My pine tree was gone! "Good grief, Stumpy," I said. "What happened to my longleaf pine?"

"You mean that ol' scraggly, lopsided pine?" Stumpy drawled. "I dug a hole and buried that thang."

"It wasn't lopsided," I argued. "It was asymmetrical. It was artistic."

Stumpy scratched his gourd head. "Well, darlin'," he said, "if that's the case, I sure have buried a lot of art in my time."

Perspective! Perspective is important in picking which trees to spare, and it's also a valuable asset in religion.

On the tenth day of the Islamic month Dhul-Hijjah, Muslims celebrate Eid al-Adha, the Festival of the Sacrifice, following the time of hajj. Every Muslim, who is financially and physically able, is expected to make this pilgrimage at least once in a lifetime. Whether or not a Muslim physically undertakes the hajj, however, the spirit of hajj leads the soul on a journey of renewed commitment to the God of Abraham. It is in commemoration of Abraham's willingness to obey God that Eid al-Adha is observed.

According to the Qur'an, God tested Abraham's obedience by commanding him in a vision to sacrifice his son. Both Abraham and his son (peace upon them) submitted to God's will. Just as the sacrifice was about to be executed, a divine voice called out, "O Abraham, you have already fulfilled the vision." A ram was then provided for the sacrifice as the son's life was spared. As Muslims observe the significance of this event in terms of commitment, obedience, and self-sacrifice, traditionally each Muslim sacrifices a food animal, but necessities equal to the cost of a food animal are also acceptable. He or she donates one third of the sacrifice to the poor, gives one third to friends and relatives, and keeps one third for the personal household.

The Biblical version of Abraham's test is similar to the Qur'anic version, and the Talmud (the Jewish book of rabbinic writings) garnishes the message of sacrifice. According to the Talmud, the wicked angel Samael taunted Abraham and warned him that, after the sacrifice, God (blessed!) would accuse Abraham (peace!) of murder. "Even so," Abraham answered, "I must obey."

Frustrated with Abraham, Samael went to Abraham's son and said, "Son of an unhappy mother, your father is going to slay you."

The son responded, "Nevertheless, I must submit."

The *akedah* motif, the sacrificial ram's horns caught in the bush, has become a symbol of Jewish martyrdom and self-sacrifice. Abraham's willingness to serve God at any cost is an important part of the celebrations of Rosh Hashanah, the Jewish New Year.

The story of Abraham and his son (peace!) is also important to Christians as the ministry of Jesus is interpreted as a reflection of the Abrahamic story of sacrifice. Jesus (peace!) is called "the Lamb" whose physical image was sacrificed for the atonement of sins. This follows the Jewish tradition of a sin sacrifice in which the death of an animal —the pitiful moans, the profusion of blood, and the gaunt stare of death— is a reminder of humanity's sins and our constant need of repentance. Christians believe that the blood of Jesus on the cross was of such value that it paid the sin sacrifice in full for all people. The Christian Bible states that Jesus was enabled to lay down his life physically, but that he remained alive spiritually. This is consonant with the Qur'anic passage that simply states that the crucifixion did not kill Jesus, who, says the Qur'an, was "a spirit emanating from Allah," but that he was raised up to Heaven as a living being.

The altar of Abraham is a consonant and integral part of the three great religions of Judaism, Christianity, and Islam. The fact that Jews and Christians believe that Abraham's sacrificial son was Isaac (peace!) whereas Muslims believe the son to be Ishmael (peace!) should be seen as a sign of personal connection to the Abrahamic story rather than a point of divisiveness. Jews trace their connection to Abraham through Isaac, and Arabs trace their connection through Ishmael. Likewise, each racial and ethnic group can find a unique link as we all approach the altar of Abraham with a commitment of personal sacrifice for the common cause of peace and goodwill. Persons of all religions and of no religion are invited to Eid al-Adha as we each make a spiritual journey of the heart to greet the ghost image of a metaphorical, ancestral child laid upon the altar of Humanity. Whether you refer to Allah, Adonai, Abba, the Great Spirit, the Universal Mind, or even the Divine Computer, or a variety of other titles, there is a power that links us all in a circle of life. It is up to each individual to find the personal sacrifice that is his or her contribution to this great experiment called 'Humanity.'

> O Lord, You have summoned all Your faithful people
> Into a single, universal family spanning Heaven and Earth.
> Bind us together with a divine love stronger than any mortal love.
> In serving one another, may we neither count the cost nor seek reward,
> But think only of the global welfare.
> *(from Mozarabic Sacramentary of 3rd century Andalusia)*

98. IT'S GOD'S SACRIFICE TOO

> Recite to (the masses) the true story of the two sons of Adam.
> They each presented a sacrifice [to Allah].
> It was accepted from one, but not from the other.
> [Cain] said [to Abel], "You can be sure that I will kill you."
> [Abel] said, "Allah accepts the sacrifices of those who are righteous."
> *(Surah 5: 27)*

One crisp autumn morning, when I was just a little squirt, I roused from my sleep and looked out the window next to my bed. I saw my daddy coming out of the woods after checking his rabbit traps. He was carrying a rabbit upside down by its hind legs. Daddy was grinning, and the sunlight glinted off the drool from his lips. He was headed straight for the chopping block! I screamed and ran outside, barefooted. "No, Daddy, no!" I raced him to the chopping block, grabbed the axe, and threw it behind the stack of firewood. I squalled and yelled and pitched a frantic fit until Daddy finally gave in and let the little bunny loose in the woods.

Daddy had several rabbit traps set in the woods, but he never got to eat any of the rabbits or possums or squirrels he caught. I couldn't let a little critter lose its life just so Daddy could have a pot of critter stew. In my way of thinking, it was just too big a sacrifice.

The sacrifice of Eid al Adha is a heavy obligation, especially for the person who has raised his or her own animal for the sacrifice. Having raised affectionate, adorable goats myself, I could understand the traumatic experience of Imam Etsamah Dudi. His father had given Etsamah, as a young boy, the responsibility of raising a goat for the Eid sacrifice. After affectionately caring for the goat, the child was devastated when his father slaughtered it. The father explained that one of the reasons for the sacrifice was so that we humans could relate to the fact that God has made a sacrifice in allowing us to eat meat.

Why was the sacrifice of Cain not acceptable to God? Why did only the death of an animal satisfy Him? After Imam Etsamah Dudi told me his father's explanation of the sacrifice of Eid al Adha, I realized that Able, but not Cain, had made the emotional bond that made his offering a true heartfelt sacrifice. Able was obedient to God and, therefore, righteous in his sacrificial act.

The pristine existence of the Garden of Eden, I theorize, was based on a system of ectropic laws (continuously evolving toward perfection and life) instead of the entropic laws (in a state of degeneration and death) of our world. The second law (that everything is moving toward a state of decay) of thermodynamics,[87] for example, did not apply to the Garden of Eden. We are now God's representatives of Plan B, so to speak, and it is Plan A that the faithful are to inherit.

The Garden of Eden was a dimension without suffering and struggle. From the Torah, we read that Adam and Eve (peace upon them), in the Garden, were allowed food from fruit trees (Genesis 2: 16), and the Qur'an allows bountiful things of the Garden (Surah 2: 35). Although inanimate objects, including plants, have a divine awareness, eating fruits and vegetables is quite a bit different from eating meat. To eat meat, one must first kill, and life cannot be regenerated from that kill. Most fruits and vegetables, however, can be eaten from the main plant without destroying the plant. There are exceptions; for example, carrots are pulled up entirely; but even then, the tops can be retained and re-rooted. Fruits and vegetables also have seeds that can be saved in order to regenerate life. When an animal is killed, all its potential descendants are killed along with it.

God commands the eating of plants, but He *allows* the eating of meat. God, in His eternal knowledge, preordained carnivorous appetites, in this dimension. He knew that the flood of Noah would make vegetation scarce for a time and that farming would be difficult at times because of changing climates. When farming is prosperous, however, we should eat fruits and vegetables most of the time and, out of respect for life and the Creator of life, limit our eating meat.

Prophet Muhammed (peace and blessings upon him) was an animal rights activist. He believed that animals have the right to security and welfare. He believed that people are responsible for making sure that animals' rights are not violated. During his ministry, the Prophet put an end to brutal, animal fights as a sport and other acts of cruelty.

Even animals used for food have the right to be raised in healthy and humane conditions. They are supposed to be killed in a way that causes the least amount of fear and pain. They have the right to die with dignity. God (blessed and exalted is He) gave us rules in how to treat the animals that He permits as food. People are responsible for making sure that all God's creatures —domestic and wild— are able to live without sadness, sickness, and hunger. We must all work together to make our planet a good home for everybody.

When God (blessed!) gave humans permission to kill animals for food and allowed animals to kill one another for food, it was not merely a way of setting the world in a balanced cycle; it was His sacrifice. Anyone who has comforted a sick or injured pet as it struggles with its last breaths has felt grief and loss. That is one of the times a person may question this world of pain and death. God has allowed us to kill *His pets* in order that we may eat. Our animal sacrifices should remind us of that and make us grateful.

Of course, in today's world, most people don't need a slaughtered goat. Most families need groceries, clean water, help with medical care, help with utility bills, and other essentials. In Surah 2: 196, the word translated to *sacrifice* means 'sacrifice, gift, or offering'. Whatever you can give to help a family is an acceptable gift, especially in areas where *tayyib* (humane/ethical) and *halal* (permissible, including the slaughtering method) meats are not available.

Someday we who are forgiven will be able to return to the Garden of Eden and the perfection in which Adam and Eve were first introduced. We must live as God has commanded because this dimension is too difficult without such precise guidance. Our prayers and religious rituals remind us of God's presence in our lives, and they prepare our souls so that we may return to God in a pure, undefiled state of being.

> We pray, O Lord, for the humble beasts
> That bear with us the burden and heat of the day
> And offer their guileless lives for the wellbeing of humankind.
> We pray for the wild creatures
> Whom You have made wise, strong, and beautiful.
> We supplicate for them and implore Your great tenderness of heart.
> You have promised to save both human and beast,
> And great is Your loving kindness,
> O Master, Savior of the World.
> *[Basil of Caesarea (329-379), a monastic hermit and bishop]*

99. IMAGINE A WORLD EMBRACED

> O Messengers, eat of the fine things, and live righteously.
> Truly, I [the Lord] am well aware of all that you do.
> Truly, your faith community is one faith community,
> and I am your Lord and Cherisher; therefore, fear Me.
> (People), however, have terminated their situation [of unity]
> and divided into sects. Each sect rejoices in its own (doctrine).
> Allow them their ignorance for the time being.
> *(Surah 23: 51-54)*

In the lobby of an office building, I was waiting to show my art portfolio to a potential client. A little boy sat nearby and waited for his mother to end an appointment. The child began talking to me about the frightening dinosaurs in the movie *Jurassic Park*. I asked him if he had read the book. He had not, so I said, "The book is a lot scarier than the movie! I saw the movie last week and was entertained for a while, but I read that book a year ago, and it's still giving me nightmares."

"How can just words on a page with no sound or pictures be scary?" he asked.

"You experience the entire adventure in your mind," I told him. "You not only see the pictures, you're in them!"

"I've never seen pictures in my mind," the little scoundrel scoffed. "You must be a crazy woman!"

Imagination! The brat had no imagination. The global, prevalent lack of imagination has perverted our world and subjected it to constant anguish and turmoil. In religion, culture, race, and society, each group of people has *defined* itself until it has *confined* itself and cannot imagine a world where all people are one.

The name of Adam is linked to the Hebrew word *adama*, which means 'dust', and also to the Hebrew word *adameh*, which means 'I will imagine'. The Biblical phrase translated to say that humanity was "made in God's image" has been understood by *Kabbalists* (Jewish mystics) as "made in God's imagination." God imagined us into being. He created us in His image in that He endowed us with the ability to imagine. Within the embodiment of one man Adam (peace!), God created Humanity with all the wondrous colors and patterns of a magnificent, human panorama. It is incumbent upon us, then, to imagine all the colors combined to make one bright light, which is the light of the One God.

Like the One God with multiple attributes, Humanity is one entity with many unique faces and many different qualities and attributes. The universe is filled with messages that speak to us of synchronized union. If the universal systems of physics and chemistry and bio-mathematics were not in perfect sync, if they were in conflict, our world could not exist but would be ripped asunder. All of nature is shouting to us that harmony is essential for humanity's continued existence. Albert Einstein said, "Look deeply into nature, and then you will understand everything better." Long before Einstein, however, the Qur'an implored people to observe nature in order to increase knowledge and understanding.

Humanity and our relationship to one another may be comparable to the flower and the bee. Just as a single flower lifts its face to God, each individual person may independently focus on the transcendence of God and ponder that person's unique relationship to God (blessed and exalted is He). The bee, however, unites many different flowers, and, likewise, the unifying factors of multiple religions can unite different people. Like the sharing of various pollens helps to recreate nature's beauty, the sharing of religious ideals can beautify the floral arrangement of humanity. Sharing means to show respect for the feelings and beliefs of others. Sharing means to focus on the consonant values of all religions and cultures and to make a collective effort in dedicating those consonant values to the glory of God (blessed and exalted is He).

Peace among various peoples cannot come from mere tolerance, because both tolerance and intolerance are based on negative value judgments. Instead of tolerance, humanity must share sincere understanding. Understanding does not mean that the individual must compromise his or her own religious beliefs or accept beliefs that are antithetical to his or her own religion. Understanding, however, leads to a person's willingness to accommodate other religions in a fair and respectful manner so that the world can peacefully unite in its diversity.

Most people are afraid to imagine a world where human diversity unites, because that would mean that a person must face the reality of how he or she has compromised the oneness of God (blessed!). An individual person or religion places limitations on God by defining God as the God of the single flower and not allowing God to be the God of the universal bee. People and religious groups tend to define God in terms of their own needs and limited understanding, and, in so doing, they practice a form of idolatry as they confine God to a fixed image. To imagine God outside a humanly devised, familiar, and comfortable image is frightening and threatening to most people. To the invitation to imagine, many people react in perverse ways, which is the reason behind global oppression, violence, hatred, prejudice, and terrorism.

Prophet Muhammed (peace and blessings upon him) was secure in his relationship with God (blessed!), so he was able to imagine a world in humanity's embrace of one another. Within the enclave in which he lived, the Prophet (peace!) established a unifying accommodation toward each community. He embraced non-Muslim believers with respect and promised them security.

In a peaceful agreement established with the Jewish communities, the Prophet proclaimed, "In the Name of God, the Most Gracious, the Most Merciful. This message is from Muhammed the Messenger of God. Truly, whoever from among the Jews abides with us [Muslims] shall be assisted and supported and will not be victims of injustice or vengeance. …. They have their religion, and the Muslims have their own and each other. The exceptions are any who are oppressive and sinful; they will thereby forfeit themselves and their families."

In the Prophet's time, Christian visitors were allowed to pray traditional Christian prayers in the mosque while Muslims prayed according to their own manner. The Prophet (peace!) prayed for Roman Christians at war with Persian unbelievers. He sent this communication to Christians in Mount Sinai:

> This message is from Muhammed ibn Abdullah. It is written as a covenant for those, far and near, who follow Christianity. We [Muslims] support them. Truly, I defend them myself as also do my servants, my helpers, and my followers, because Christians are citizens, and, by the will of God, I withhold anything that would displease them. No coercion is to be on them. Their judges will not be replaced, and their monks will not be removed from their monasteries. No one is to destroy a Christian church or damage it or remove anything from it to put into the Muslims' houses. If anyone does such a thing, he would spoil God's covenant and disobey His Prophet.

Truly, the Christians are my allies, and they have my secure agreement to protect them against all they hate. No one is to force them to travel or to fight; the Muslims are to fight for them. If a female Christian is to marry a Muslim, the marriage cannot take place without her consent. She is never to be prevented from going to her church to pray. The churches are to be respected. Christians will not be prevented from repairing the churches, and will not be prevented from the sacredness of their own covenants. No one of the nation is to disobey this covenant till the Day of Judgment and the end of the world.

Notice in the foregoing message that, even though the Qur'an criticizes monasticism, the Prophet (peace!) accommodated the same. Prophet Muhammed (peace!) imagined a world without strife, prejudice, and rivalry. He was a humanitarian who respected the unique characteristics of various religions while focusing on all faith as one divine truth. He admired each individual believer as one would admire a single flower, but he was able to see the beauty of variety in glorification of God (blessed!). Seeing beauty in human diversity is the same as scanning across a field of multi-colored wildflowers and seeing one beautiful landscape.

As we try to follow the footsteps of Prophet Muhammed (peace!), we must imagine the future of Islam as he wanted it —a religion peacefully uniting all religions of light. Imagine the many voices of prayer rising to Heaven as one harmonized sonnet of praise. Imagine the prismatic shimmers of faith streaming together to make one, brilliant, white light. Imagine a world decorated by a human tapestry of love, peace, and charity. Imagine a world in which all Humanity embraces one another in friendship. Imagine one world cradled in the arms of the one, loving God. Imagine.

> Our Sovereign and Wonderful Lord,
> You gave us the potential to do wonderful things on this planet.
> Forgive us for failing You so miserably.
> Inspire in us a global, spiritual renaissance
> In which people of all faiths will glorify You
> In one fantastic symphony of voices celebrating Your praises.
> May the whole world, O Allah, know of Your awesome deeds.
> May Your mercy and grace be realized in the lives

Of those who are struggling, hungry, abused, and oppressed.
Energize us so that we may be Your instruments of comfort and healing.
Provide opportunities for us to share the blessings and bounty
That You have provided to some to distribute to others.
In accordance with Your will,
Keep us from danger, evil, accident, injury, and illness.
Bless the children, and rescue those being abused and neglected.
Bless the elderly, and may they live and die with dignity and grace.
Bless the chronically ill and disabled; may they find comfort in faith.
Bless the animals, for the struggle is difficult for them.
Inspire us to connect to nature in amazing ways
And to be constantly aware of the union of all Your creation.
Help us to be responsible stewards of Your planet
So we may repair the damages we have done.
Help us unite to make this world according to Your vision
Of peace, harmony, goodness, and justice.
Amen.

ENDNOTES

[1] Shamim A. Siddiqi died in 2018. He was a theological intellectual who dedicated his life to acquiring Islamic knowledge and sharing Islamic principles and perspectives with those thirsting for truth. He was founder of Dawah in Americas and authored the books *The Commitment, Methodology of Dawah Ilallah in American Perspective, The Dawah Program, The Greatest Need of Man, Looking for the Book of Wisom, Dawah and its Objective, The Revival, The Provision of Akhirah, and Al-Fatihah & its Significance*. May he be rewarded in Heaven.

[2] The words I have shown as "scholars and devout parishioners" are from words possibly borrowed from Abyssinia. They are often translated to "priests and monks," and Abdulla Yusuf Ali translates them to "men devoted to learning and men who have renounced the world."

[3] Abdulla Yusuf Ali, <u>The Holy Qur'an: Translation and Commentary</u> (original 1934 version) (American Trust Publications: Washington DC, 1971), from the Introduction to Surah 93.

[4] Ibid, Yusuf Ali, nn 6182 and 6187.

[5] Daniel Moore, <u>The Blind Beekeeper</u> (Kitab: MD, 2001), pp 154-155. Used by kind permission of the author.

[6] RuqaiyyahWarisMaqsood, <u>Muslim Prayer Encyclopaedia</u> (Goodword Books: India, 1998), p 21.

[7] Ibid, Yusuf Ali, n 137.

[8] Ibid.

[9] Hadeeth: Abu Hurayah: Bukhari.

[10] Sunnah: Bukhari and Muslim.

[11] I must mention that there is a hadith that indicates that one should not go back to bed if he or she has to get ready to go to work. Good point! "Just five more minutes" always seems to last longer than it should.

[12] Muhammad Asad, <u>The Road to Mecca</u> (The Book Foundation: Kentucky, 2005), pp 88-89. Used by kind permission of the publisher.

[13] Ibid, Yusuf Ali, n 145.

[14] The word *apocalypse* is from the Greek *apokalysis (revelation)* in reference to the visions of John in the Christian book of Revelations, similar to the visions of Daniel in the Jewish texts. The Greek word *armageddon* is from two Hebrew words, *har (mount)* and *megiddow (rendezvous)*; the literal meaning is *mount of the rendezvous* and refers to a battle preceding the destruction of planet Earth. Zionism is a modern, political movement inspired by Rabbi Zevi Hirsch Kalischer in his 1862 book *Derishat Zion*. Kalischer insisted that the Messianic Age could be brought about only by human initiative and not dependence on God's promises. Part of the Zionists' plan is to destroy the mosque in Jerusalem and create a Jewish political center in Palestine. Zionist Jews instigated the Schofield Bible, which promotes Zionist views. When the Hadeeth and Qur'an tell of oppressive and violent acts of Jews, we should understand that these were, not all Jews, but specific tribes. We must not be guilty of fearing and opposing the Jewish people as a whole. The majority are peace-loving and not in agreement with the violence of the Zionist movement.

[15] "The *dajjal* [anti-Christ] will appear in my Ummah..." (Hadeeth: Bukhari, reported by Abdullah bin Amr bin As). After one of the ritual morning prayers, "The dajjal will be waiting outside [the mosque in Jerusalem] along with 70,000 armed Jews. When the dajjal sees Jesus, he will seem to melt [with fear] like salt in water and will try to escape. Jesus will warn him, 'I shall strike you with a fatal blow.' Jesus will overtake the dajjal at the eastern gate of Lod..." (Hadeeth: Ibn Majah, reported by UmamahBaheli). Lod (or Lydda), thirteen miles southeast of Tel-Aviv, is now the most important airport in Israel. "Then Jesus will descend, and Allah will cause the dajjal to be killed near the mountain pass of Afiq" (Hadeeth: Musnad Ahmad, reported by Safinah, a freed slave of the Prophet). Muslims also believe in the Mahdi, which some Muslims, including Abul A'laMaududi, believe is the same as Messiah Jesus; other Muslims believe it will be a new messiah. To read Maududi's arguments and the supporting hadeeths, read his Tafseer in the Appendix that accompanies Surah 33. The referenced Appendix is entitled "The Finality of Prophethood," and the specific paragraphs are "The Reality About the Promised Messiah," "Traditions Relating to the Second Advent of Jesus Son of Mary," and "What Do These Traditions Prove?"

[16] Hadeeth: Bukhari.
[17] Jeremiah's Grotto was located at El Edhemieh, just north of Jerusalem. I do not know if it still exists. British occupation and Israeli/Palestinian conflict have destroyed many such places.
[18] It is also said that Jeremiah's donkey was later admitted into Paradise and united with one of its ancestors, which had been cruelly beaten for refusing to convey Satan into the ark of Noah.
[19] Hadeeth: Tirmidhi.
[20] Commonly translated to "rested," the Hebrew word *sabat*, from which *Sabbath* is derived, has a variety of meanings including 'to end,' 'to finish,' and 'to celebrate.' God has no need of rest, but as the Master Artist, He finished commanding His creation into existence and celebrated its beauty.
[21] Hadeeth: Darqutni.
[22] www.beliefnet.com, quoting from The Power of Prayerful Living (Rodale). I could not get permission to use the original, so I rewrote it.
[23] Renée Miller's prayers "Living With Purpose" and "Stillness" used by kind permission of www.explorefaith.org.
[24] Robert Van de Weyer, The Harper Collins Book of Prayers (Castle Books: New Jersey, 1997), p 287. I could not get permission to use the original, so I rewrote it.
[25] "2003 New Year's Day Prayer," used by kind permission of the author.
[26] Hadeeth: Bukhari.
[27] The Biblical account is given in 2 Samuel 12: 1-9. The Qur'an confirms that David had ill intentions and states that God humiliated him by sending two messengers (angels?) acting as litigants in a legal dispute. In the Qur'anic story, a ewe is used as a metaphor for Uriah's wife and ninety-nine ewes represent the wives of David who had been trying to get Uriah's wife for himself. "Have you heard the story of the litigants who climbed into the private sanctuary? When they entered to face David, he was startled by them. They said, 'Do not fear us litigants; we two are feuding with one another, so judge honorably between us without injustice and point us in the right direction.' [One explained,] 'This is my brother who has ninety-nine ewes, while I have only one ewe. He demanded that I give him my ewe, and he won the argument.' (David) said, 'He has wronged you by demanding your ewe to be added to his ewes. Truly, many business partners transgress against one another, except those who believe and act righteously, but they are few.' David realized that We had tested him, and he asked for forgiveness. He prostrated in repentance. We forgave him for that, and for him is a position near Us and a wonderful destination" (Surah 38: 21-25). In the Tafseer of Abul A'laMaududi, he explains, "This shows that the Prophet David had certainly committed an error, and it was an error which bore some resemblance with the case of the ewes. Therefore, when he gave a decision on it, he at once realized that he was being put to the test" (from Maududi's n 27 to Surah 28). He continues, "When this story was so well known among the people, there was no need that a detailed account of it should have been given in the Qur'an, nor is it the way of Allah to mention such things openly in His Holy Book" (from n 28). Maududi, however, does not accept the entirety of the Biblical account, but only that David desired and demanded Uriah's one wife when David himself had many wives.
[28] A new Muslim wrote to me with great concern because a vintage Muslim had told him that he had to get rid of his three dogs, which he adored. There are some hadeeths that suggest that Muslims should not keep dogs as pets, although farm, hunting, and other work dogs have always been allowed. Such hadeeths must be understood within the context of the time, place, and culture. Dogs could create health and welfare threats in a society where food was sometimes scarce, where rabies and parasites were almost impossible to control, where hygiene and good health were difficult to maintain, and where breeding was difficult to control. In our world, there are rabies shots, flea, tick, and mosquito repellants, medicines for parasites, grooming products, spay and neuter procedures, and pet food products. If someone cannot afford to properly maintain a dog and still provide for his or her family as well as meeting his or her zakat obligation, then it would be a sin for that person to have a dog. That is my opinion. Pet dogs today do provide services for their human families. Pets are wonderful companions who treat and guard against depression. They also warn of intruders and other dangers, including evil spirits *(jinn)*. I think the Prophet

(peace upon him) would be disgusted at the way animals are treated by senseless, evil people, but I think he would be delighted at the humane laws designed to protect animals. Certainly abusing and neglecting animals are evil acts, so giving good homes to dogs and cats in a society that kills unwanted pets is, in my opinion, a good deed.

[29] Prince Arjuna is a major character in the great Indian epic poem "Mahabharata."

[30] Ibid, Yusuf Ali, Appendix 12, para 11.

[31] Muslims Weekly, 2006.

[32] The rising sun and the East are symbolic of knowledge and enlightenment. The Prophet (peace upon him) predicted that someday the sun will rise in the West. This may be interpreted to mean that the Islamic renaissance will begin in the western hemisphere.

[33] This prayer was at the door of a Christian hospital in England.

[34] Bart Ehrman, Misquoting Jesus: The Story Behind Who Changed the Bible and Why (New York: Harper Collins, 2005), pp 153-154.

[35] Marcus Braybrooke (ed), The Bridge of Stars (Duncan Baird Publishers: England, 2001), p 169. I could not get permission to use the original, so I rewrote it.

[36] Ibid, Yusuf Ali, n 663.

[37] www.giveshare.org/health/porkeatdanger, 2008.

[38] www.moseshand.com/studies/eatingpork, 2008.

[39] Used by kind permission of the author.

[40] Used by kind permission of the deceased author's son.

[41] Used by kind permission of the author.

[42] Adrian Butash, Bless This Food: Amazing Graces in Thanks for Food (New York: Delacorte Press, 1993), prayer 89 (adaptation/editing mine).

[43] Under normal conditions, guns should be stored unloaded, with the safety on, and in a locked cabinet inaccessible to children, adolescents, and anyone with a problem in anger management or substance abuse. The ammunition may be stored in a separate cabinet as an additional precaution. Anyone, including children (as age-appropriate), exposed to a gun should be properly trained in gun safety and handling. If a gun is kept for protection, the owner should be totally committed to its use as a weapon; otherwise, the owner may put him- or herself at more risk.

[44] Ibid, Yusuf Ali, Appendix 12, para 11.

[45] Hadeeth: Muslim.

[46] Another interpretation —and both can be true— is, "(Jesus) is a sign of the Time [of Resurrection]...." In this case, Jesus' resurrection from the illusion of death is a sign that our own deaths are mere illusions, although in a less remarkable and mysterious manner, and that we will each be resurrected in a reality beyond this temporal reality. I accept both these interpretations, and there are others about which I am merely open-minded.

[47] Hypno-birthing is the use of clinical hypnosis to prepare expectant mothers for delivering their babies in a natural and joyful manner. By tapping into the amazing power of the brain, a hypno-therapist can help a mother deliver her baby in fifteen, pain-free minutes. It really works!

[48] Hadeeth: Anas ibn Malik.

[49] Hadeeth: Mawdudi.

[50] Thomas W. Lippman, U. S. News & World Report, Collector's Edition: Secrets of Islam (2005), p 14.

[51] Jesus was referring to the tendency of men to abuse their wives instead of reconciling their differences. As to Matthew 19: 9 and Mark 5: 31-32, Jesus was referring to men who divorced their wives without the proper Jewish *gett*.

[52] Hadeeth: Abu Dawud.

[53] The wives of the Prophet (peace!) were extremely valuable to the welfare of the faith family of Muslims, to the understanding of the Prophet's teachings, and to the spread of Islam. They shared the most intimate thoughts and feelings of the Prophet and, therefore, were the most qualified as mothers of the faith. After the Prophet's death, his widows were responsible for ministering to the Muslim family. God gave them

the charge of devoting their lives to the Ummah, without the distraction of new husbands and more children.

[54] Hadeeth: Anas ibn Malik, transmitted by Tirmidhi and Ibn Majah.

[55] Used by kind permission of the author Michael Wright, copyright 2021. Michael Wright is author of *Our Love's Rivalry with Religion* (Amazon, 2021). His work, including poetry, is available on his website www.thewrightauthor.com.

[56] Hadeeth: Bukhari.

[57] Hadeeth: Bukhari.

[58] Ibid, Braybrooke, p 106. I could not get permission to use the original, so I rewrote it in my own words.

[59] Ibid, Yusuf Ali, n 951.

[60] Indigenous to the Island of Mauritius, the last dodo bird was killed in 1681. The quagga was a zebra-like animal of Africa. The last quagga died in a zoo in 1883. The spectacled cormorant, a bird of the Aleutian Islands, was extinct by 1840. Some other losses within recent centuries include the thylacine, a cat-like, carnivorous marsupial, all killed by hunters over fifty years ago; the English wolf, extinct since 1770; the Caspian tiger, native to parts of Asia and the Middle East where the last one was shot and killed in 1957; and Steller's sea cow of the Aleutian Islands, all killed by hunters by 1775.

[61] Ibid, Braybrooke, p 207. I could not get permission to use the original, so I rewrote it in my own words.

[62] There have been other holocausts, including the Armenian Holocaust, also denied by blockheads.

[63] Muslims Weekly, 2006. Used by kind permission of Yousef Drummond.

[64] A reader's comment on "War Stories": Dr. Hasan Qazi Muizudin (originally from Dharampura, Patiala): "You are lucky, in a way, that you are a US citizen. Your soldiers have cameras. Your media lets you report all. In contrast, I refer you to a holocaust about which you may never have known, heard, or read. It was Patiala holocaust —seven days of massacres, rapes, and humiliating horror by the military units of Patiala of fellow citizens, Muslims, children, women, and elderly within their own homes. Patiala was my birthplace in Punjab, a part that is now in India. A million at least (no actual count was possible) lost their lives in August and September; six million lost their homes and everything forever. They were forced to save their lives by marching on foot toward the border of Pakistan as refugees. Few actually did reach the border. Many were killed on the way. Bism'Allah, I am not comparing it [to the Jewish Holocaust], but I could not help but to recall my own misery, which the world does not know. It happened after August 15, 1947, the day India was partitioned. To this day, I painfully recall my friends and relatives who could not reach Pakistan."

[65] This is the explanation presented in A Brief, Illustrated Guide to Understanding Islam (Darussalam: TX, 1996), p 8, p 9 (illustration): "The Arabic word *mudghah* means 'chewed substance.' If one were to take a piece of gum and chew it in his or her mouth and then compare it with an embryo at the *mudghah* stage, we would conclude that the embryo at the *mudghah* stage is similar in appearance to a chewed substance. This is because of the somites at the back of the embryo that 'somewhat resemble teeth marks in a chewed substance.'"

[66] Hadeeth: Bukhari.

[67] The Arabic word *mawaleekum* has been rendered 'allies,' 'friends,' 'clients,' 'members of your family,' 'your freed slaves,' 'those entrusted to you,' 'those under your sponsorship,' 'companions,' and 'comrades.' I felt that 'dependents' fit the context as it concerns foster and adoptive children.

[68] Ibid, Abdulla Yusuf Ali, n 3672.

[69] Ibid, n 3673.

[70] Hadeeth: Muslim.

[71] Hadeeth: Bayhaqi, according to Sa'ib ibn Yazid.

[72] Hadeeth: Ahmad.

[73] Hadeeth: Bukhari.

[74] Hadeeth: Bukhari.

[75] Hadeeth: Mu'jam al Kabir, as told by UmmiSalamah.

[76] Hadeeth: Ibn Abbas.

77 The *daff* is a narrow, hoop-shaped drum held in one hand and struck by the other hand, creating a cheerful beat for singing and dancing.
78 Hadeeth: Al Muham al Saghir, according to Anas ibn Malik.
79 Hadeeth: Bukhari.
80 Readers' comments on "Jive Talking From a Rock 'n' Roll Dervish": Dr. Jerald Dirks: "I arrived at the same conclusions you did with regard to music. It even looks like we used pretty much the same source material in reaching our conclusions." Dr. Omar Afzal: "The clash between 'music is halal' vs. 'music is haram' is an old one and relates to the core question, 'What kind of human society/civilization does Islam want to build on earth?' As long as the Muslim mind is tied to Arab culture instead of universal and timeless Islam, we will keep wasting our energies on trivial issues." Dr. Habib Siddiqi: "Any act that brings one close to Allah and also encourages others similarly is a good deed and encouraged. Many of the great Sufis of the Middle Ages were great admirers of music. Imam al-Ghazzali, one of the most astute scholars of Islam, did not have a problem with music either, as long as it was for those who could not be swayed by lowly inclinations of *nafs* [self-interests], ego, lust, passion, etc. To him, music was not okay for vulgar people who find in it a way to detach themselves from their duties or obligations to their Creator and others. Maulana Rumi was a great promoter of music; so was Khawaja Mainuddin Christi of India. Then there are many others. Unfortunately, most people abuse music for all the wrong reasons. So, if one's intentions are good and the music helps one and others to relax and come closer to their many obligations, then music is good, just like poetry can be." Imam Khalil Akbar: "My sentiments about music mirror your statements. I am in total agreement with your thoughts regarding music. We [at the mosque] encourage good, decent music. In fact, at most of our public gatherings, such as banquets, we have music. Thanks for sharing your thoughts."
81 The Lawful and the Prohibited (American Trust Publications: IN, 1994), p 110.
82 "Contemporary Muslim Artists: Tradition, Faith, Image," Muslims Weekly, January 14, 2005, p 2.
83 At one time, there were 7,100 named varieties of apples.
84 In translating the Qur'an, Abdulla Yusuf Ali and a few other translators use the word *mansions* for the phases of the moon.
85 Hadeeth: Bukhari.
86 Ibid, Braybrooke, p 161. I could not get permission to use the original, so I rewrote it in my own words.
87 The second law of thermodynamics is that everything is moving toward a state of decay. The first law of thermodynamics is that energy cannot be created or destroyed, only transferred. The energy of the soul, then, cannot be destroyed (except, of course, by the One who first created it); instead, the soul of a deceased body is transferred from this world into the next.

www.ingramcontent.com/pod-product-compliance
Lightning Source LLC
Chambersburg PA
CBHW022040290426
44109CB00014B/929